God
Save
the
Quarterback!

G⬤d
Save
the
Quarterback!
American Football Goes to England

Michael Globetti

Random House

New York

Library of Congress Cataloging-in-Publication Data

Globetti, Michael.
God save the quarterback! : American football goes to England / Michael
Globetti.—1st ed.
     p.   cm.
ISBN 0-394-57564-4
1. Birmingham Bulls (Football team : Birmingham, England)—
History. 2. Globetti, Michael. I. Title.
GV956.B57G57   1991   796.332′64′0942496—dc20   90-53142

Manufactured in the United States of America
98765432
First Edition

To Mama,
a middle linebacker in anybody's league

"But—but—there must be some mistake. Can you have come to the wrong island?"

George A. Birmingham,
Spanish Gold

Acknowledgments

The first game of American football in Great Britain kicked off in 1910 between the crews of two visiting battleships, the U.S.S. *Georgia* and *Rhode Island*. Dreadnoughts and spirals arriving about the same time, Britannia not only ruled the seas but could stake as much claim as anyone to the forward pass. When our brand of football again was shipped abroad, almost a century later, the Brits had fallen into our wake but seemed to be catching up in a hurry—thanks chiefly to people like Frank Leadon, without whom this book wouldn't have been possible.

Frank and his generous energy for it exemplified the game's new dawning. His cooperation on *God Save the Quarterback!* was yeoman. Thinking of him, I hearken to a remark by the character Jimmy Porter in John Osborne's *Look Back in Anger:* "I must say, it's pretty dreary living in the American age . . . unless you're an American." Frank tried awfully hard to be. Typical was how, the year before I joined the Birmingham Bulls, he ran up a transatlantic phone bill to tell about the team's latest victory and how he'd figured into it. Other sportswriters with whom I worked for a newspaper in Boston enjoyed hearing from him, too. "It's that guy," they'd say, "with the funny American accent."

Without him, I wouldn't have gotten this golden chance to see a sport take shape—nor to play it again. I'd long entertained a notion to become an overage freshman and play under a fictitious name at a remote college in the Cascade Range, then compare it to when I was an actual frosh. As it turned out, Frank also could have been a great help furthering a plan to be somebody I wasn't.

The Bulls' hierarchy also contributed enormously. I'm grateful to former co-owner Denton Thomas for his theatrical insights and flourish. The exclamation point at the end of the title belongs almost solely to him. "My favorite Shakespeare character is Macbeth," Denton once said, "because he was somebody who got set up." Know what you mean, old boy, know what you mean. Thanks, also, to Bulls' founder Gerry Hartman, a great ambassador for football, at whatever the cost or verbiage to get it across. To Peter Biddulph, another whose syllabicity so enhanced the season and made it memorable. A salute to the Webbs, David and his son, Andy, for whom the Bulls might not have been the investment of a lifetime but surely made for an endless return on humor. And to John Eyre, whose near-heroic name could have earned him the nickname "Everywhere" Eyre for his genuine help to the team. The Bulls' Supporters Club also fit that niche, or defined it: namely the Greenwood brothers, Ian and Terry, along with Paul Forrester, Peter Spencer, and Peter Robinson, who infused cash and cheer without surcease.

I commend my gridiron support group: Well done, pardner, to Chris "Jago" Pee, the undefeated retired British quick-draw champion (200 straight notches for his Colt Dragoons) and his wife, Alma Pee, whose apple pie à la mode made a Yank feel right at home. To the greengrocer known as Mr. Nice 'n Fresh—nice for the nourishment, and fresh dollops of levity. To the Duce family, who personified British hospitality, and to West House School's kitchen staff for the best cafeteria lunches in academia. To the Warwickshire County Cricket Club, for taking an interloper to heart, and vice versa. And te deum to conductor Simon Rattle, whose baton supplied sanity much needed over the season, and to the cities of Birmingham, Alabama and England, for being the inimitable Brums.

Also, a bow to Gabriel Miller for his unstinting Anglophilia; to

Richard Zacks, for getting the ball rolling; to Kristine Dahl, my agent, for huddling and encouragement throughout; to my editors, David Rosenthal, Susan Bell, and Durrae Johanek, for diagramming the play to make it work; to Rick Rosen and Diane McWhorter, who advised the light handoff instead of planting it in the gut; to A. E. Rancatore, world champion confectioner, whose prunes and armagnac ice cream made coming home something to look forward to; to Robert J. Sales, who will have a hell of a time saying "nurtured" in Brooklynese; and to the Chief, Bill Lumpkin, who, better or worse, first anchored me to a typewriter.

Finally, to the Birmingham Bulls. I'm thankful to my American teammates—Bobby Shoop, James Thornton, Russ Jensen, and Steve Pisarkiewicz—who were especially kind with their time and patience. And the biggest bravo of all to the Britain Bulls— for whom the season's encumbrances might have been enough to send them off their chump, were they not so good at reality. "All part of the Brit psychology—our backs to the wall, the stress syndrome, like how everybody in World War Two helped everybody else," once averred Malcolm Byron, the Bulls' equipment manager and team melodramaturg. "That's when we're at our bloody best." That they were.

Newton Corner, Massachusetts
April 27, 1991

Introduction

For football, the compass of improbability swung to one name on the map: Birmingham. When last I'd seen Steve Pisarkiewicz play a football game, my view from a front-row seat in the pressbox, he was the star quarterback who led a stunning upset of the top-ranked college team in America. This was the game as meant to be played: before a national prime-time television audience and in front of 80,000 fans in the self-proclaimed football capital of the South, Birmingham, Alabama.

Now, fifteen years, a travel epoch, and three professional football leagues later, Steve Pisarkiewicz again found himself in Birmingham—that improbable place on the map—for a football game, this time leading a top-ranked team of his own. No return to past glory, however; he was in another country and another Birmingham, though he was seemingly playing the same game. Zark, as he liked to be called, had signed on as quarterback and new coach of the Birmingham Bulls of the British American Football Association. Another coherence to that compass: I had vacated the pressbox to join him on the playing field as the Bulls met the Dublin Celtics to open defense of our British championship.

Even as a 35-year-old veteran, Zark wasn't above admitting to jitters. Maybe not so jittery as when he started his first NFL game, and faced as his opposing quarterback another newcomer, which naturally helped balance anxieties. Two new QBs in an NFL game, moreover both of them having been first-round draft choices? Nobody could recall such an occurrence. Yes, it was one for the history books and, until he landed with the Bulls, maybe the zenith of a career. The rival quarterback would go on to win four Super Bowls and guarantee his immortality in the game, but his debut against Steve Pisarkiewicz was one Sunday when Joe Montana came out second best.

Now, for the first time Zark himself would be playing in what amounted to a postseason game. Rules made football abroad a strange new world. Both the Bulls and Celtics had last played a game six months earlier, when each won its country's championship. The reward was a maze of future competition. For the Bulls, start of the regular season was still a month away when we lined up against the Celtics. Victory would send us into something called the Euro Bowl—played for the continental championship—but also send us, with the championship game's summer playing date, into direct conflict with the British season.

By then, a Yank like Zark might be playing with his second, even third team of the season. It wasn't trades that caused him to move on, but personnel raids, or dissatisfaction, or a preferred change of climate, or peregrinating to a town that offered a better brewery. Better yet: He might be playing simultaneously for two teams in different leagues.

But if rules were wacky, if not incomprehensible, Steve Pisarkiewicz, of all people, having had what could only be called a pigskin panhandling career, was right at home with them. Here he was, back in action, with another team, in another city, another country, camped beneath another set of shoulder pads, and sporting jersey number 18 just as he had in the old days with St. Louis. Except there, or in Green Bay, where he'd also played, or Philadelphia, or Orlando, or Winnipeg, he'd not had the opportunity to go up against a pair of linebackers a full head shorter than he was, brothers with the humble but distinguished names Billy and Declan Peat.

. . .

Alexander Stadium in the British Midlands had never been more boisterous. Some of the noise got generated by traffic from the M6 motorway, one of the country's busiest, which ran directly behind the stadium—jammed on a holiday weekend. But most of the buzzing belonged to the grandstand. Much ado about the game was made by Birmingham's Irish community, Britain's biggest, and it didn't hurt to have the game slated just after conclusion of the city's annual St. Patrick's Day parade, which was bigger even than what took to the streets in Dublin.

Gridiron, as American-style football was known abroad, had come into a new cynosure, and this was the day Brum, as Birmingham was called, would establish itself as a leading outpost, a city that aspired to international status hitching itself to a sport that was internationally ambitious. The game was the biggest in Bulls' history, with more riding on the outcome than for any British team since the sport was born in the United Kingdom, or got grafted.

We were seen as the team expected to give the sport legitimacy. Gridiron had become more than a fad, more than the latest incarnation of Yank wannabe, and the Bulls, Britain's best team, were building an organization to compete with anyone on the Continent and possibly—our visionary owner dared dream—the world.

With betting legal in Britain on everything from who would be named archbishop of Canterbury to the likelihood of Elvis still being alive, bookmakers were well aware of the Bulls' preeminence. Wagering for this game was out, though, since too little was known about the Irish for the bookies to lay down a point spread.

But the spread would have been generous, Bulls players knew, because we'd beaten it ten straight games a year ago and now entered the new season a stronger team. Much stronger, from having an ex-NFL player, an influx of Americans, and the best indigenous athletes. Not to be overlooked, the Bulls also boasted the man who had arguably done more to promote gridiron abroad than anyone, Frank Kalili, as our owner and showman.

A Supporters Club had sprung up around the team, and given it mythical backing. What they contributed couldn't be measured in cheers alone, and club members fancied themselves as so essential to the team that the Bulls could not operate without them. Long before the game began, they brayed a favorite chant, "We're so good, it's un-be-LAY-vable!"—dum-dum—"We're so good, it's un-be-LAY-vable!" That our two-man Bulls mascot—designed by Frank Kalili—went missing after having been dismantled one time too many by opponents did not quell them.

But they met a match in the outpouring of support for the Irish team, whose fans who had come from far and wide and waved tricolored flags like they were at a liberation day. Many more on hand were impartial fans from throughout the country, who had come from Brum to see if the Bulls could duplicate our improbable championship, won by a team that started the season with just 13 players.

More than a game, it became an occasion, this being the season that showed the world, showed the United States, and more specifically the National Football League, how Great Britain had adopted this newfangled sport and would support it in an international league the NFL had proposed for Europe. American flourishes, among them a yellow Checker cab and a huge inflatable beer can, adorned the field. There was a coaching conference in conjunction with the game, with British coaches having correspondence course diplomas validated by a visiting group of assistants from the Ivy League.

In just five few years, gridiron had grown from two-hand touch on London greenswards to comprise almost 300 teams throughout the British Isles. Called the biggest new sport Britain had ever seen, it began with a weekly NFL highlight show aired opposite British religious programming, called the "God-slot," by an independent network. Soon the show had six million viewers, more people than attended weekly church services in England.

Now the future for Britball, as the game had come to be called, looked gilded with NFL's putative involvement. But prosperity was yet to filter down to the British champion Bulls. The reason there'd been but 13 players to come out for the team the previous season was because nobody knew if there'd be a team—such was the penury. One of the football tabloids referred to us weekly as "Raging Bulls" on the pitch; off it, we were ragamuffins. For weeks Frank Kalili counted on a good gate from the Dublin game to help extricate us, and himself, from longstanding financial woe. We needed to start the season not just with a compelling performance but also pump a lot of pounds back into our perforated pursestrings.

Giving a battery of interviews before the game, Frank punctuated each with a reminder of where it was being played. By nature he was a worrier, but there was no need for it even if Zark, as Bulls general manager, had oddly camouflaged posters for the game, tacking them to the utility poles and pillars ringing the stadium rather than having them arrayed around town. Getting there was simple enough: Fans should drive past the newly built Saddam Hussein mosque (named for the donor who'd given $3 million toward construction), and from there any hearse driver in town could provide directions. To reach Alexander Stadium, come straight to the city crematorium, bang a sharp right, continue past a plot of victory gardens, and a little further beyond an AstroTurf-covered car park. That was guaranteed almost to land a fan at midfield, which in Britain was likely to be the 45-yard line.

Spoils of the championship aside, it had been a difficult preseason for the Bulls . . . namely because there hadn't been any spoils, particularly in the way of team sponsorship. Sport survives in Britain through sponsorship—from the lowliest nonleague rugby side to Football Association soccer power Liverpool, which took the pitch not with its proud name across players' shirts, but the incongruous word CANDY. The Bulls were now playing in old jerseys that bore the name of a brewery that last sponsored us three years earlier. Internal problems also hampered us. Particularly jarring was an off-season en masse arrest of our starting secondary, on charges ranging from armed robbery to assault. They had spearheaded the best defense in the country a year ago, but we would play Dublin, maybe play the entire season, without them; their trials weren't scheduled for months. Worse, after earning the nickname Uncle Frank for almost single-handedly saving the team the previous season, the owner had begun to alienate his players.

Frank Kalili was a chattering, flattering owner, which befitted the former entertainer that he was. But a year removed from his Uncle Frank status, a groundswell of resentment had begun against the man who'd bought majority interest in the team for a pittance, if that, and parlayed it into becoming a leading figure in Britball. The Bulls had tired of being the most bedraggled team in the country and thought they should have been better served by winning the championship. It was indignity for them to take the field in tatters as their owner went around Alexander Stadium handing out three-color, embossed business cards with Union Jack over a red, white, and blue football helmet.

On the surface, we seemed a dominant team; beneath it the Bulls seethed. That lack of sponsorship, which Frank nevertheless bandied with tireless theatrical resolve; the shunning of his jailed players; a management feud with another American, lineman and coach James Thornton—it all made for a foreboding cocktail to toast the new season.

But as the opening kickoff neared, everything deferred to the occasion. I personally hadn't seen such a festive atmosphere for a game of football since *John Goldfarb, Please Come Home*—one of the worst movies ever made but, it would turn out, an uncannily prescient epic about international gridiron—in which two expatriates help an emir's football team beat Notre Dame's Fighting Irish in the desert to win their way home to the States.

What we had at Alexander Stadium in this reprisal was James Thornton—who swore daily he wanted to be deported to America because of his unhappiness with the Bulls—as one expatriate, me the other, assisting him on the sideline, and Frank Kalili letter-perfect as emir, all joining forces against an authentic, if underwhelming Irish opponent.

The Bulls won the coin toss by calling, as loyal subjects, the queen's head, and everyone stood for the national anthems. The Irish version was scratchy, but acoustics proved kinder to "God Save the Queen." The anthem was as ceremonial as the game itself, accommodating the players' propensity for posing. After they stretched and strutted, Bulls defensive captain Colin "Diesel" Nash ran from the center of the field and hurled himself ritualistically over the top of our pregame huddle.

"United"—he shouted to an echoing by the Bulls—"we stand!" These were chemists and car painters and carpet installers, all with inherent hope gridiron might offer them something better someday, not cachet of playing a sport, but pay them for it. Posing was the only compensation at the moment—posing and a constant greeting they bestowed on one another as "champions."

"Divided"—concluded Diesel Nash, himself an electronics engineer—"we fall!" We hemmed and hawed and then, with skyward thrust of fists and stomping of cleated feet, came the coda of "Boooools! Booools! Boooools!" The British gridiron season was ready to begin.

As an assistant coach, I trained my attention on the Bulls special teams and our nosetackle, Andy Webb, whom I'd been assigned as position coach, and whom I exhorted to stay low charging across the line of scrimmage. Andy knew a thing or two about staying low in a stance; he'd once been Army of the Rhine heavyweight boxing champ. But his mobility on all fours was a matter of concern to the Bulls staff. When the ball was snapped he must have thought he was answering the bell for the first round, because invariably he stood straight up.

The special teams gave me more consternation yet, given the Brits' reluctance to join them. I gathered they might have had their fill of shock-combat during King Arthur's era and were not yet ready to resume it with the modern-day equivalent. Perhaps I might have gotten more enthusiasm calling them speciality teams, as in speciality teas.

Odd, their bashfulness, given how Britball's participants were innately theatrical, and not just participants on the pitch. The atmosphere that afternoon was charged throughout Alexander Stadium, with a huge electronic scoreboard that exhorted cheers and explicated the game for fans—even those who might be following the sport for a third or fourth season.

Public address duties got passed around, quarter to quarter, to the sport's pooh-bahs. One of them was a perpetually grinning and genial buffoon named Mick Luckhurst, who'd been among the few Brits to play in the NFL. He was a special guest of the National Division Management Association (NDMA), which governed Britball, and graced the P.A. with slightly inane comments gleaned from a game that once saw him kick a field goal during a bowl game in the United States without ever removing his warm-up suit.

In the grandstand sat a middle-aged expatriate from Philadelphia and former security man for Howard Hughes named Gerry Hartman, reputedly founder of the Bulls. Hartman was unemployed, and as befitted Bulls' mythology, liked to joke that he was on the dole when he founded the team. A crew cut and an aviator jacket were about the only things in the world he owned, along with his memories of the Bulls, poignant as they were. At his side, cheering without cease, was David Webb, a fleshy, flat-faced chap, and father of our star lineman. Before taking early retirement he'd been a superintendent with the West Midlands police, and now, looking for a new interest, he thought this gridiron might have a bloody fine future and he'd like to be a bigger part of it.

Fifty-seven players dressed out for the Bulls, or at least attempted to dress, since a dozen had to be returned to civilian clothes with Euro Bowl limitations on how many could kit for a game. James Thornton, as co-head coach, had delegated me a duty of giving rejection notices to unlucky ones. My duty was made easy by an outpouring of unfamiliar faces, faces I'd never seen before, not once at practice, until they turned up in uniform expecting, like a snap of the fingers, to play in a football game.

One of the rejections was a distinguished spoken man named Radcliffe Phillips, who volunteered as a backup quarterback and long-snapper on punts and field goals. Phillips I truly hated to turn away; the Bulls could have used him, not on the playing field, but on any contested rulings by the referee—he'd been a founder and commissioner of one of the first British gridiron leagues.

Of the players picked to stay in uniform . . . well, uniform wasn't quite the word: No two pairs of socks matched; sometimes one pair didn't match. Helmets were shared by up to three players, and pairs of shoulder pads got exchanged several times over during the game. A vigilant referee refused to let two of our linebackers into the contest because they weren't wearing hip pads; they didn't own hip pads, which made for more communal outfitting. A dozen variations of football pants and five different kinds, not to mention shades, of black jerseys were on display. Three players simultaneously wore number 59, one of them a shaven-headed 43-year-old, Son Tustin, trimmed from the Bulls' roster a year ago only to come back as one of football's oldest rookies (abetted by steroid consumption in an effort to get himself competitive). Frightful sight, the Bulls—right out of *The Omen,* a horror film in which Tustin, outfitted in rugby togs in his previous athletic highlight, had appeared dashing across the screen during the opening credits.

But dire circumstance might soon be a thing of the past, since several jerseys bore the boldly stenciled name of one of the country's largest Rolls-Royce dealerships. Had the salvation of sponsorship come about at last? A colorful full-page advertisement on the match program's back cover touted it, and in the locker room players got chirrupy at this anticipated good fortune. Having figured, given the Bulls' condition, I might have to buy into the team to help save it, I, too, grew jubilant. Flowery script trumpeted how the Bulls were "going places," our name twinned with the Rolls dealer's, connecting us to the yellow brick road of sponsorship.

Spirits projected to the pitch, too. Quickly, the Bulls got a couple of touchdown passes from Zark, grabbed a comfortable lead, and seemed en route to Euro Bowl. Conquest of the Continent lay ahead—yes, with sponsorship, ownership, and partisanship, we had everything going. Still, some of our deepest thoughts lay elsewhere. Middle linebacker Gary "Bush" James was one of many players to remember his incarcerated teammates—the three defensive backs stuck in Winson Green Prison—by dangling a waist towel scribbled: "Nos. 23, 32, 34—There [sic] Here."

Then there was Locksley "Animal" Roberts. He was one of four brothers who'd played for the Bulls, but due to indiscretions with the law, never played concurrently. Animal himself, given his canon of crime, was something of a surprise playing for us; having been recently questioned in connection with the murder of a police officer was the kind of thing that often kept him off the roster. He was detained overnight, because, as James Thornton would say, "He gave the cops some shit when they tried to question him, so they locked him up to let him cool off."

Now, with Animal returned to the lineup, from the opening whistle it was an auspicious outing for the Bulls, even better to my personal satisfaction for the Ragtime Rambo Big Every Time Posse—the nickname Animal had pinned on our kickoff team. It was a nickname undoubtedly arrived at one night after he drank a little too much champagne, his libation of choice, whether he was in training for football or not. Now, a trip to the Continent to look forward to, a former NFL quarterback leading us, an owner back in harmony with his boys, the Bulls might be inclined to pour out our nasty cocktail to join him in that champagne toast.

God
Save
the
Quarterback!

February

14

How strange was football's strange new world? Nobody else in
the history of sport had ever awakened on Valentine's Day in
Birmingham, England, to find himself swathed in purple passion
sheets, held hostage by an aging Don Ho impersonator. My first
glimpse, and scent, of Britball—the sheets were perfumed—and
it all went beyond my powers of ratiocination, way beyond
them.

I cast off the sheets and ambled into the drawing room, where
an old album was spinning on a turntable. My host smiled and
lit a cigarette with aplomb. "Now listen to this and tell me it's not
Don Ho singing Sinatra," he averred. "How about it, babe, eh?
Is that a voice for you, or what?"

Frank Kalili was vocalizing in stereo, accompanied by "the
best Polynesian band in Europe, bar none, son," his own easy-
listening, bubble-twisting group, the wonderful Waikikis.
"Never believe it's me, and not Sinatra, eh, babe?" he said, patting his chest—patting it a little too hard, because he provoked
an awful coughing spell.

Frank Kalili and the wonderful Waikikis. Yes, an apposite welcome to Britball. All stand for the anthem of "God Save the
Quarterback," or should sheet music be unavailable, a few im-

promptu stanzas of luau music. The band will not march at half-time, but may take requests.

Many innovations for gridiron would come from Frank's artistic touch; he would orchestrate it as he had Polynesian music on the Continent. The NFL's international offshoot was expected in Europe any day, and he saw himself at the front of the receiving line. With his milky, melancholy eyes, he had great vision for the game. No serving tea with time-outs, either. No, something of a more pecuniary nature.

One of his proudest possessions was a magazine clipping from America, headlined FANTASY FOOTBALL IN THE YEAR 2001, and he got ecstatic from skimming it: "The Miami Dolphins in the Super Bowl XXXVI against the Birmingham Bears. It'll happen, babe," he allowed with more chest puffery.

To land a franchise in the WLAF, the fine acronym for the new World League of American Football, he was competing with many others out to capture the same prize. But Frank knew he'd win it, and had a sizable head start on how he could out-American them, from a fondness for Tiparillos to making Aunt Jemima pancakes. From having knocked around the Pacific Northwest, he had usurped Jimmy Porter's credo in "Look Back in Anger," spoken, incidentally, in Brum's Bull Ring market, where Frank got his start as a peddler: "I must say, it's pretty dreary living in the American age . . . unless you're an American." By Jove, he was as American as one could get without citizenship papers.

He would outdress the others, too, having earned from a newspaper sobriquet "the Uncle Sam of Elan," for he had the finest owner's wardrobe in sporting quarters, light years, if not light shows away from Saville Row, his spiff entailing Nehru jackets and gooseberry green leisure suits.

His ownership on and off the field was equally impressive. He'd recently dismissed from the Bulls a middle linebacker who was purportedly gay and had shown him the back door even though he was not only a starter but also the team's surest tackler. "He's been coaching our youth team," Frank declared. "Doesn't look good, if you know what I mean."

Uh, one more thing, babe, his eyes hooding as he spoke: About those Bulls players who'd gotten themselves locked up, imprisoned on an assortment of charges—he had no choice but disavow them, at least until they were acquitted or paroled back into the lineup. Should the press inquire, he had rehearsed for months stating unequivocally how he threw them off the team upon learning that they committed their heinous crimes.

Now I was working with him—in management, in the front office, and as an assistant coach and player, too. Surely all this was my entitlement from a lifetime of loving gridiron. Polynesian music, I'd never much cared for.

But my appreciation for it grew, sitting at a magnificently anointed dining table, insisting on second and third helpings of paella graciously spooned onto my plate by a bejowled chap with wild and wildly lidded eyes who wore a gold pinkie ring embossed with a "$" insignia, and told me in a hybridized accent to save room for Spanish brandy. Frank Kalili, owner-entertainer-chef extraordinaire, at my service. Yes, and all on account of my wanting to be a football player again. Thanks to Frank, I was the newest addition to the Birmingham Bulls' front office, fairy tale and active roster.

As a sportswriter for more than 15 years, I'd become jaded by the predictable outcome of American football. The Bulls couldn't have been a better cure or opportunity to redress my jadedness. I first heard of them in a pressbox, flipping through a program before I covered an NFL game. I was idling time, trying to keep my face from falling asleep—a common affliction when assigned to a brand of football that's less sport than automation.

Often I daydreamed for a last chance at putting on a helmet, the playing field a felicitous world for me, and didn't care where I had to go to play. Soon it transmuted into wanderlust. Birmingham, namesake of my own hometown in Alabama, where not only was football a religion, but where I'd never gotten my fill of plenary indulgences, having begun playing there as a boy like everyone else, but unlike anyone I knew, as a tackling dummy for a future Heisman Trophy winner, before making a linear progression from one end of the bench to the other. Yes, Birmingham obviously was the place for me to be reborn as a football player.

I was on the telephone to Frank the next day, hatching what I wanted to pursue and do. "You're joking," he said at first, with a phlegmy laugh. But he gradually warmed to the idea—not only for enlisting a food tester and wine taster—but deduced it as possible entrée with the NFL.

There was no curtailing his enthusiasm as he began relaying the Bulls' season with marvelously narrative phone calls; imagine a bibulous Richard Burton giving an account of birdwatching from in front of a pigeon coop.

"Hell-ooooo, babe," he'd begin, then exhale, await transatlantic feedback, then pause a little longer for sublime effect. "Well . . . touchdown last play of the game . . . we've done it again, 29–27." With Frank Kalili, I was at a fountainhead of vicariousness. Week after week, one victory after another, his reports came across, sonorous syllables all, until the Bulls became British champions.

What would I encounter on the pitch when I got across to join him, and the Bulls? Britons had leapt into the game, into that global diaspora of gridiron, early on, not only with zeal but with the nearest approximate pronunciation of playing positions. Say, as opposed to introducing the sport in Nairobi, they weren't totally unfamiliar with armor. And they also were a country clinging to yards as measure, even if for football they seemingly could count only as high as 90 of them. Yes, this British version looked altogether attractive to a man of my sensibilities.

What first caught my eye in the article inside the NFL program was a staged photo of a British player as he dashed onto the pitch past a rather nonchalant bobby. As it turned out, he couldn't have been a member of the Birmingham Bulls, or that bobby in all likelihood would have been handcuffing him, or, as it also turned out, handcuffing somebody much higher up in the organization.

There was, in fact, something a little strange about our owner. Not until I saw his picture on an old album cover, in a floral shirt with a lei spangling his neck, did I learn he had gone by the name

Frank Kalili. On his innumerable phone calls to me in the States, he'd always introduced himself as a Mr. Frank Leadon.

He possessed other names, too, depending on which of the proper authorities was asked. The most colorful came from a global hunger relief benefit for which he'd printed up and sold T-shirts: He became, to Bulls players and others surrounding the team, Feed-the-World-Frank.

I was perfectly willing to testify Frank Kalili-Leadon did a great gustatory job feeding me from the moment we met. "Most of the Indian restaurants in this country are crap," he said in the Americanese he was so good at. "Just crap. They make me want to puke. That's because they hire the Bangladeshis to cook for them. Bangladeshis are peasants. Here, have some of mine," he said, handing over a sumptuous plate of korma, a creamy coconut and cashew dish. "That's the real Indian cuisine, son." And after he'd thrown together a platter of rigona al jerez, a Spanish dish of kidneys in cream sherry, he would provide the evening's entertainment by playing his old records for you.

Usually, you didn't even have to ask.

Social hour never expired at Frank's house. "Scrumpy," he'd explain, serving an aperitif. "My father used to say, drink enough of that stuff, lose the key to your asshole. Now black velvet, a beautiful drink, ah, just beautiful."

Scrumpy was fermented cider, black velvet champagne and Guinness. But the Spanish brandy that always followed: pacharan, it was called, distilled from Catalonian blueberries. Frank kept a private stock, and be you deemed in his good graces, or instrumental to his football team, he'd break it out.

After one of those fabulous curry dinners he enunciated my first duties as Bulls general manager. "We'll dispatch you to Majorca for more pacharan, babe," he said. "You can never have enough of it in the liquor cabinet, so bring back as much as you can get through customs."

He contrailed cigarette smoke from a Silk Cut. "Of course, you'll have to pay for your own trip."

Normally, I wasn't much of a drinking man. Normally was long gone, for normally I wasn't three thousand miles from home benevolently incarcerated by an aging Don Ho impersonator. I tried to go by the maxim of eat, drink, and don't be the least chary—seriously decanting pacharan all the while. But the pacharan was dwindling, and I got a feeling that much, much more of this enchanting captivity lay ahead. I was the general manager who came to dinner . . . and couldn't leave.

February

15

Gridiron couldn't quite be called a cultural reciprocation for the Beatles. Still, the Brits—except at catching passes, which was as alien as carrying a burden atop their heads—had long enjoyed a feel for the game. Especially in what had become Birmingham. A millennium ago Brum was the Forest of Arden and host to the shock-combat tournaments by King Arthur's Knights of the Roundtable—and what was this new foofaraw but bipedal jousting? Okay, so maybe they didn't have chinstraps.

That it had ever diverged from rugby seemed a twentieth-century concession to the plastics industry. The "cocoon" was how Jess Rodgers lampooned a football uniform; skin and bone were plenty sufficient in British sports. Jess, a linebacker, was the most veteran of the Birmingham Bulls. He had gotten in on the game from the start, when the Royal Navy's Faslane nuclear sub base, where he was stationed, accepted a sporting offer from some American sailors at another sub base in Scotland. They'd play rugby, then for the second half have a go at this American football. Townsfolk who saw the teams emerge after halftime from the dressing room fully kitted probably took one look and figured there'd been a nuclear leak nearby.

· · ·

9

More than a decade later came the Bulls. By then Jess's excitement threshold was running high. He had gone from playing wing forward on the Royal Navy's rugby side to a stint in military intelligence in Northern Ireland then into the Special Air Services. What brought him back to gridiron was possibly ego-dependency, because he could recall the stares, the fascinated looks on British faces, how those posers at this game got ogled like no other athletes, what with their futuristic garb.

Native games—soccer, rugby, and cricket—had gone unchanged for centuries; now the port of sporting entry was open for something new. That Americanization of the country started it. The weekly TV highlight show from the NFL nurtured it. The thousands of available players—young men out of work and, in the Thatcherite immobilization of a work force, looking for something to do with their lives, with their aggression—fed it further. And when sociologists got around to analyzing why gridiron went abroad, they might see it as an underlying metaphor for the British Isles, 22 men crammed together on what was called the line of scrimmage.

Gridiron's allure ranged from athletes eager to test their skills and hostility quotient, because clearly this wasn't a contest for curtsying, to others who'd never before played a sport, given how there wasn't much demand for 300-pound soccer goalies. Novelty, narcissism, and something to do on Sunday afternoons, and what with that growing aggro of Thatcher's masses, it found the right social climate, for there were a lot of able-bodied young men throughout the country to whom mayhem with impunity appealed. Maybe its physicality seemed a strange pursuit for the British, given how George Orwell once denigrated physiques and braggadocio of his countrymen—how'd he put it—"pansified"? Not anymore—not with the homicidal tackling, and with those 22 men doing their damnedest to level each other every time the ball got snapped.

It had begun in a clubby way. Groups gathered in greenswards tossed around an actual oblate spheroid when they could find one, or a rugby football if they couldn't, and spoke of playing the exotic-sounding positions they'd heard on the telly—quarterback or strong safety, or outside linebacker.

Hundreds of teams, thousands of players had taken it up from throughout the most remote of those isles: More than a craze, it was a movement called, in British delectation of consonants, gridiron. Teams originated on rugby pitches, infields of race-courses, or bicycle tracks and, in the case of one London team, something called Flower Pot Fields.

Teams came from junior rugby clubs, from pubs, from police forces. They liked to say about themselves things like, "We were formed the week of Super Bowl XX." They carried over terms: equipment was kit; cleats, boots; running backs didn't gain yard-age, they plopped it up. But nothing so British as nicknames of the teams: the Horsham Predators, the Poole Sharks, the Staines Removers (later to become the Euston Oilers), the Ayr Burners, Black Country Nailers, Buckley Hangmen, Cheshire Cats, Edinburgh Emperors, and Ness Monsters were but a few.

Polyglot, it was, too. One team, the Slough Silverbacks, boasted Iranian, Japanese, and Maori running backs. The Silverbacks had been the 43-year-old Son Tustin's first team; Son came to it after almost three decades of rugby, and from his age and some of his contemporaries', they could just as well have been called the Slough Silverhairs.

Pat Roach was another who could have played for them under that name. Frank Kalili entreated his friend Roach to join the Birmingham Bulls, to play his first sport since he quit pro wrestling for acting. In the movie *Raiders of the Lost Ark* he played the Giant Sherpa who confronts Indiana Jones in the Cairo markets. The scene, as with his play in the defensive line for the Bulls, was pure improv. He never managed anything so dramatic on the football field, but did garner good early publicity for the team, though all of the stories made one rather significant omission: Pat Roach didn't take up gridiron until past his 58th birthday.

Even if they had the externals down and an outpouring of men to play it, a lot went beyond the British ken. The melding of wild emotion and organization was a tough enough undertaking. The

Brits were all lathered over this peculiarly American sport, with its bombast and complicated strategy, the endless stops and starts as opposed to the seamlessness of rugby and soccer—games that carried on for 90 minutes, almost straight off the clockface. How different it became once incomplete passes and out-of-bounds plays entered the sporting vocabulary. For gridiron, spectators cawed, you didn't pay admission, you rented it.

Teams from the largest cities, with expatriate communities of Americans, fared best at the outset. The London Ravens, who in 1984 had played the Norwich Spartans and defeated them 48–0 in the first game between British teams, went five years without losing a game and their first three years without getting scored upon. (The first touchdown against them, pushed across by the Birmingham Bulls, was cause for celebration: In the Bulls' official team history, a bold notation read: "Down 61–6 against the Ravens, and the chanting was getting louder and louder, but from Bulls' fans, not Ravens'. ")

Naturally the game had growing pains, teams always in flux and looking to America for inspiration, not to mention largess. After an overture to Baylor University of Texas, one British team was rewarded with a care package of jerseys and shoulder pads, and thus did the Gloucester Boars become the Cotswold Bears in deference to their benefactor's nickname. An Irish team called the Carrickfergus Cowboys wore a uniform of Harvard helmets, Yale pants, and Princeton jerseys. Another team, the Thames Barriers, lacking for equipment, scraped up money for a television advertisement and then took in enough donations from it to last a season. A rival team, the Thames Valley Chargers, having learned the coach of the San Diego Chargers, Al Saunders, was born in London, cajoled him into used equipment and old uniforms from the NFL team. The Vestavia Hills High School state championship team from Birmingham, Alabama, sent red neckrolls to the Birmingham, England, Bulls.

In the early days a team called the Heathrow Jets decided to go cost-effective with their gear. Luckily, the Jets survived the utilitarian misdirection—and without serious injury—after they played several games with face masks affixed to motorcycle helmets. Exaggerated prices for football garb meant many teams went two years or longer before kitting, and players got frustrated at the wait. Kit, which authenticated the posing, was everything to them, and some of the best athletes at gridiron gave up when patience wore thin at not getting it.

Player nicknames were another prerequisite for playing. The British knew all about the Refrigerator, the Chicago Bears' William Perry, and the cachet his monicker had given him. So flip open the London Ravens game program and what jumped off the page was the likes of Jude "the Baptist" Ugwuegbulam; Jona "Copy" Carbon; Ian "Mr. Moto" U-Chong; Merek "Greystoke" Raczynski, and Paul "Spearchucker" Johnson. Even the coaching staff insisted on them: Ravens top assistant was Llew "Emperor Ming" Gittens. Then there were those with no need of them, such as Joe St. Louis, who still insisted on Joe "Dangerous Hombre" St. Louis—though from how he ran the football, it more accurately would have been Joe "Meet Me on the Sideline" St. Louis.

The Cardiff Tigers took a more secretive approach; number 57 on their roster, perhaps typifying the ilk of early players, was listed simply as "Aka." Nothing conclusive, but according to his former head coach, he was believed to be a fugitive Iranian linebacker. And what to make of the Brighton B-52 Bombers, who boasted players with jerseys emblazoned by numbers 2A, 46A, and 60A?

At community functions, street fairs, Rotary Club meetings, these players of gridiron were much in demand. One of the Bulls, a running back named Desi Taylor, signed 500 autographs at a team appreciation day at a supermarket. It may have taken decades to master the game, but the players quickly mastered gridiron comportment. Wristbands, two or three to a wrist; neckrolls; lampblack applied meticulously to the eyes all added up to a Charles Dickens-cum-Arthur Koestler look. As aesthetics went, another Irish team sported "No Smoking" logos on its helmets. Cheerleading squads, which did not exist in other sports, were formed, though cynics cruelly appraised that British women had the ankles to absorb the catapulting.

The Brits also brought to the game their own ideas, and innovative some of them were: The losing team would come to the sideline at the end of a game to cheer opposing fans; free hotel rooms for referees who would agree to travel to the Isle of Man and work games there; or, as a Leicester Panthers director suggested, the game might generate more enthusiasm if teams changed uniform colors every other year.

The game had no aristocracy; Frank Kalili's climb from 52-year-old waterboy to dispensing a team payroll typified it. Save for the orbital cost of kit, it was a commoner's game, particularly in purported ownership of teams. A Don Ho impersonator wasn't unusual in this sporting realm. The former proprietor of a British hot dog stand now owned the team with the highest payroll in the country. Several teams were owned by comedians; a stuntman in low-budget British films was another owner, as was a dustman who headed a team gaudily called the Washington Presidents.

Britball: It was George Halas meets George Orwell. But above the logistics and, later, the machinations, it was showing up to play—often showing up the day of the game, with nothing else but their presence to recommend them. Until the first American coaches arrived, preparation might consist of coming onto the pitch with a cigarette in one hand, pint of lager in the other. "They knew nothing about calisthenics, the mentality was who needs it?" an Ivy League coach recalled. "It was, let's all muck about. But did they love putting on a uniform!"

Players gravitated to the game from every corner of the country, from every walk, or style, of life: Twin safeties for a team in the Midlands were brothers, though not twins; one of them a hairstylist, the other fresh from having won something called the Mr. Supercool male modeling contest. Clive Loftman of the Bulls had just started a job as stage technician at the Birmingham Repertory Theatre when he got insight into the game from an American actor who was touring a play. As they talked the sport one night after a performance, suddenly the actor asked, "How about if I suck your cock?" Clive wasn't sure about gridiron for a while after that.

Teams boasted clergymen on their rosters—not to pray for them but to play for them. One shoulder-padded padre was an Anglican priest, the Reverend John Hardaker. The kicker-ecumenist had strong feelings about football: He "believe[d] converting an extra point as important as converting an atheist." Asked by a sportswriter how he justified getting out of priestly vestments on a Sunday and into kit, he declared: "I've come to the conclusion that if Jesus had played sports, he would have played this game. That may sound odd but when you think about it, it is a very Christian game. It's very much about teamwork."

And with soccer hampered by hooliganism and rugby sinking in popularity since the last war, the time for gridiron seemed ripe. So it began, with a vengeance and proliferation. Newspapers carried public service announcements for teams seeking players, ran stories to fit the gridiron stereotype—of behemoths and brutality—though, thankfully, you could leave it to tabloids to get it right. The *Sunday Sport* ran pictures of the West London Aces alongside topless women in satiny football pants. In one photo players cradled a woman as if she were a perfectly delivered touchdown pass, and no doubt Britball was enhanced by descriptions of the Aces as "hunky iron-hard." The crux of the game, as explained by one of the *Sport*'s "stunnas," was: "Some of them try to catch the speeding ball before the whole of the other side knocks him over and jumps on him. The coach then calls time-out, and they trot off the field and stand in a circle talking about which cheerleaders they would like to score with."

The Birmingham Bulls didn't have that concern; our cheerleading squad had been disbanded two years earlier after one of its members got in the family way via, she claimed, one of the team's coaches.

At the vanguard of the game, the Bulls were a group of workday lads, when they had work, which once had been exceedingly rare. Now a fair number of them had jobs, but how many were within the legal limits was uncertain. Minority players largely comprised the team, many of them saddled with form, which was British for criminal record. Thus the violence they brought to gridiron was ingrained. Yes, the Bulls came with their own perception of the sport: "Break somebody's arm without going to jail for it, ain't that the idea, mate?" one of them, Animal Roberts, said almost gleefully.

February

17

The Bulls' owner was more a pacifist—or given his former profession, Pacificist. His players called him in Midlands coinage "a star, a case," and that was irrespective of a career in pseudo-outrigger canoes across the Continent. "They say oysters are an aphrodisiac," Frank Kalili cracked. "Not true: I had a dozen last night, only six worked." He was a titan among talkers; paragonish host, a presence. Probably it started as a boy in India, where, in Jean Renoir's film, *The River,* he'd been half-caste as an extra. He'd drop the name of a famous rock star to his dinner guests. "The singer, babe? Beauuuu-tiful girl. For two weeks we had a torrid affair."

Now, owner of a gridiron team, director of the European Football League, self-styled American, he was jollity's boy. His nicotine-stained teeth would configure into a big smile, and in an alcove of the drawing room a chipped ceramic Buddha grinned back. So did a 14-carat, gold-plated Oscar statuette and a fertility goddess, among gewgaws in a tastefully arranged room whose centerpiece was the Budweiser Bowl trophy, symbolic of supremacy in Britball.

But Frank Kalili was, for all his charm, a disciplinarian. The 250-pound fullback, Steve Harvey, who'd defected the year before to a rival team, was hoping to rejoin the Bulls. He had made overtures in the off-season only to be rebuffed. Now before training camp came a last plea. "But you're a terrible person, Stevie," Frank told him over the telephone. "The team's scared of you. You run bloody wild out there, threatening to punch people out. I've heard about the javelin thing, too. I won't have you back with the Bulls. No, won't do." Frank Kalili wouldn't be bullied, not even by Steve Harvey, who happened to be ingesting large doses of steroids and could be prone to illogical behavior.

Frank's voice trembled with staunchness as he hung up. "He's done ten years in prison and you can't control him," he whispered, syllables interspersed with gulps for getting his breath. "Just cannot control him. . . . Beat up the directors of the team he played for last year when they wouldn't pay him. One threw a javelin at him, but it didn't stop him. Won't have that with the Bulls."

Authoritative when warranted, Frank, but congenial as they come. He shared his postprandial brandy, culinary talents, wealth of expertise on football, and the luxuriously smoky, smelly confines of his house. So acquainted did I become with those confines, a stucco abode on a sloping corner of a suburban street called Yew Tree Close, I got to know every square foot of it. Good thing, too, since it turned out to be nothing less than the front office, training table, and training camp for the Birmingham Bulls.

Neither his daughter, Debbie-Jean (a former Bulls cheerleader), nor his spouse, Sue, who came off as a modern-day Good Wife of Bath, was impressed by the sport or his stories about it. But if he was on song, as the lovely British expression goes, it made for sheer listening pleasure. "When the Bulls won Bud Bowl last year, just as the final gun was going off for time, the Concorde flew over the stadium and dipped its wings," he said. "Purrrrfect, babe. 'How'd you manage that, Frankie?' everybody wanted to know. Heh-heh." And it was worth remembering, as has been stated: "His remininescences are not meant to be edited, but enjoyed."

Frank fancied himself quick with a quip, and his favorite re-

frain, "True quote," came when he thought he'd spoken something epigramatic about Britball, which got reprinted verbatim in
the newspapers. The first of them for the upcoming season had
just been voiced to a sportswriter, expressing Frank's great dissatisfaction with the schedule handed the Bulls. "Write it like this,"
he emoted. " 'You're forever asking my boys to climb mountains,
but why's it always got to be Everest?' True quote, just like I said
it, babe."

He lived for Thursdays, when the latest edition of a tabloid
called *First Down* came off the press, to see how many times his
name got into print. *First Down*'s literate headlines would read:
GASTY-NO! about former New York Jets' star Mark Gastineau giving up football for his bosomy main squeeze, or SCHRAMMBO MUS-
CLES IN! about an executive with the Dallas Cowboys selling his
interest in the team. Next to these stories, readers would be
treated to a weekly paean to someone known as "the Wily Midlands Fox." It took little imagination to twig Wily Midlands Fox
was yet another appellation for Frank Kalili, himself.

Frank Kalili-Leadon: Not enough that he had given, as he put it,
his "good name[s]" to his football team, he had, he reiterated a
half-dozen times daily, even mortgaged his home for it. Not once
mortgaging it, but twice. He could be overheard on the phone
enumerating like an abacus run amok the personal debt he had
incurred for the Bulls.

How he incurred it he never stated, the specifics amiss but
unimportant, for Frank was a gridiron pioneer, as one of his
clippings called him, not a bookkeeper. "Don't know why I do
it anymore, I really don't need football," he'd say with a wave of
his cigarette. "I could get by without it, or start a new league in
Spain. Could do." If in his weaker moments he resented the
pressure the game put on him, he vowed not to succumb. "Everybody always wants to put a pound of rock up your ass," he would
say, acquitting himself by serving up the thickest lamb chops I'd
ever seen.

Once, he did painfully reveal how his partner in ownership of
the Bulls, a government tax agent, had taken a lengthy, costly trip

to the Caribbean; meanwhile the partner defended himself by allowing how his sister owned a hotel in Jamaica and "I could stay there all year if I liked."

Another problem with a game so young as Britball, Frank declared: too many charlatans, and more drawn to it every day. Frank himself didn't command a salary with the Bulls, another daily reiteration; he just owned, promoted, and true-quoted the team. Since he got nothing from the game but lighter pockets and a possible loss of the roof over his head, why should anyone else make money from it?

I got to know this spiel by heart, and surrounded by such selflessness, ensnarled in its smoke, quickly conduced to it. So when Frank informed me the £50 weekly paycheck I'd been expecting from the Bulls couldn't be issued in the foreseeable future because we were so financially strapped, I gave a shrug of companionable munificence.

Hey, babe. We'd get by.

February

18

Frank's modus operandi from the very first at gridiron was getting by, but by any calculation, getting by with style. As at an international match at Alexander Stadium—Britain versus Holland. The stadium's record player fritzed after the playing of the Dutch national anthem, which, no stirring British refrain forthcoming, likely would mean a swoon in the home side's spirit. But Frank dashed into the pressbox, instinctively seized the microphone, and in patriotic a cappella, belted "God save our gracious queen, God save our noble queen."

"Everybody forgot about the game and looked up at the box," a Bulls player named Davey Parkes would recall. "They could tell right off it was Frank, you know, because he was coughing before he got started singing."

Yes, babe, we'd get by.

"And let's hope nothing gets out in the press about the three boys in the nick," Frank said. "You know, prison. That would sink our sponsorship deal for sure."

As he aired notes of precaution about the Bulls, I had some of my own. Save for that grotesquely beautiful faux-bronze trophy in his drawing room, it got difficult to remember that he owned a British gridiron team or had anything to do with one besides

serve it as a human megaphone. Evidence, say an actual football
or two, didn't seem to be in supply.

As swell a stay as I was having at his house, a couple of
questions began to override everything but the aroma of saffron
curry from his kitchen. Had the Bulls ever existed anywhere but
in his fertile imagination?

There once had been a slashing Chinese halfback from a small
polytechnic in Maine, Johnny Chung, who'd run for a slew of
touchdowns—had run and run, till his creator gave up the ruse.
Johnny Chung had done his running only in Saturday afternoon
phone calls placed to the sports department of *The New York Times.*
Had not my knowledge of the Bulls begun with a spate of melo-
dious transatlantic telephone calls to another newspaper sports
department? Could I, as a sportswriter, have fallen for the old
pseudo-Polynesian owner trick? What was to say Frank Kalili
hadn't made me a prisoner, albeit a happy prisoner, of his deceit?

I found myself turning sedentary, not what I had in mind when
I signed on with the Bulls. Through a triptych window in the
drawing room, I watched English ladies push prams along Yew
Tree Close and envied them their exertion . . . until my host
announced the latest batch of fresh, buttered scones were ready.
But what was he serving up with the Bulls? The season was but
a month away, but Frank kept insisting that management sit
tight. If we sat any tighter, steatopygia was likely to set in.

I began to wonder hard at my predicament. The Bulls, if there
was such a team, seemed in stasis. Only sign of reality I'd seen
was a yellowed envelope postmarked Sarasota, Florida, that lay
on Frank's dining-room table until he chucked it to put down a
clean tablecloth. The letter inside sought payment of a fee to a
sports agent who last season had sent a player-coach to the Bulls.
Frank broke into a guffaw when asked about it; the sports agent
was a septuagenarian named Sam Ketchman who ran a football
placement agency out of his kitchen, nobody to be taken seriously. Especially not by a former Don Ho impersonator who
owned a football team from his foyer in Birmingham, England.
"Ah, babe, old Sam and his clackety typewriter," he laughed,
holding up the letter. "See here," he said, showing off the enve-

lope, "how the capital letters jump? Hah! You think I'm going to pay any attention to somebody doesn't even have a decent type-writer?"

If having a decent typewriter that boasted a properly aligned carriage was the key to getting Frank Kalili's attention, at No. 10 Yew Tree Close, credibility was about to come through the front door.

February

20

The Bulls' minority owner, a Jamaican emigre named Denton Thomas, spoke in what throughout the Midlands was called a whinge. Denton's was a superior whinge, nervous and hasty; vowels playing bumper cars with syllables. He pronounced the name of the Bulls' new general manager in an appropriate and endearing way: Steve Bizarre-kivich.

He had been the first quarterback taken in the 1977 NFL draft, a first-round choice by his hometown team in St. Louis, and then began a sporting odyssey. "Win some, lose some, and some get rained out," this man with the topographical-map nose said upon the latest impromptu stop on his world tour of gridiron. "But," he smiled crookedly, "you got to dress out for all of 'em." And without question he had dressed out as often as was humanly possible, had put on more pairs of shoulder pads than any player in history: three professional leagues and seven teams throughout North America, now four more teams and three leagues in the eighteen months he'd spent in Britain.

He also happened to be my new boss, having supplanted me as Bulls' general manager before I even got the chance to find out what kind of coin gets flipped at a Britball game—as if the Bulls had a spare one lying around to flip in the first place.

"Zark," Frank Kalili declared from the foyer in the official announcement, "more fits our needs."

Despite a life in football, he arrived in Great Britain from the streets of the Magic Kingdom, from Disney World, where he was driving a limousine. Before that he was also delivery boy, beer truck jockey, and health club instructor. Then came the offer to play more football. He had spent two years in Wales before turning up in Brum with a flimsy suitcase, flimsier shoulder pads, solid portable typewriter, and a petrifying fear of a fiery Indian spice called vindaloo. "Somebody slipped me one once and I shit for five days," he said at Frank's dinner table, refusing curried chicken. "That hot shit ain't for me, man."

I tried to be ticked off over having been usurped as GM. But given the only skill I'd brought to the job was typing, and how the new chap obviously could make hay with the home keys, too, I had no squawk. "Nothing personal," Frank Kalili assuaged, "but Zark is a name people know. We're very lucky to have him, babe. I see big possibilities here with him, er, for him."

With one's palate won over, by Frank's reckoning, the rest of a person would follow. For me, slaveringly so. As for Zark, vindaloo made him reticent, but Frank knew what it would take if his cooking wouldn't do the trick. Feed-the-World-Frank fed Zark the future. And given where he'd been, it wasn't unkind to say that future was just another word for nothing left to lose.

For hours at a time, with Frank's little Yorkshire terriers in their laps, they conferred in the drawing room, lifting the roof with expectations about Britball. Or, if they sat up into the night, lifting it with their concordant snoring.

"British football's a happening thaaaang, man," Zark stated first day on the job. "Yeah," he reiterated in his nasal midwestern twang, "a happening thaaaang." To entice him, Frank offered 10 percent of his own limited company, FLA, acronymn for Frank Leadon Associates, which had been formed a year earlier to save the Bulls from oblivion. Within hours the new GM (and acting head coach as well as emergency quarterback) had agreed to the terms—everything settled in the 11-page contract that Zark, impressively, had typed up himself.

.   .   .

As the Bulls owner saw it, the day-to-day, or hand-to-mouth operation of the team would fall to Zark, to develop and invest with everything he'd brought with him from the NFL, USFL, and CFL, not to mention Disney World. Zark may have known better than to get comfortable. He'd had more than his share of disappointments. In St. Louis, a new head coach refused to play him even in exhibition games, telling a newspaper he knew Zark's capabilities on the football field just from looking at him in street clothes. And the coach's look, make no doubt, was a look of scorn. Then, during the players' strike in 1987, his agent called every NFL team—all 28, many of them desperate, signing semi-pro quarterbacks and 40-year-olds long out of football, and he wasn't even offered a tryout.

His British experience hadn't been very pleasant, either. His latest team, the Cardiff Tigers, had refused a promotion into the stiffer Budweiser League, in which the Bulls played. The team had met, announced themselves overwhelmingly against it, and voted to disband. Zark, who had built the team from scratch, and chiefly through what was left of his passing arm, was once more a nomad.

But jaded wasn't his nature; in spite of everything, he could still screw his blank, blemished face into a smile. Frank cottoned to him right away, and assured him how together they would further the sport. "Ah, Stevie, to the future," he said in the drawing room, handing him another pint of Tennant's Extra lager. "Who knows where we'll go. Here, take a good look at this." Frank produced a page sheared from a Spanish newspaper and full of gridiron coverage. "That's the long range, Stevie," he said. "Spain—no place like it. Stick with me, babe, we'll go places there."

I wasn't about to disagree. Having enjoyed his lovingly concocted paella, which had taken all day to prepare, I knew if gridiron was a failure for them in Spain, he and Zark, who held a college degree in food service and lodging, could always open a tapas bar. But for now, Steve Pisarkiewicz, at 35 years old, clung to his jockstrap and coaching clipboard. And, tenaciously, with strong fingers for the home keys, his portable typewriter. Surely, there was still a place somewhere in the sport for a man of his unique background. His résumé, self-typed, of course, read:

Since becoming a first-round draft pick of the St. Louis Cardinals in 1977, I've built an 8 year career from backing up some of the most prominent quarterbacks in the game today. We all strive for opportunity in the world of professional sports, and determination is the common key. My qualifications and confidence are at a career peak, as I am eager to contribute to your program.

But what Zark could most contribute, and a giant contribution it was as Frank Kalili saw it, was his name. Just be careful about the pronunciation of it. As for the Birmingham Bulls, we were about to be pronounced gravely ill.

February

22

Maybe to the naked eye we resembled a football team. As accoutrement went, no team was better equipped. But it was difficult to tell if we were kitted for football or our owner-choreographer's stagings: After each game, win or lose, we performed a "Bullrush" to the sideline. Further along that theme, bullfight music blared at home games, and Frank Kalili once considered staging an actual corrida on the field, to stoke the crowd. "I know a woman bullfighter named Betty who was a close friend of Ava Gardner's, babe," he said. "Bet I could've gotten her."

"Bullfighting," Zark assayed in the drawing room while Frank showed it on videotape. "Not exactly a sport where you can afford to go 0-and-1, is it?" I tried not to laugh too hard, for in my euphoric wheezing within No. 10 Yew Tree, all the smoke and dustiness, I'd sucked on asthma inhalers until my ribs hurt.

Now the oxygen supply dwindled with the bunking in, or flooring in, of another Yank, of whom as many as three more might be en route. White the ever-growing crowd played to my asthma inhaler fetish, eventually Frank put a halt to my happy housebound status by expanding my duties as assistant GM.

Till then they encompassed tea kettles and cozy placement. Now he dispatched me to London to fetch the newest Bulls import. "This one, can you believe it, has paid his own way," I thought I overheard him remark on the phone.

"Who's paying his own way, Frank?" I asked later.

"No, heh-heh, babe, you misunderstood. What I said was, 'This one's going to go a long way.'"

The newcomer, Bobby Shoop, was variously referred to within No. 10 as Shawp and Shop and Shope. The walls so reverberated with stretched vowels one could be forgiven for thinking he'd walked into a synthesizer testing studio.

Robert Shoop III: Dyed-in-the-tweed Yalie, football star, he'd also been captain of the school's baseball team, as had George Bush exactly 40 years earlier. Fresh from college he was on the backroads of New England as a disposable diaper salesman, only to find it unfulfilling and realize how badly he wanted to play football again. He pegged Britain the place and began entreating Frank Kalili to join the Bulls. Eventually Frank came around, and let the press in on having discovered Shoop, whose attributes as a receiver were excellent. One in particular stood out. "I'm willing to play for almost nothing," the Yalie told him, and within a few days, Bobby Shoop's signing was announced.

He was a sweet-dispositioned, impressionable young man who had led a sheltered life behind the neo-Gothic walls in New Haven. His trip from London to Brum was his first time ever riding the rails. He'd never drunk wine before sitting down to Frank's dinner table, nor enjoyed a cuppa, coffee or tea. He didn't have to shave, unless practicing. He exuded enthusiasm from the start. Whenever it rained in Brum, he couldn't wait to go out into the street on Yew Tree Close and pass the football around with Steve Pisarkiewicz. "When it's wet is really the best time to learn to catch the ball, man!" he gushed. "My brothers and I used to get spanked by my dad because we would always go out and play in the rain."

He was preternaturally likable, the kind of kid who seeks out people to open the door for. When he got hurt once, the star quarterback at Yale, who happened to be his best friend, tried to take the field next game wearing his jersey, number 17.

He also was Ivy League from every angle: At one of the Bulls' first practices, he almost kicked a player off the team for wearing blue socks with his football boots. "I told him there's no place for him out there," he said emphatically, "till he comes back with some white socks."

Only reason Bob Shoop couldn't have been Frank Merriwell at Yale was because he was too spindly. Beloved on campus, too, and the school's longtime football coach, Carm Cozza, promised him a coaching job if he got good experience abroad. Carm Cozza, of course, couldn't have predicted Yale's School of Psychiatric Medicine might be interested, too, given the experiences Bobby Shoop was soon to encounter with the Bulls. Frank Kalili, meanwhile, instantly made plans to utilize his Ivy League education: He put him to work at his sporting goods shop, Great American Sports, behind the counter.

Soon a grudging impatience came over Shoop, fed by a dislike of where he was and what was happening, or not happening with his new football team. He became bored, sequestered inside the owner's house; he loathed Frank's smoking; the little dogs annoyed him; he didn't care for the constant offerings of Indian food, and pined for a McDonald's menu. He sat around the house, his hands continuously clutching a football, his politesse tested. He wasn't outwardly impressed with the Bulls' organization, namely because there wasn't much outward about it. In frustration he would kick an inflatable jukebox in the drawing room, or curse the Yorkies.

He began to worry seriously when he realized how his gig with the Bulls might lead to foreign diplomacy problems. Playing baseball for Yale, he had toured the Far East and thus knew a bit about passports and immigration. Since landing abroad he'd noted he could not coax from Frank an application for working papers, required for Americans who played gridiron in Great Britain.

"Don't go worrying, son," Frank said with characteristic caginess in his voice. "We'll parcel you to one of Europe's sin capitals for a few days, and you can get your passport renewed when you come back through customs."

"Oh. OK."

But what about a playing contract with the Bulls? He hadn't seen one of those yet, either. Nor had I, for that matter. Unless you typed it yourself, the team, it seemed, operated on the premise that if a contract's as good as the paper it's printed on, then a verbal agreement from Frank Kalili must be better. The most binding thing about it was, "Come and get it, babe."

Not that Frank meant to manipulate us, force our schedule to revolve around his own; just that he had other priorities, like making sure the Americans were culturally attuned. One morning, he spent an hour rummaging through a secondhand record stall at the Bull Ring Market. The tips of his fingers were blackened from flipping through old album covers. "Ah, here it is—come have a look, lads," he said when he found what he'd been looking for. "See any familiar names on the back here?" He patted his chest again, lightly. "See? Arranger and vocals: yours truly, Frank Leadon . . . er, Kalili."

"No fucking way!" Bobby Shoop imploded, throwing his voice in the opposite direction from Frank.

"What'd Bobby say?" Frank asked.

"He said, 'Isn't that just great?' " I translated.

"Why, thank you, lad." He transmitted a big smile.

This constituted the last appreciation he'd be getting anytime soon from the Bulls or their immediate kin, especially American cousins. Bobby Shoop had been thrilled to come to England. But not for the first time, an American abroad began the refrain "I'm going home."

Beset by his darkening mood, he telephoned his father back home in Pittsburgh, only to get a cryptic word of encouragement: "Remember, son, when Art Rooney started out in football he was no choirboy himself." Art Rooney, late owner of the Pittsburgh Steelers, was no waterboy-cum-retired Don Ho impersonator, either. Zark also spoke up on his partner's behalf. "Good thing Frank ain't like these other NDMA bastards," he allowed of

31

Britball's guiding hands. "It's everything for themselves, and nothing for the good of the game," he said. "They'll stab you in the back, cut your damned balls off, grab whatever they can, and do nothing for the good of the game. Whole thing's ego and for themselves. Hey, man, Frank cares. Frank genuinely loves football."

Maybe so. But had we been wearing Wellington boots when Zark came out with the remark, we would have felt much more comfortable with it.

Bob Shoop clung to his countervailing notion, and began alluding to the Bulls' owner as Fraud Leadon. Frank was facing malcontent elsewhere on the team, too, chiefly from linebacker Jess Rodgers, who had been with the Bulls from the beginning. To Jess, he was "Frank the Wank"—wank an abbreviation of wanker, a nasty little term for onanism, a jerk-off. Actually, it sounded like the title from one of Frank's old songs.

But Jess was strident about it: The Bulls' owner wasn't "a general good guy," as he often called himself when feeling American, but smarmy and "an empire builder."

Frank did his best to take the impugning in stride. "There are all kinds of wild and woolly things in British football," he said softly. "It's the business, babe."

True quote, terribly so.

February

25

Another of my duties as assistant GM was making a weekly trip to Brum's bustling Bull Ring market, to see a friend of Frank's about the bounteous vegetables he donated to the Bulls. The markets man was an affable chap called Mr. Nice 'n Fresh, who'd once lived in San Francisco. "Will James Thornton be returning?" he asked as he sacked Swedes and fresh greens. "Beautiful boy he is, ah, beautiful."

Thornton was indeed due back, about to become one of the first veteran Yanks in Britball. A second Ivy Leaguer fielded by the Bulls, out of the University of Pennsylvania, he'd arrived circuitously, he claimed via Wall Street from the Wharton School after having worked on the Atlanta Braves baseball ground crew. Though it was the personal opinion of the Bulls' majority owner that he hailed from the more southerly clime of Hades.

Frank again dispatched me to London to pay in advance his airfare across. Only after much trepidation, almost ulcerization, he confessed, had he decided to rehire Thornton. Mr. Nice 'n Fresh might be moved to classify him a beautiful boy, but for Frank Kalili he was the biggest, baddest bête noire imaginable.

During the previous season, over the length of it, there'd been mortal enmity between the two of them. They had argued salary and living conditions. Medical insurance. Transportation. The weather.

Even with the markets man's encomium to him, Frank was all but disqualifying Thornton from the human race, saying, "He's a bridge with the black players, but a bad bridge."

Everything about him was unsettling; from quarrelsome nature to fragile physical condition to his divisiveness with the players. He also was Locksley Roberts's best American friend. Locksley was, of course, Animal, and never more so than in Thornton's company. But Frank knew too well that key players had vowed not to rejoin the Bulls' roster unless James Thornton returned to Birmingham.

Frank, of course, prided himself on getting along with Americans. Why, he was practically one of them. A Bulls' import from the previous season even had referred to him as "my transatlantic father." Transpacific, anybody could have bought. But transatlantic: a real compliment, that. With James Thornton, though, he was nothing but nemesis. For all his capacity at impersonation, Frank Kalili could not pretend otherwise.

Now Big James hastened back, and Frank braced himself; it was like fielding a request on the bandstand he had no desire to play. He did it anyway, took that microphone, squeezed the living amplification out of it, and sang on. Grumbling, he trudged upstairs at No. 10, foraged beneath a mattress, and shocked me by coming back with a sheaf of £20 notes as big around as a Benedictine Brothers fruitcake.

"This money ought to be going into my pocket, not paying Thornton's way over," he said, modulating his voice with lament before he made a metronomic peeling of the notes into my hand. Then he retracted the money, counted it out again to be sure it was all there, put a rubber band around it, and blew it a Polynesian kiss goodbye.

February

27

An ailing wallet wasn't the half of it. Three weeks before our opening game most of the players came off noncommittal: They were concerned over the scarcity of kit and over a snagged sponsorship deal, which hastened the absence of their American star quarterback from a year ago, Russ Jensen, who had been the best player in Britball, but vowed not to return to Brum unless his salary was paid in advance.

Frank Kalili's face told of all the Bulls' woes. His cheeks were in need of a forklift; his eyes conveyed his feeling that, with sporting interests, he should have stuck to mah-jongg. The team troubled him, and not only the acute shortage of free safeties and shoulder pads. For months he'd maintained sponsorship was sealed, only to see it dematerialize before his rheumy eyes.

Players began slagging off. One of the more troublesome complaints, made by an offensive guard named Michael Maynard, was how the Bulls' owner had begun selling pornography out of the Great American Sports store.

Maynard was incensed because what he called "porno" consisted of a personal picture of him taken in the shower of a jubilant locker room after the Bulls won the championship. "Yo, man, I might sue," he said. "People come up saying, 'Seen the picture Frank's showing everybody? Of you naked? He's, you know, taking the piss on you.' "

Frank felt impugned. For a man who wore his generosity like one of his gooseberry leisure suits, who prided himself on that label "Uncle Frank," the players' anger toward him would not do.

"I'm living on nerves," he said.

To which I would have added the nourishing condiments of curry and pacharan.

Zark, his partner, consoled him with another story from the NFL. "Had a teammate in St. Louis who'd say, 'Go home, rub your paycheck on it, and it won't hurt so bad.' "

Of course, Frank, as he would let you know daily, had no paycheck.

He failed to see why everything bogged. In a fit of desperation he'd asked me to call Charles O. Finley—the former owner of baseball's Oakland Athletics, and another off-song paragon, not to say unsung paragon, of sport, who hailed from Birmingham, Alabama—to inquire if he might not be willing to help bail out the Bulls of Birmingham, England.

Finley and I, about 50 years apart, had gone to the same high school. Finley's uncle, the first All-American in football at Auburn University, had been my next-door neighbor, and as a boy I had raided his backyard for soft-shelled pecans that fell from his tree. To Frank, it made for a plausible financial linkage. "O'Finley could be the man who saves us, babe," he said.

Yes, he'd intuited how he and the man he called O'Finley were nothing if not kindred spirits—the owner of a world champion baseball team who'd begun as a batboy for a minor league outfit called the Birmingham Barons, and the owner of the British champion gridiron team who'd gotten his start squirting water on the sideline for the Birmingham Bulls.

March

1

O' Finley failed to bite, dissent from players grew and creditors came calling; Frank Kalili's spirit, as the Brits say, was beaten into a cocked hat. But only Frank would fight the cataclysm by buying British rights to the Arena Football League, a gimmick game that had gone defunct in the United States.

Bob Shoop, having majored in business management at Yale, was duly impressed. "You know how you're talking and somebody says, 'She's the prettiest girl in the world,' but you don't believe it?" he hooted. "With Frank we've found him—the absolute worst businessman in the whole world."

He also kept pestering the Rolls-Royce dealership about sponsorship, and to help him at it, he recruited an outfit called Sterling Management, and then insisted they were on the verge of succeeding. Sterling was run by someone named Bob Breen, or Preen, a close friend of Frank's, who reportedly had cosigned for the home mortgages on No. 10 Yew Tree.

The sponsorship check was to be cut any day, for who in the United Kingdom could resist a company that went by the name of Sterling Management? The infusion of cash would guarantee the return of Russ Jensen, whose re-signing was a priority Frank Kalili claimed he had plugged away at for months. But little if anything had changed, with the star quarterback still sitting home in California and likely to miss the opening game against Dublin.

But for an incoherent phone call in the middle of the night, Jensen had been incommunicado. "He didn't seem to remember who the Bulls were," Zark said after speaking with him. "But he said he was ready to play football. Oh, yeah, man, he just wants his money first."

Frank Kalili quailed slightly at the sound of that. Jensen, it turned out, was troublesome and abrasive, and for Frank, more enervating even than Thornton. Worse, sponsorship money expected to patch over his personal mortgages probably would have to be funneled instead into Russ Jensen's stonewashed denim pockets.

Frank also was unnerved to contemplate the league's Most Valuable Player's return, his physical return; Jensen—who had played professionally in America—didn't like the way the Bulls were run from the first day he got into town, and laid blame brusquely on the front doorstep at No. 10 Yew Tree Close. Once, he threatened bodily harm to Frank. And cowering wasn't an impersonation Frank had fully mastered. More disturbingly, and this really hurt, he'd banned the owner from smoking on the sideline.

"It's the sponsor that wants him," Frank rasped. "Look, babe," he said flatly, "win a Grand Prix in a Jaguar, even if it's the worst car in the world, people still expect to see you the next year again in a Jaguar. He's who the sponsor wants." Even if the sponsor's assembly line was turning out Rolls-Royces.

"The king, this Jensen is, that's what he thinks of himself," Frank said. He began a colorful impersonation of Russ Jensen's British girlfriend el flagrante delicto: "Yes, Russ, oh, yes, you are the king!" he moaned convincingly, without aid of estrogen. As he spoke, Silk Cut smoke swirled like a funeral pyre.

As it happened, Frank's fatalistic if not morbid bent was in perfect pallbearer step with the new practice site chosen by the Bulls. Or, more accurately, foisted upon us. The Moor Lane Sports

Ground was directly adjacent to the moss-covered stone walls of one of Britain's biggest cemeteries.

Frank looked very restful there, amid the gravestones. He was closer, in fact, to the gravestones than to football, and not just figuratively speaking: After delivering us, reluctant to get out of his car, he would watch practice from his parking spot near the cemetery gate.

Having fallen out of favor with the players partly explained his distance. Then there were other people he didn't wish to come in contact with. "The Supporters Club," he said with a huff. "You can't talk to them, you won't get anything done with them, they're on tangents of their own."

One of the more prominent Bulls' supporters, whom he took pains to avoid, was known to players and fellow club members as L.B. Peter "L.B." (for "Local Businessman") Robinson was a little man with a lot of fervor for gridiron and the Bulls. He attended every practice and every game, donned a black Bulls jersey, and when the players were strapped, opened his wallet to them.

Rumor persisted that Frank Kalili had been partners with L.B. in buying the Bulls, which was where the nickname came from, but when asked, Frank quickly disavowed it. "I'm owner of this team, he has nothing to do with it," he said, his irritation rising. Robinson was just another pesky supporter now, with whom he dealt accordingly—which meant shunning him.

The Supporters Club raised money, he claimed, not to benefit the Bulls, but for their own loopy causes, from their backing of unionized California grape pickers to starving Sandinistas. Frank couldn't control them, so in the best interests of Britball he had no choice but revile them. Who knew what they might be up to, and how nefarious? Once they even gave money to an opposing team whose bus broke down in Brum and left them stranded without transportation home. They sported buttons that read BOYCOTT SOUTH AFRICA, NOT NICARAGUA on their Bulls' windbreakers—windbreakers bought incidentally not at Frank's Great American Sports, official merchandiser of the Bulls, but elsewhere. "At the end of the season they bought satin jackets for the

Americans," he decried, "when the money could have gone for something good for the team like new helmets." Those satin jackets hadn't come from Great American Sports, either.

Disdain was mutual by now, for the supporters weren't exactly lining up to put their feelings for Frank on compact disk. In an uneasy truce, the situation threatened to become ugly. Club members even hinted in the off-season of trying to wrest control of the team from him, a hostile takeover if he wasn't willing to sell. Frank thought I would become a liaison. "Maybe you can tell them how fan clubs operate in the States," he suggested. "Let them know who the money really ought to go to."

Shaky to begin with, his personal finances had grown more precarious with a sharp hike in rent on his sporting goods store, which was moving to a new shopping mall. He had another business, a clothing concern, that was eating up capital, too. The phone bill was still something else; safe to say British Telecom's profits for the fiscal quarter depended on whether he paid it or not. And Zark—his partner, cohabitant, and employee—wasn't living on air or getting paid in smiles.

But just when it looked bleakest, Frank somehow scraped up the resources, called in the chits, to throw the Bulls a celebration, called by the British a presentation party, for winning the championship. Unsurprisingly, the Supporters weren't invited, but nevertheless, unwelcome sentiment for Frank Kalili would be there.

The purrrr-fect person for hosting it, this shindig, was the man who had taken his stage name from Don Ho's tune, "E Lei Ka Lei Lei", which translated in Hawaiian to "Beach Party Song." The players indulged in free food and beer, as great quantities were donated from Britball's sponsor—awful American stuff but a good hedge against a world shortage of horse piss.

The party, at a once-mediocre hotel, took place on a Sunday night, usually a time of respite by the social schedule of one Locksley "Animal" Roberts. Animal, who at that moment was not wanted by the law, and who had some sterling he needed to get rid of in a hurry, went around ordering up champagne for everyone. His mates were most receptive of his offer; it was a free bar only for the American beer, and from the looks of unopened bottles and cans lining the bar, it was going down like castor oil, by the teaspoon.

Appetites were well provided, too, all kinds of hors d' oeuvres, but mostly plate upon plate of pancakes drenched with orange sauce. "Ugh, terrible, man, terrible," Michael Maynard flinched to teammate and safety Clive Loftman. "Pancakes no good without lemon juice on them, know what I mean?"

Maynard also refused the free beer. "Wish I had some sexy, know what I mean?" he said.

"Yah, the best—ragga!" Clive replied excitedly. "Better than carrot juice."

Sexy was a Caribbean concoction that sounded like a genuine threat to pacharan, although it must have reassured Frank Kalili that if either of them had a hankering for flapjacks they'd come to his house for Aunt Jemima's.

Fraternizing was intense; few of the players had seen each other since the season ended, for except at Frank's dining table, the Bulls were not a particularly close-knit team. Poignant moments were aplenty. Linebacker Colin Nash, the team's Co-Most Valuable Player, showed up with a cane and wrapped in bandages, having been burned in a gas heater explosion while on holiday in Wales. A big man for bonhomie, Nash, as witnessed when he went to the podium for his MVP trophy: "It will be very tough to repeat as champions," he said into a microphone, "but my desire is strengthened because I've just learned it was one of our rivals that tried to have me bumped off with that explosion—yes, the dastardly Leicester Panthers."

Next came thunderous applause when the Bulls' other co-MVP, a tight end named Errol Perkins, was announced. But he made his way up to claim his trophy only to learn there'd been an oversight, and he would receive nothing for now but cheers from his teammates.

Frank Kalili gave him a protean clap, too, and clandestinely, perhaps, gave him some incentive. To claim his trophy, Perkins would have to wait—maybe wait all season. Could it be the Wily Midlands Fox afoot? Frank knew Errol Perkins had threatened to retire from the Bulls two years running. If, when he had borrowed money to buy the trophies, he failed to order one for Perkins, mightn't it have been a psychological ploy for delaying his retirement? Good tight ends were at a premium in England, even if they stood 5 feet 10, 174 pounds, as did Perkins. He could hardly exit with the embarrassment of not getting a trophy. So Errol Perkins signed on for another season, one less worry on the Bulls' depth chart, thanks to the wile of Frank Kalili.

. . .

To the Bulls the fete prefigured a new season, the best yet, a healthy, wealthy season, another championship, maybe even matching jerseys if we made it back to the Budweiser Bowl. Sponsorship, of course, was the dominant theme. This was where the deal culminated, right? Sue Kalili-Leadon, in her protesting incarnation as a football widow, had stenciled the Rolls-Royce dealership's name across several jerseys in anticipating the big announcement.

No more scrimping, the team now finally able to afford a tackling dummy or two, players got giddy thinking about it. "Champions!" a group shouted in the lounge, usurping a Supporters' chant. "Cham-peeeeons!" Frank nodded, trying not to work too much smarm into his smile. But where was the car man with his hefty check, anyhow?

Kerchiefs with the jailed players' jersey numbers, "23, 32, 34" emblazoned on them, hung from lapel pockets of several Bulls. Such togetherness Frank Kalili didn't really like to see. Let any leading questions get asked, with answers falling into the wrong notepads, and the sponsorship, that desperately needed infusion of cash to save his team and to save himself fiscally, would, as Frank might have put it on this Americanized night, "go bye-bye."

A cameo by James Thornton was more affirmation the Bulls had arrived, had become a "legit" team. This not only marked the first time an American had come over for a second season but also announced to them that there must be some fiscal clout for getting him back. Thornton's luminous smile also conjured the good times of hitting helmets and of postgame concupiscence, and with his descent of the hotel stairs—well, even Frank Kalili had to admit it'd mightily impressed him.

"Cuz," the big man said in greeting each Bull. "Can't believe I'm back, can you?" Back as walking, talking apocalypse, Frank brooded, going out of his way to avoid him.

For Frank, being an impresario was taxing, and he slumped into one of the lounge's fake Chippendale chairs, its sage upholstering

43

matching his pastel blue gaberdine jacket. Why not take a few moments to appreciate what he'd done? The Bulls had always been a sturdy team on the field, the conundrum, of course, getting onto the field or even getting a field to play on. But during the last season, with his pacharan keeping the British boys fueled, his having assembled a nucleus of Americans, they'd become juggernautical. Best measuring was how they demolished the London Ravens, who hadn't lost a game in the five years since gridiron first was played in Britain, before falling 51–13 to the Bulls. Other games had the same one-sidedness, as bad as 93–0, and to his chums at *First Down,* the headline Frank always suggested, and which usually materialized, was RAGING BULLS.

But his best work was away from the pitch, where he had been a contortionist with his wallet. Once the Bulls got rolling, the Yanks started demanding more money, more amenities—they were nothing but a greedy outstretched hand of want, want, want, and Frank had no choice but benevolently siphoning from wherever he could find it. How benevolent? The home mortgage—not the first, mind you—a hundred pounds here and there borrowed from a friend, proceeds from concessions at home games: Frank Kalili, by any account, kept his football team together with charisma, saffron curry, and kite cord.

Yes: Everyone was indebted. Unthinkable it had all been a year ago, the skeletal remnants to start with, just 13 players and less spirit, until he asserted himself. What was the new nickname he had been given: Mr. No Problem? Right-o. Even if, unappreciated then, he'd considered himself not just a free workhorse but as Orwell wrote, "only a poor drudge muddling among an infinity of jobs." But now—this party, that ornate trophy at his side— came remuneration for all his muddling.

He surveyed the room, gave a good listen, out of habit as an entertainer, for acoustics. He had something to say and wanted to reap his own words, wanted them to come off well. He calculated; in a cellar lounge, the bounce of his voice, the feedback, would have to be neutralized. Finally, he got up and walked past co-owner Denton Thomas, himself hugging the lounge's pièce de résistance, a circular sofa of plush pink. Just like Denton, adorning something, though he had to admit, in his red bow tie and white dinner jacket, adorning it impeccably.

The players were caught up in a buzz of wine, women, and why there no longer would be a shortage of chinstraps. Their fair city, too, was in full swing, throwing itself a centenary, with 700 events scheduled around it, though, alas, none of them had anything in the least to do with shoulder pads. It made no never mind to the players. Some wore gold medals presented after the championship game. Mike Maynard, like the pulling guard he was, had been first to arrive, and softspoken and personable, became a magnet for camaraderie. The young backup QB Andrew Jefferson brought three women, all older and bigger than he was. Nizzy Nisbet, a receiver, dangled his medal—it'd become his second most prized possession next to a photo from the Falklands, where he'd seen action with the Royal Navy.

Suddenly, there was tapping on a hastily stationed microphone at the mezzanine. When that didn't work, Animal Roberts bellowed "Yo!" with the shrill of the all-clear.

The mike went to a factotum from the Birmingham City Council who offered praise to the Bullets—"Bulls!" came a chorus—as "fine representatives of our great city."

"Bullets, er Bulls"—he fumbled with his glasses—"er, yes, I'm sure you'll have another prosperous year." Players could be forgiven if acoustics turned what he said into "preposterous year."

The Bulls clapped and stomped, acknowledging the team's good fortune as the little man rose; music had been playing so loudly when he was introduced, some mistook him for the general manager of the Rolls-Royce dealership, who they knew to be on hand for awarding the sponsorship check. He was still unseen, however, though Frank had eyes out for him, rheumier than usual from looking so hard. Or maybe his eyes clouded from something else as the owner himself seized the microphone.

"Let me welcome . . . ," he said into it, and listened for feedback as he gauged those accoustics, ". . . welcome everyone." Imperceptibly he angled his ear; just right.

He began again, whorled hair in rhythm. "And while it's a

happy occasion, recognition for winning the championship, there comes a time to . . . to . . ." He stepped back from the microphone, turned away, and sniffled.

"Comes a time . . . ," his voice strained, face a pseudo-Polynesian bas-relief of pain, "to . . . to wind it down."

The players may have thought he was telling them, with entertainer's manufactured grief, the party was over; it was getting on toward midnight. But Denton Thomas, near the dais, shook his head; he knew what came next.

"To wind it down," Frank reiterated, "after all we've been through, all we've accomplished. What I will remember are the good times, and, boys, you know there've been many of them." Now—now, they were catching on.

"We did it together, when everybody gave up on us, said there wouldn't be any Bulls, laughed at us about winning the championship. But now . . ."

Why now? Debts were caving in, lots of personal liability. But how much was an act, escape by manufactured grief? The man before us, stoop-shouldered, sallow-cheeked, agonizing, was an impersonator. But it sure looked real.

"I will always be your Uncle Frank. But now I have passed it on to someone else, and it's time, time for me to go." He sat down dabbing at his eyes.

Denton quickly took the microphone, his own voice more elusive than usual to follow. He gave it an emergency grip and almost shattered the hotel sound system by sputtering at close range: "Ah, Uncle F-F-Frank, we know you will al-always be part of Birmingham Bulls!"

Denton blathered a few more incoherent but equally compassionate sounds, then took a seat and began rubbing his forehead. Another of those damned headaches, poor man. When the going got tough, Denton got a migraine.

Frank watched him with watery eyes. Partner, daily phone communicant—friction be damned. Touched by Denton's display, he grew conciliatory. When he stopped to think, Denton cut a fine figure on the sideline in his white windbreaker, by Jove, they both did; had videotapes to prove it.

46

Zark spoke next, Frank's heir apparent. Except for a bout of snoring, he'd sat up all night drafting an acceptance speech, drawn on past speeches, during his playing days in America, at restaurant grand openings for Red Lobster. But, whatever was said, however he said it, he didn't want to upstage Frank. Nasal syllables made damned sure of that.

Frank sat head in his hands, his thoughts elsewhere. Wife Sue put a consoling arm around him. He was oblivious to that, too. How could he know a mere ten minutes of true-quote abstention would hit so hard? Already he felt he was ancient history. A story at that moment was going to press in the Birmingham *Evening Mail,* announcing his resignation as supremo, but much as he liked publicity, he couldn't envision headlines, much less enjoy them, for regret getting the better of him.

Palmy days, palmiest since his tours with the Waikikis, his time with the Bulls had been for Frank Kalili-Leadon, and there would be plenty more of them, you betcha, babe. He not only would remain the team's majority owner but also continue to have sway in the front office, in his foyer. Zark might be the GM, but majordomo credentials for the Bulls belonged to only one man.

That farewell would have to be recanted, the newspaper story retracted. "Uncle F-F-Frank will always be there," Denton stammered. Little did Denton know. He'd bloody well be there all right. For he'd built this team, practically from ground up, running it from the dining table at No. 10 Yew Tree Close. He was the team's symbol—forget the Bull. No, he wouldn't let go.

The mounting debts, of course, he'd let go of in a second, just needed to find somebody dumb enough, or rich enough—or if he really hit the jackpot, babe, both—to take them on. But while the Bulls' future was firmly back in his hands, the sponsorship check wasn't. Just where in the name of Jenny Churchill was that Rolls-Royce man, anyway?

March

6

Before practice at Moor Lane, Frank Kalili, chary of his own supporters and players, cracked a car window to offer jocular advice to quarterback Andy Jefferson, who stood 5 feet 5 and weighed 145 pounds. "Jeffo, lad! Stay off the steroids!"

Frank permitted himself the slimmest of smiles. On this day James Thornton was due back in uniform, and he could only damn the thought of it.

"Won't you tell us, please," he said, turning to the Bulls' physiotherapist, Jeff Kahn, who was in the car with him, "about Mr. Thoooorn-ton?"

"Mr. Thoooorn-ton." He modulated his voice; might have been an emcee introducing a cabaret act at a low dive in Blackpool.

The physio chortled. "Oh, yeah," he confided, "the goy, he's always hoiting, hoiting something owful."

Hailing from the Bronx, but having lived for more than a decade in Brum, Jeff Kahn gave a colorfully inflected diagnosis of Thornton's maladies. "He demanded a brain scan last year when he detoimined his football helmet was fowlty," the trainer continued. "A brain scan, hah!"

Scan sounded like something to nibble on at high tea. "Noiss

48

asked if he'd had any previous brain scans and he said, 'Yeah, a couple.' Noiss said, 'I thought so because you got more radiation up there than anybody I ever saw.' "

"Thornton loved medical attention, all right," volunteered the assistant physio, John McGowan, who'd jumped into the back-seat of the car. "Never one for training, either. Got tireder as the season wore on. Amazing that he never missed a game."

Nor a meal, by Frank Kalili's gustatory scoreboard. "Ate thirty-five cupcakes last year before the championship game, babe," he said. "Every one of them, in one sitting."

Thornton was perpetually hungry, but maybe not for playing, or coaching, any more gridiron. On this Sunday he was nowhere to be found. Having avowed to the players how determined he was to reconnect with the Bulls, his behavior proved perplexing. Since coming across, he'd remained almost incommunicado with the team.

This surprised the players; earlier he had promulgated his intent to become head coach. But he seemed less than committed to the job until he saw some of the money owed him. Eventually Thornton might accede to the job, or it could be someone entirely new. Frank, in a moment of grandiosity, had spoken of bringing in the deposed Ohio State coach, Earle Bruce, because "he's certainly got the first name to catch eyes in this country." The currently indisposed Russ Jensen was strongest candidate as coach, should he return. The players took perverse pleasure in recounting how, when Jensen alighted the year before in Brum, another American was, nominally, the head coach. "Yeah, well, you might be head coach," Jensen snarled, "but I'm the fucking boss."

But strapped financially, and ever sponsorless, the Bulls in seeking a coach had only the smorgasbord from Frank Kalili's kitchen as enticement. For now we were stuck with Zark—a decent working arrangement, because, what with his aversion to curried food, he wasn't costing anything in food bills.

If he could tone down the technologizing in the huddle, where he seemed to make most everything beyond players' ken—if he could tone it down, the team's promise might flourish. He'd posted an 8–1 record the year before in Cardiff, though his play at quarterback contributed a hell of a lot more to won-loss record than his coaching in a province where they'd never seen a passed ball, much less had to defend against it.

Flushed to have again a team of his own, Zark blew a whistle for practice, which began with a lap around Moor Lane. The players ran along the cemetery, went over undulating athletic grounds and a crown bowling green, past a vast industrial park strewn with dismembered seagulls, then along one of the sewerage ditches that Brum proudly considers to be canals that outnumber those of Venice; all told, a sightseeing trip for the Americans. Lap over, Zark hustled out front of the team for calisthenics. "Stretch 'em!" he chirruped. The Bulls loved this; it doubled as a posing exercise for them.

Next he huddled together an offensive team. "Receivers, be sure to watch out running your pass patterns," he instructed, "for those light poles over there." A keen admonition. One of the Bulls best running backs had almost been paralyzed for life the year before after colliding with a light standard that bordered the pitch. His name was Desi Taylor, and from the looks of his hair, a miasma of ringlets, he'd gotten a severe jolt of voltage upon collision.

In the off-season Frank Kalili had foreseen 75 players vying for the roster; fewer than half that many turned out. But Zark was elated; at his other stops in the United Kingdom he'd gotten but a handful onto the pitch. "Just give me enough bodies to scrimmage," he said, "and I'm a happy camper."

The Brits, he intimated, loathed training. To be expected, for football practice was gnashing and meting out punishment, three hours of it, and having this kind of thing sprung on them in adulthood when they were used to mucking about, just showing up for a match of soccer or rugby—why would anyone, unless of a sadomasochistic nature, enjoy football practice? "No givens in this game, that much I can tell you from the start," he'd averred. "First thing you find out over here is lead by example." Such exemplar was Zark, he'd even put on his kamikaze face, running downfield in Wales to cover kickoffs. Moreover, his proboscis and old quarterback's ego withstood it.

One innovation he brought to Britball was his procrastination strategy. He established a time practice was to begin, and he actually intended it to start an hour later. For not only did the Brits have a determined air of lollygag about them, they also bristled when reminded of it. At least they didn't ask for tea in the middle of a scrimmage.

Stragglers were coming onto the pitch an hour after practice commenced; from the dressing cubicle they passed other putative players who'd stayed for a few snaps, then left abruptly. It struck me as a practice that could have been organized by Peter Sellers. A few players, fully kitted, weren't sure they wanted to train except on a selective basis. Or perhaps they didn't want to practice until having sufficient time to size up the new coach, which might take weeks in Britball, and stood resolutely on the sideline and watched. Of anyone, Zark could appreciate it, his personal motto that dressing out was what counted, not how, or if, you played the game.

Scrimmaging started from the outset, Zark bypassing blocking or tackling drills, and it came off as feckless, though as a social occasion the Bulls devoted themselves to a bloody marvelous time. The huddle was pure pageantry. When they broke from it, I expected spectators to cheer. Sometimes they did. Particularly conspicuous on one side of the football was a linebacker who wore a jersey that read, simply, DEFENCE. He, of course, was going up against the offensive center.

The receivers, who weren't quite comfortable with that description of their position or the hands at the end of their arms, seemed to catch the ball as if it were a violin case, but they, too, were willing. Coach Bobby Shoop had brought with him from America a drill he hoped would help them overcome the fear of catching. He ordered the receivers to lie on the ground, flat on their backs, then stood over them and threw the football straight down at them. He almost caved in a couple of chests with his drill, not to mention how they blenched at the ball.

Zark warned about getting too close to his players.

"But it's the only way they'll ever learn to catch the darned ball," Shoop protested.

"I'm talking about off the field, man," Zark replied. "They all want to be buddy-buddy, and once you start letting them, they'll lose respect and run over you."

"Oh."

One player, defensive end Kenneth "Spats" Lewis, excused himself from the huddle for a conversation with two young women strolling through the park. It had to be a British variation of the lonesome defensive end play. "Spats, come back, you've got outside hook coverage on this play," I shouted, losing out badly for his attention.

"Mind yourself, you," one of the women cautioned.

"Ain't done nothin' . . . yet," Spats said with a sly smile before finally returning to the defensive unit.

Spats was key, defensively and to team spirit. Excepting Animal Roberts, a recidivist, he was our first prison alumnus to assimilate back into the lineup—having done time last season—and he was looked to for leadership.

Spats was conscientious. The coaches just never knew where his conscientiousness was trained. A year ago, he'd led the team in quarterback sacks. But if he made one, he might spend the next three plays scanning the stands, seeing who best appreciated it. If a pretty face, he appreciated it back—sometimes as a running back blew right past him.

Most reassuring thing about practice was that the distance from the pitch to the nearest pub was less than 100 yards. As an assistant coach when not practicing myself, I worked the sidelines, sending in substitutes, quizzing new players about their experience at gridiron, asking veterans what they had done in the off-season to get themselves ready to play again. Most admitted to having gone to the pub a lot.

One newcomer I was put in charge of attempted to get into a four-point stance and fell flush on the most awesome array of tattoos ever seen on two forearms. It was one of my first chances to coach, sitting him in a stance so the brunt of those tattoos was turned against our opponents. But alas he must have felt his tattoos inferior compared to some of our other players'; he was never seen again. Our kickers made some orbital boots, only to have soccer players on a adjacent pitch outkick them when they returned the football. But in a sense we bore pretty good resemblance to a gridiron team: At practice not a single player went cross-eyed peering through his facemask.

Still, we were defending British champions. If the players would commit themselves despite the team's travail, if we could keep from getting shunted onto a gravel pitch as Moor Lane's management threatened us once soccer season began, and if we could curtail the Supporters' wacky urges, the situation stood to improve. Sure enough, as Frank forewarned, they were everywhere, meddlesome, including one who happened to be pop-eyed and kept trying to infiltrate the huddle while calling for "more play action" from Zark at quarterback.

Against the secondary his passes zipped through the air with impunity. A year ago, impunity wouldn't have been the label. A year ago the secondary not only was a ball-hawking bunch, having led the league in interceptions, but based on allegations, it also had been markedly criminal. Now its three most prominent members were behind bars. In their absence, Trevor Carthy, the best indigenous gridiron player Great Britain had produced, was making a transition from breakaway runner to defensive back, but even his talent couldn't compensate for en masse arrest. "Shoot! I got nobody back there," decried secondary coach Bob Shoop. He was right; we damned sure had to hope jurisprudence could be worked into our game plan.

March

9

When James Thornton failed to report to the Bulls, Frank Kalili dared speculate that without working papers he'd been sent back stateside. Pendulous bags below his eyes perked at the possibility: glory, glory, aloha, babe. But Thornton was lodging with a friend—a friend on whose blouse was sported nothing less than a customs and immigrations badge. When a belated urge to contact the team coincided with the rare chance to get through by phone to No. 10, he and Frank began an acrimonious roundelay of whether he would again play for and coach the Bulls.

Mundane stuff of sports contracts: Thornton had flown over with five extra bags of luggage, insisting Frank absorb the cost as money due him from last season, salary he claimed he was never paid. He also sought a sizable insurance policy for the many injuries he expected to sustain.

"Over my dead body, babe," Frank told him.

Doing her ironing upstairs, Sue Kalili-Leadon could only look over the balustrade with sloe eyes and consider the ramifications of the remark. Thornton would be all too happy to do the shoveling atop the grave, and make her husband Britball's first martyr.

Thornton was another Yank who had come to Brum through old Sam Ketchman's kitchen placement agency in Sarasota,

54

Florida. The scoop, straight from Sam's jumpy typewriter: TRICKY
AFOOT, HARD RUSHER, GIVES ALL HE'S GOT. HEART NOT TO BE OUTDONE.
Now, for a second season with the Bulls, Thornton wanted his
salary doubled. "Really," he allowed, "because of all the promises
made last year but never delivered." The big batch of cupcakes
from his teammates to lard their plea for him to play in the
championship didn't rate consideration; he would have much
preferred glazed doughnuts (of which he'd been known to eat 30
in six minutes).

He knew resentment awaited, given the storminess of the previous season, and how, with his wolfsome appetite, he'd almost
eaten his way through another mortgage for Frank. But his buffer
was Zark, with whom he had developed a camaraderie from
having both played on two continents and in three countries as
pros.

Actually, Thornton hadn't played in Canada; he had shown up
there once at a training camp, one of the many he'd visited,
without sticking at any of them. He maintained he'd played pro
in the States, too, but his memory may have been selective, or else
he was impelled to keep up with a horde of other alleged ex-
professionals in Great Britain.

Instead of the pros, he'd found himself in a last resort situation
with the Bulls, for whom he quickly became the best offensive
lineman in the country, a punishing blocker. You had only to ask
any of those 192-pound defensive tackles he'd gone against. But
he wasn't very happy. Bad enough in Brum not to get paid regu-
larly and to have his life strewn with lies and deceit. And those
British defensive tackles having the build of Queen Victoria was
something else to contend with. For now Frank outposted Thornton and his caravan to a nearby economy hotel. Though there
were three Yanks and two dogs already hugging the floor at No.
10, Frank's citing a space shortage was just a dodge—Thornton's
quasi-exile was a move born of diplomacy and more than a little
dread.

Thornton liked the hotel, quickly restruck old acquaintances,
some of them paying nocturnal visits. But a few days later when

Frank failed to pay his bill, he found himself evicted—a ceremonious eviction that later would become known as the first gallery opportunity for British gridiron in the Imperial War Museum.

The two had backbitten each other often, were regarded by the team as a dueling concatenation, but always maintained a semblance of decorum. Now they went over the line. After Thornton was given his ouster by the hotel manager, he telephoned Frank, who vowed to come right away to the hotel, a few blocks from Yew Tree Close, and spirit him to new lodging elsewhere.

Right away, he repeated. But Thornton should have known better.

He was left embarrassed, stranded in a hotel lobby for five hours, until his anger built so that he pounded on the bell at the front desk and demanded the manager call the police and have Frank Kalili arrested.

When Frank finally arrived, gingerly espying the situation before he set foot outside his car, he managed to forestall things without the police being called. He promised the money soon, and the hotel manager agreed.

But in the parking lot, he began berating Thornton, a feckless berating, in which he failed to make him flinch. Frank blustered on, heatedly, and Thornton let him talk. Then he calmly repeated transgressions against him.

"Got nothing on paper, babe," Frank said firmly.

Right on that account: With the Bulls, unless you typed up your own contract, clearly you didn't get one.

At length, Frank, having heard enough, most of it from his own lips, shambled to his car. He got in, ground the ignition, and began to drive off. He went only a few feet, then threw the old orange station wagon into park and jumped out; there was some unfinished brouhaha to take care of.

He accused Thornton of plotting against him, and tore into him for general invidiousness. Frank was going to quash Thornton once and for all, even at grave risk to his health.

Thornton again tried to hold off the verbal charge, but Frank's

Silk Cut slipped in a parry. "I'll run you off clear back to America," he shouted, gasping it out.

"Nothing against you personally, you just don't got the foggiest how to run a football team," Thornton replied, almost staring at the ground. "And lookit, your family's crumbling around you, man. Crumbling, man, crumbling."

For Frank Kalili, it was a seismic moment. "Son," he shouted at the top of his abused vocal chords, "I'll send you home! I won't have your trouble again this year!"

Ideally he would have traded James Thornton to a British team that played on the Outer Hebrides, but alas, trades could not yet be made in Britball, even by pioneers.

He jumped back into the car, threw it in reverse, and peeled away. But as he was leaving the parking lot he skidded to a halt, threw open the door, and again jumped out to confront Thornton.

"Why I ever agreed to take you back . . . if you keep bothering me, not only will I not have you back with the Bulls, I'll have you deported!" he shouted, inches away from Thornton's mountainous face.

"If Jimmy gets sent home," Bob Shoop scowled, "I'm going to wear an armband with his jersey number on it and a towel on my football pants with F.L.A. (Frank Leadon Associates) on one side and SUCKS on the other." Those Ivy Leaguers stuck together, even in Birmingham, England.

Once more Frank stormed off. Back in the car he slinked so in the seat, his head barely visible over the dash, there was almost an emergency urge to run through the hotel shouting for digitalis pills. But no, it was just his James Dean driving style, low-slung, laid back, among his best impersonations yet.

March

10

A deportation order had in fact been placed for James Thornton, not by Frank Kalili, but Thornton himself. No, the owner needn't have expended precious energy threatening him, for from the instant he sized up the situation, Thornton declared himself a goner from the Bulls, from Brum. Demoralized by a reprisal of what he'd gone through a year earlier, calling himself victim of deceit and fraud, he planned to leave first chance he got. Even if it meant strapping himself to an aileron.

That, in fact, appeared his only way home. "I'm broke—stone broke," he said. "But I can get myself deported. You know, commit some petty crime. I'm not a criminal, but can I tell you, it's how to do it. They have to put you on the first flight out. Might even be first-class if that's the only seat available. Only thing—you can't come back into the country. Do I look like I can handle that?"

Soon Thornton drafted out to Frank, in calligraphic hand, an ultimatum for back pay and expenses—a writ the Bank of England would have accepted in a split second, and declared: "Minute I get my money I'm history, cuz." But the Bulls weren't willing to lose him. At practice that night, the team captain, a defensive tackle named Steve Trow, pressed into his hand a £5 note. "We've got to get you solvent, mate," he allowed.

"Hear, hear!" shouted a chorus of Bulls.

There was a rapprochement of sorts when Frank Kalili billeted the Bulls' imports into a four-star hotel ten miles outside town. Distance between it and No. 10 Yew Tree Close and the stadium was symbolic: With no car, we were so far out of town, if we had started walking toward the stadium yesterday, we'd almost make the opening kickoff of the season against the Dublin Celtics more than a week hence. Frank had finally gotten us out of his whorled hair, and could get down to pioneering again with his partner Pisarkiewicz.

But who would pay for it taxed our imaginations. A football team unable to provide a player with a new chinstrap surely couldn't reimburse the lap of luxury. How he managed it, we hadn't a clue; perhaps he and the Waikikis had been the lounge act there, and he was entitled to a senior entertainer's discount. "Just say I've got a good name in this town, babe," he confidently told Bob Shoop as we checked in. "A good name—and leave it at that."

But Thornton was far from mollified. Frank continued to shun him, and the star player vented it one night by running up a huge food bill and ordering six bottles of a decent vintage brut to go with his dinner. "Bill's in his name, cuz, not mine. And can I tell you? Still owes me twenty-one hundred pounds from last season." He stuck a loaded fork in his mouth. "Hmeh ccmapayn frr effeebddy!" he clamored.

A waitress set before him his fifth order of fried whitebait. "Can I tell you?" he said, vigorously attacking the plate. "If I can't get my money from him, I'll eat my way through it." Coming from someone who was supposedly listed in the *Guinness Book of World Records* for one of his eating feats, that was not a threat to be taken lightly.

March

11

Now, at long last, my kit having arrived by steamer and with a new pair of British cleats on my feet that made me feel a little like a telephone lineman, it was time to play football. But just as I geared toward making myself top special teams player in the British Isles, I was beset by the specter of the Fourth American.

That would be me.

As the Bulls' roster now stood, I had little choice but to think of myself as an imitation Graham Greene title: *The Fourth American*—the extraneous Fourth American.

The rules of Britball, unlike "Rule, Britannia," were ephemeral. No, ephemeral was too kind; they were made to be broken—on a daily basis. Trying to fathom them, as put forth through the dubious National Division Management Association, was like snorkeling through pea soup. "They change them fuckers in a minute," Zark said as I listened with a blend of sympathy and rage.

The newest rule dictated a reduction in Yanks on each team. The year before four had been the limit, which led me to believe I'd be spending a season on the Bulls' roster. But for the upcoming season—as of 10:07 A.M., March 11, 1989—the number was three, leaving me out.

For a brief, dejected moment, I considered jumping to another Britball team. Names of the Brighton B-52 Bombers and the Glasgow Diamonds came immediately to mind—well, maybe not immediately, but I knew who they were. It was befuddling as to why they might want to preclude someone like me from playing a spot of football. I wore allegiance to the old Ealing comedies, even enjoyed bread pudding, for crying out loud. I was leveled. Was there no place on a roster I had traveled 3,000 miles to crack? What kind of xenophobia was this? Not long ago the Brits couldn't get enough Yanks to join their side. Now we were discriminated against because of the way we wore shoulder pads. Crikee, had they not heard of the old Statue of Liberty play?

I tried to be undeterred. Great Britain was a measure of how far I was willing to go to play football. It was edifying, in fact, to know that I could now be credited with having gone further playing football than anyone in the history of my high school; another alumnus, Cornelius Bennett, had very recently signed a $1 million-a-year NFL contract, but he'd only gone to Buffalo to play.

I would do almost anything to play, anywhere, my spirit untrammeled by lack of ability. My creativity was the kind of thing Frank Kalili ought to have admired, such as when I'd tried out for the World Football League, at age 18. Prospective players were required to have medical permission before they were allowed to practice, so I got a quick physical from the family doctor. Before handing over the results of it to the Birmingham Americans—as my hometown team was called—I took scissors and beneath the doctor's signature, carefully snipped off "pediatrician"; impersonating an adult. Of course, the coaches must have known by looking at me that I was a youngster from the way I got run over by the other players. So the shun from the NDMA wasn't something to be taken personally, just the kind of thing to which I'd become inured. On the bright side I might be the first Britball player ever made redundant, and that would be something to tell the folks back home. It would be, I confess, one more dubious distinction. Because from the very first time I'd ever picked one up, the football had always been prone to take elusive bounces for me. If Frank ever got around to doing a Polynesian rendition of "Drop-kick Me Jesus Through the Goalposts of Life," it was almost certain I would be on the bandstand with him as a kind of pathetic kabuki figure in my new cleats.

Of those funny bounces, this pigskin purgatory and gustatory heaven was just the latest. My career, if it could be called such, had begun when I was six years old, playing in something called the Toy Bowl, in a suburb of Birmingham, Alabama, named West End (an inherent sign I was preparing myself for the theatrics of Britball). There, I'd been picked out by a Benedictine religious brother for the privilege of serving as a tackling dummy for Pat Sullivan, a future Heisman Trophy winner. Seldom did my involvement with football get any more illustrious.

But whether it was as special teams player of the year for the semipro Brooklyn Mariners (acclamation given largely on my taking the D train across town an entire season without getting mugged), or playing under an assumed identity for a team of convicts against police in something called the Pig Bowl, my career, if never prominent, damned sure added up to persistence. Whenever and wherever I wanted to play, I found a way, and circumventing the NDMA's flimsy rules looked but a formality. Maybe I'd apply for naturalized citizenship, or better yet, have Frank Kalili teach me to impersonate a Britisher.

I didn't figure to go a whole season and not get into uniform; might not even go one game. The Bulls' roster was in serious flux for Americans. With James Thornton, who'd officially retired a year ago—only to retract it when he was unable to find work in the States—you never knew: He leaned toward going home in a huff and in a hurry. Zark, at age 35, might not want to play again; as much as he loved dressing out, he'd hinted his playing days were over. Bobby Shoop, with a history of injuries, could get hurt at any moment, particularly the way the Brits head-hunted Yanks.

But not wanting to sit and wait, there was but one thing to do: formally declare myself the team's taxi squad. I envisaged a P.A. announcer: "Followed by the balance of the Bulls, and hailing from Birmingham, Alabama, six foot, two hundred and three pounds, the taxi squad." This, of course, gave cachet in a country where taxis are widely esteemed, never more so than in the second city of Birmingham, its marble-columned Victorian town hall built by Joseph Hansom; yes, the same man who invented the hansom cab.

Yet though confident I would get to play, I couldn't help feeling unsettled at practice, imagining my jersey had no numerals on it, but a great big IF on one side, and WHEN on the other.

March

13

Taxi squad set, our search was now for a quarterback. As acting head coach, general manager and presumable QB, Zark wore a haberdashery of hats. Hats were nothing compared to the clothes he wore, or how he wore them. Serious preparation for the Dublin Celtics began the night of practice when he slipped shoulder pads over shirt and tie, and had it allowed his passing arm mobility, he might have gone all the way to a Harris tweed jacket.

But as indefatigable as he was at dressing out, Zark seemed to prefer not to play against Dublin. The Bulls preferred it, too, NFL first-rounder or not, and hoped against hope that Russ Jensen would cross the ocean to pass a football again for them. But negotiating to bring Jensen back to Brum at an impasse, we found ourselves counting on Zark.

Even on days he considered kitting, he was at best iffy, and his indecision put us in a bind. If he chose not to play, our quarterback likely would be the third-stringer from last season's youth team, the irrepressibly punked-out Andrew Jefferson.

Jeffo was a likable kid who had earned approbation from Bob Shoop as the "littlest guy I ever saw with a potgut," but was considered somewhat unstable as a leader because his voice still seemed to be changing. Actually, his mannerisms at quarterback resembled a Pleasbottom from *A Midsummer Night's Dream* on speed. Teammates put no confidence in his haircut, either; his head looked like a Rototiller had run amok; new thunderbolts outcropped weekly. He'd just lost his job as a bank clerk, reportedly because of that hairstyle.

We hadn't a lot to choose from, though Shoop himself was another possibility, having in high school been a quarterback in the wishbone formation—which, with its resemblance to a rugby scrum, might make him an instant crowd favorite in Britain.

A more remote possibility was Pasco, a Sicilian immigrant and refugee from a defunct minor team, the West Bromwich Fireballs. He had a great moustache, and it was high time a QB with a lip brush made an impact on the game. Especially if the mustache looked like Trevor Howard's, and was sure to come off as another big British hit. But Pasco, whose Christian name was Pasquale, had a small problem: He still hadn't learned to grip a football.

Further concern was pronouncing his last name, Lamedica (Luh-med-EEKA), bound to be troublesome in a country where P.A. announcing was in its infancy. (Then again it might give the Bulls an edge, for if the announcer sped pronunciation— "Lamedica at quarterback!" as in "Lamedica the Beautiful" or "God Bless Lamedica"—the Irish would quake in their boots, given how in Britball a Lamedican quarterback is instantly deemed most dominant player on the field.)

Our uncertainty clouded more when, a week before the game against Dublin, Zark up and left suddenly for Oxford, to become offensive coordinator for the British national team. The Bulls were caught by surprise, left not only without his services off the field in the front office but on it as well.

We flicked our foreheads, and wondered why he would devote himself to another team, abandoning the Bulls, by whom he was, after all, being paid. We could point to his contract, which bespoke conflicting loyalties, making him beholden not only to the Bulls, but to F.L.A.—Frank Leadon Associates—and its ancillary outfit, Sterling Management, which also promoted the British national team. I suspected, above all, Zark was fattening up his cherished résumé, in which he took enormous pride. His self-typed sheaf of past experience was legacy to him, and putting in with the national team was a golden opportunity to embellish it. How could anyone in gridiron possibly top a résumé that listed both Green Bay and Oxford? As the Brits would palaver, "That's some curriculum vitae, old boy." No, there couldn't have been a more perfect place and pairing than Oxford for a road scholar like Zark.

He also welcomed there a reunion with a fellow NFL alumnus almost as well traveled as he. In a brief conversation at national team practice, this particular fellow, whose many travels and exploits had been the fruit of a side career in covert intelligence, impressed Bob Shoop with his shadowy reticence.

"Sure is cold out here today," the man said, getting out of the rain by squeezing officiously under Shoop's bumbershoot.

"Yeah, sure is cold out here today," the man repeated. "Like Green Bay, eh?"

A tip-off he was wanting to come in from the cold?

Shoop only nodded politely.

"Green Bay . . . Packers."

Again Shoop gave a nod.

"Packers, you know?" the man said.

"Yeah, the Packers," he continued. "I . . . was . . . with . . . the . . . Packers . . . played for them for ten years."

Now Shoop's eyelids rose like an opening-night curtain at Stratford-upon-Avon, catching on, but to what he couldn't be sure.

"Before that I was in Nam—Southeast Asia—under a different name—you know how it is with the, uh, agency. Don't really like talking about it." He got around to revealing his name as Dick Capp, who went by the alias "Andy" to friends and "colleagues" and to the, uh, intelligentsia of Britball.

For further insight, one had to depend on investigative reporting of the gridiron tabloids. One story about him read: "[Despite] a 1–9 record . . . Bournemouth Bobcat coach Andy Capp is full of optimism. . . . He won't talk about his years with the Green

Bay Packers under legendary coach Vince Lombardi. He's reluctant to discuss his year serving with the U.S. forces in the hell of Vietnam."

But Andy Capp, or Andie Cap, as a second alias was disclosed, had more to divulge. Here he spoke from the gut. Of his team's record, he admitted: "Sure, it's frustrating. I've been in football for thirty years and I've only ever coached fifteen losses. And nine of them were this season."

Maybe he had a legitimate excuse for that sorry season. The Iron Curtain was crumbling, new borders opening daily, and who could expect a man of his pedigree to devote every minute to coaching at such a cataclysmic time?

The article continued: "One day, Capp promises, he'll stop talking about his team . . . and tell about what it was like to win a Super Bowl ring, play with Bart Starr and Forrest Gregg, and study under Lombardi. . . . 'I don't want any personal publicity, I want publicity for my team. When we have a winning season, I'll tell you everything.' "

The Green Bay Packers acknowledged having had a player named Dick Capp who stood 6 feet 5 and weighed 250 pounds. The Dick (aka Andy, Andie) Capp Britball knew and loved was, being generous, 5 feet 4, 150 pounds. The Packers probably weren't more forthcoming on instructions from "the agency." Another story about him began: "All Dick Capp wants to talk about is the Bournemouth Bobcat American Football Club. And the art of the fake."

The Birmingham Bulls were learning a little about that art, and having it foisted on us, too, from a foyer.

March

14

The Bulls' money woes worsened and put us on the brink of going under. Nobody, least of all Frank Kalili (unless he got a windfall of song royalties), had a clue where our next bob or two might come from. Actually, that was a propagandistic thing to say, and not quite a true quote, either.

For, while quaffing soda and shandy inside the Moor Lane Lounge after practice, Bob Shoop and I teamed to crack a video game's jackpot, in the category of sports trivia—the machine squirting out so many 10p coins we needed a sack to lug them back to the hotel; it was money judiciously spent, on six-packs of soda to satisfy Shoop's sugar craving and bus fares to practice the next week.

We Americans now had everything going for us at the fine hotel turned branch front office of the Bulls, but room service coming 'round with a nightcap of milk of amnesia.

James Thornton bided his remaining time in company of Animal Roberts, going to nightclubs, getting in gratis at most of them, from having worked, to supplement his salary the previous season, as a bouncer around town. Lots of women remembered him, and the story the next day was always "Sex and the Single Tackle." After entertaining his concupiscence, he entertained his teammates. When he'd awaken around noon and recount it, we could only exchange glances of awe.

Though depressed by the Bulls' plight, Thornton was glad to lend a little animation to our lives. One evening I got back to the hotel from the theater, having seen *The Glass Menagerie*. "Tennessee Williams, huh? I was in that play in high school," he said with a smile. "As the Gentleman Caller, of course."

Shoopy wasn't so sanguine. Besides his mantra and bemoaning of everything about the Bulls, the ordeal of a near-nonexistent team, he was irked at having been misquoted about his beloved hometown. During a newspaper interview, the Americans were asked about Brum's appeal, and being a veteran of one Birmingham already, I'd responded to a question about the other, only to have the next day's editions attribute to Shoopy how he'd come to Great Britain expecting to find "a sister-hellhole" to Pittsburgh, Pennsylvania.

That we were a team rapidly dematerializing also grated him. After he took a hit at practice from a defensive back named Jock "the Flying Scot" McManus, it was hard to tell which hurt more, the tackle or our off-the-field reality. "Dammit," Shoopy shouted, "we don't even own an ice pack!" Another gripe was serious enough to bring tears to players' eyes: During our training sessions, management at Moor Lane Lounge had begun burning caustic potash in a lot bordering our pitch.

But these were just petty exercises, warm-ups, before the big bleat about money, or our continuing shortage of it. We decried the continued absence of Russ Jensen, and fingers started to point toward Yew Tree Close.

Uncle Frank was no longer in a state of grace, and a clique formed after practice to oust him or even fold the team if unable to; it included Jess Rodgers, Andy Webb, and Billy the Club Mills, a Brit who'd played college football in the States, and got his nickname from a character in *One Flew Over the Cuckoo's Nest*. He'd been in constant touch with Jensen, who vowed he was yet to hear the first word from Bulls' management.

"But Frank said they talk to him a lot, and he'd be coming over any day," Trevor Carthy protested. Carthy was the Bulls' best player and it took little imagination to guess who had curried friendship with him from the beginning. He'd often worked in Frank's business and several times been a holiday guest at his condominium in the south of Spain.

"He could be here any day . . . any day," Carthy repeated—showing mimicry gave nothing to impersonation with the Bulls.

With the team practicing but twice a week, we coaches had a surfeit of time on our hands. We slept late and slept a lot—not atypical behavior for Americans who found themselves in Birmingham, England. Washington Irving, for instance, during a visit with his brother-in-law 150 years earlier, had given outlet to his somnolent bent in Brum by penning "Rip Van Winkle."

One afternoon sprawled on his hotel bed, watching a Pink Panther cartoon on the telly, Bob Shoop buried his face in a pillow and sighed, "Man, I'd do anything for an NBA game." I, too, craved culture, wanted to enrich my adrenal cortex during the day before shoving it into a football helmet at night, and we had only begun to find what a cornucopia of it Brum boasted.

Though it had been around in some incarnation since the tenth century, and incarnation indeed was a key word in describing it, Birmingham ranked among England's newer cities, only now celebrating its centenary. It had been an industrial bastion, and become known as the city of 1,001 trades—now 1,002 with gridiron having come to town.

The second city's population had surpassed 2 million as it gobbled the Midlands. Still it came off as one of the best-kept secrets in the country, if not the Continent; for instance, in its 450 pages, Frommer's *Travel Guide for Britain* mentioned it not once. Even maps of Britain seemed to break off indiscreetly before their cartography got to Brum.

When I was growing up in Birmingham, Alabama, the few people who didn't find it a paradise might remark, "This is a place hell would turn a cold shoulder toward annexing." I never understood it. And so the proud residents of Brum South were quick to point out that it had more shopping centers per capita than anywhere in the United States.

Denizens of the British Brum were equally unrestrained in their enthusiasm over where they lived. They referred to it as the Big Heart of England, and unquestionably that heart pumped best by pouring concrete. The New Street rail station, among the grandest in Britain, had been flattened, and, in a spirit of progressivism that Birmingham, Alabama, could appreciate—having torn down its own Gothic train station to replace it with a vacant lot—a vibrant shopping center developed overhead. Architectural critics knew not what to make of either Brum. But residents would always tout the rebuilding of Birmingham, England's, city center, which got demolished and erected again in stranger and stranger conurbation every decade or two. One-way streets called ring roads, which made for turn-signal hysteria, circled the city's centerpiece, a breathtakingly concave Holiday Inn, the tallest building in town.

Another of the city's higher and longer-standing buildings, the Rotunda (which resembled a tumescent R.F.D. mailbox) was the embodiment of longevity, in its third decade. Wide avenues led to the Bull Ring, Europe's oldest shopping vista, avenues that needed their great width to accommodate the stampede shopping that occurred as a favorite parochial pastime.

A landmark clock tower, naturally enough called Big Brum, loomed as aerie to the city's finest adult bookshops and massage parlors. While the streets went one way, buildings went another, and a few years later, still another. On the whole Birmingham, England, conjured the words of Frank Lloyd Wright when asked how he would go about improving Pittsburgh: "Abandon it."

Not a spotless city, Birmingham, but clean, because detritus never collected, never had time to, as the newest urban re-renewal was always starting. A far cry it seemed from when Queen Victoria, while passing through, would order windows of the royal train tightly drawn, leaving her appreciation of it to the imagination; or when Kenneth Peacock Tynan, the critic who'd disowned and declaimed it as his hometown, called it a "satanic cemetery without walls"—probably a jest wherein he meant Brum was devilishly attractive.

But there was no disputing its impact on Britain, and the world. Its many illustrious, or at least renowned children could stagger the mind: Arthur Conan Doyle got out of town just in time to make Sherlock Holmes a great detective instead of a tradesman; J. R. R. Tolkien stoked a fecund imagination with what he saw of Brum while growing up there. He, of course, would have been a good team historian for the Bulls. Alan Napier, the butler Alfred in the *Batman* television series, hailed from Brum, and was a cousin of another indigenous personage, Neville Chamberlain of the Munich deferred-kickoff fame.

The best of the city could be seen from my bus window aboard the West Midlands Transit No. 51 Walsall local into town. (Walsall was a neighboring burg with the world's best prices on boxer shorts.) Just off the Walsall Road sat Alexander Stadium, the newest phase in sporting spectator luxury, with its AstroTurfed car park.

Further on was the grand crucible for postindustrial Britain, a confluence of motorized traffic called Spaghetti Junction, where enough carbon monoxide was emitted daily to choke an entire football team. Some thought Spaghetti Junction a cruel joke foisted by the ghost of Joseph Priestly, another famous Brummie who was run out of town as a radical scientist belonging to a group called the Lunatics, but went on to discover oxygen after moving to America. Just below the junction lay a condemned velodrome called Salford Park, whose pocked infield served as a last resort for gridiron teams with nowhere else to play.

March

16

Our road scholar was back. Almost as suddenly as he'd left, Zark returned from Oxford and rejoined the Bulls without explanation or any mention of an adjunct chair in geography. He now journeyed to our hotel headquarters nightly, by train or double-decker bus, after Frank Kalili fell further into a funk and couldn't be budged into driving him over.

Now he wanted to be one of the two Americans to play against the Irish. His case was bolstered by James Thornton's first practice outing; he'd needed almost as long as the Brits to get into kit, a bad sign from the outset. Then, after the lap around Moor Lane, Thornton tumbled into a soccer net—"like a big ol' beached fish," Zark said, and had to be extricated from it. Moreover, Thornton had done no contact work, not wanting to commit until medical liabilities were settled, maybe get scheduled for another brain scan or two. And thanks to free rein with Frank Kalili's hotel bill, he'd also begun to eat himself into the size of a house.

Yet Thornton was determined to play as his reward for having spent the championship season with the Bulls, and having been instrumental in helping them win it. He bristled and began using the term "cuz" a lot, insiderish, bridging again with the players. He also informed Steve Pisarkiewicz, in a country where there was a dearth of them, that a good lineman, going against the tenacity of those 192-pound defensive tackles, was worth two, maybe three Americans elsewhere on the field.

But what to do with Zark, now that he had flip-flopped himself back onto the roster? Frank was pushing him to play, to justify his salary, Britball's highest. But money, it turned out, was not Zark's motivation to play. His abrupt return from Oxford came only after he'd been sacked by the national team, ignominiously dismissed by people who knew a fraction of the football he did.

And with Frank an emotional and financial mess, Zark took charge with renewed zest. He was out to restore his belittled manhood, it seemed, and playing one more game at quarterback augered better for it, yet. He practiced hard, and handed out countless memos, all flawlessly typed. They foretold new formations, new plays, playing dates, duties—everything but the weather.

He also insisted that he play against Dublin. "What the hell you think I'm getting paid for?" It was a question often asked, by the players in particular. When he chattered away in the huddle, fashion plate and technician, his play calling caused them to look quizzically at each other. The nosetackle Andy Webb grimaced and said, "This bloke really played in the NFL?" Tolerance of him till now had a great deal to do with their suspending disbelief. "Good thing for us," one whispered, "that they've only been playing football for a year in Ireland."

But above their aversion to the Yank now running the team, the players demanded to know where negotiations stood with Russ Jensen. Zark claimed Sterling Management had been communicating daily with him; next he said it was Frank doing the talking. Then, pressured, he admitted neither was true; nobody had spoken to Jensen in weeks.

"Do we look like fools, man?" fumed Femi Amu, a defensive back as he turned on a stunned Zark. "Do you take us for fools?" Femi was renowned for his blunt parries except when he got beaten by a wide receiver, which was rather often. "Nobody's called him, and you and Frank are probably calling us fools behind our backs. Don't be calling us fools too long."

Pisarkiewicz's pale face reflected his concern. The mood turned ugly, tempers shortened. One of the players called him a noodle. Another challenged him to go outside; I had to hold him, er, myself, back. A threatening situation, and the tic of fingers flicking his temple didn't alleviate it.

Poor Pisarkiewicz. From Frank's fiscal dystrophy, his own techno-blunder, he was like a movie projectionist tripping over unspooled film. But he not only snubbed collaboration with the other Americans, he treated them as if they got Ivy League degrees majoring in coloring books. He could not finally keep the players from regarding him as a pariah. They saw his salary as eating up good sterling that could have gone to get Jensen back.

On the pitch were faces punctured by uncertainty. Another sport, become champions, and circumstances stand to improve in a hurry. The Bulls had only gotten more derelict, and it demoralized the Brits. They couldn't understand why. If you had an American face, they looked imploringly at it for answers. But now when they looked at Zark, all they felt was contempt. The most emotion he'd raised among them was when he absconded to Oxford, carrying off a sack of footballs and leaving us with only a scarred youth model with which to conduct practice.

Desperate, he tried to quell things by bringing Shoop and Thornton into the Bulls' front office (the figurative front office—such an assemblage impossible in the physical space of Frank's foyer) as tri-general managers. But then came something that made him out a real rotter; rather, would have made him a rotter if he hadn't been an American, to whom the term is never applied.

A newspaper story appeared about the Bulls' new GM, a single person named, with quotes making clear he'd reneged on letting the others share the job as "authorized by Frank." It was only going to be a title for them, anyhow, since he never listened to what they had to say. But Thornton couldn't confront him quickly enough in the hotel lobby, amid a coaches' conference there. A hundred British correspondence course coaches must have been wondering to themselves if this was their dramatized lesson in dealing with disgruntled players.

March

18

Opening kickoff of the season less than 24 hours away, Bob Shoop did sit-down comedy by telephone from his hotel bed. "Enthusiasm of the players has been a pleasant surprise to the coaches . . . but we're not overconfident because of all the adversity we've faced in the past," he said. "We know what we got to do . . . but as they say, on any given Sunday."

After I gave him an imbecilic look for clichés fresh to British ears, he cupped a hand over the receiver. "It's the laughable *First Down*, he allowed, "and Frank said you got to tell those guys what they want to hear."

That night I'd seen at the theater *The Importance of Being Earnest*, whose theme of self-inflation Oscar Wilde called Bumbryism. In the hotel lobby, where the convention coaches were milling, I stumbled onto Bumbryism en masse. One coach, whistle around his neck, gesticulating with a clipboard, informed a colleague: "This is a play that worked extremely well for us last year." He elaborately scripted the *X*'s and *O*'s, and said, "We call it the down-and-out."

"Ah, beautifully diagrammed," praised his mate.

Frank Kalili, of course, hated such practitioners of self-importance; he thought they trivialized Britball. Frank himself had made a last try to cast off his lassitude, having shown up at the hotel, and seemed to be ubiquitous at the coaching conclave, except when he caught sight of the Bulls' player-coaches.

When one of us made a step in his direction, he waddled away. His flinching countenance was so far removed from that charisma-curry-and-kite-cord character who had kept the Bulls afloat, who had almost basked in the fresh ink of home mortgages, and had definitely basked in the ink, fresh or stale, of true quotes, that it looked once and for all as if football had emasculated him.

The term "beautiful corpse" came to mind; or maybe requiem for a gridiron governor. Last time he looked so glum must have been the day the Feed-the-World-Frank story broke.

Yet, the next day, as the Bulls' lineup was being called out over the loudspeaker against the Dublin Celtics, he overcame all that ailed him to join the team beneath the grandstand at Alexander Stadium.

The Bulls had chosen to have names of our starting defense announced, with each player cheered on by teammates as he ran through two lines of them at midfield.

On the sideline, I was plotting kickoff coverage, when all of a sudden, out of the corner of my eye I saw a frumpish figure, bedecked by white skimmer cap shading a deranged angelfish face, as he superseded the tannoy's next player introduction by going through the receiving lines straight into a maw of TV cameras and photographers.

Through the players he went, shambling, fists held high, then carried on down the sideline acknowledging the cheers of the crowd.

It was, of course, Frank Kalili. Outdoing himself with his most lifelike impersonation yet of owning a gridiron team.

March

19

Frank's jaunt helped. With no American hired hands in their lineup, the Dublin Celtics, neophytes at gridiron, doubtlessly intimidated facing a former NFL quarterback whose name they could ill pronounce, and imbued with Irish spirit but little else, made meager opposition. An actual rainbow appeared over Alexander Stadium in the second quarter, but it betokened nothing except to make easier to appreciate how the Celtics were the size of leprechauns. We won in a teacakewalk, the outcome so predictable that a reserve defensive back, George "T" Nisbet, spent halftime in the grandstand signing autographs.

Even little Andy Jefferson got to play near the end, threw a few passes, completed none of them, but sounded outstanding when shouting his cadence of "Blue—40! Blue—40!" Our place-kicker, Spider Webb, made a lovely 51-yard field goal between the jerry-built wooden uprights facing the M6 motorway and twice helped the Bulls' kickoff team pin Dublin inside the 10-yard line. Yes, all in all, an auspicious debut for the Animal Roberts-led Ragtime Rambo Big Every Time Posse.

Most important, from the 25–3 victory, the Bulls drew a fortifying spirit that might let us carry on to Euro Bowl in Holland.

But where was the sponsorship to fund us through? Despite

the program advertisement, of "Going Places," not a pound of it had materialized.

Sponsorship aside, no denying we were a team on the upswing. Kenneth "Spats" Lewis, in prison this time a year ago, started the new season not only as a free man but also by being selected the game's Most Valuable Player as voted on by the experts in the pressbox—though somehow they failed to notice he was yanked from the field five times by coach Thornton for blowing pass coverages. As someone who had voted for MVP's in the past, I felt certain the acclamation had come Spats's way not for what he'd done between hash marks, but from how he endeared himself off the pitch, with winks and words to fans in the first row of the stands, particularly those of the distaff persuasion.

Others also were deserving, among them the brilliant Trevor Carthy, who on his only offensive play of the day ran 80 yards for a touchdown. Trevor could run like a roebuck, all right, but unfortunately he also played pass defense like one. As a defensive back, he got victimized by the Celtics' lone successful offensive play of the game, a wobbly halfback option pass that came down over his head like a dirigible and got caught right in front of him. We still had a huge cavity back there in the secondary, and he wasn't helping to fill it very well.

I had been begging for involvement on the pitch, and finally got it. Responsibilities as an assistant to James Thornton ranged widely, chief among them managing the Bulls' Rastafarian fans who insisted on watching the game not from the stands, but from the sideline, and traipsing onto the field to register dismay when a penalty went against us.

Many of the Rastas once played for the Bulls before giving up gridiron on philosophical (they didn't believe in practicing) and physiological grounds. I really couldn't blame them. Dreadlocks proved an impediment when they got tackled—and that was only after they succeeded in getting a helmet over their heads in the first place. If the dreads were of deluxe length, oh, the misery.

Had they stuck around and had an influence on the game, manu-
facturers no doubt would have devised a model with a rear vent.
But after a couple of seasons the Rastas opted to be fans.

They also hadn't liked it very much when head coach Russ
Jensen ruled out smoking ganja on the team bus, even after a
victory, which they thought rather brusque of him.

I wasn't as inflexible as Jensen, and on the sideline the Rastas
and I began an uneasy alliance; how could I, certified white bread
and probably the only 33-year-old male in captivity who had
never in his life smoked a marijuana joint but who enjoyed the
smell of the stuff, feel anything but hypocrite telling them to
douse their joints? So, with Jensen not around to rebuke them,
I resolved to let them light up, toke away, but only when the
Bulls were on offense.

Still, I couldn't give their ganja the attention it richly deserved,
because, as we were scoring so often, special teams preoccupied
me. Special teams, in fact, were going on or coming off the field
almost every play, and given that this was Britball, going on and
coming off at the same time. But they generally excelled, except
when we failed to count off and put eleven men on the field. The
thought crossed my mind that maybe, as sporting a people as the
Brits are known to be, they had handicapped themselves to give
the Irish a better chance.

As the electronic scoreboard at Alexander Stadium blinked the
final score, the Bulls took a good, long look at it, not only because
it might be the last scoreboard we saw all season not operated by
hand and chalk, but also because we should have won by three
times the margin. Good thing, as the player remarked, the Irish
had been playing gridiron for only a year. (Actually, they'd been
at it two years, but were trying hard to forget the first, embarrassed at having lost another Euro Bowl qualifier to the Germans.)

But we couldn't have asked for a better opponent, and not just
because they were so effortlessly dispatched. The Celtics had a
civility unforeseen in gridiron, gentlemen to the point of twice
picking up and folding a penalty flag after they'd been called for

infractions. They were heroic as well. Almost as strapped financially as the Bulls, if such was possible, they had, during their brief history, been uprooted from four practice sites, finally forced to work out on the strand, which was fine so long as a practice schedule got coordinated with solunar charts for high tide.

As for sponsorship, the deal was real as convertible Corn-iches for the coaches to tool around town in. But having lived bare-boned for so long, the players were more caught up in victory, and to fans' delight, we lined up for another Kalili-choreographed Bullrush. Frank was too tuckered from his elegant cameo, from exerting and propounding himself, to join us. For him the afternoon had been one long bow, followed by the blare of a headline the next day: BULLS GIVE SUPREMO [KALILI-] LEADON FITTING FAREWELL.

So he was quitting again, aye? The Bulls couldn't be bothered to waste good eyestrain on that one. Broken record by now, Polynesian swill at 16 rpm.

Victory did allow James Thornton temporarily to cast aside his discontent; he scurried about Alexander Stadium shouting how he was "a big 1 and 0" as a head coach. From the look on his face, victory might even have put his self-deportation bid on hold.

Shoop also got excited. "Oh, man," he exulted after scoring two touchdowns, "I'm going to get laid tonight!"

"Ah," Denton Thomas said as he squired the Yanks to a post-game party, "a standing cock has no conscience."

Zark, two years abroad with teams that folded or showed him

the door, restrained his jubilation; something seemed to be both-ering him, surprising for a man who'd once again resurrected his career. He spoke to a portly Irish supremo, who was irked about the Celtics' lack of lodging and repast in Brum as promised by Frank, becalmed him, and they began getting along splendidly. Then he showered, and with his public transit savvy, awaited the Number 51 bus to take him to New Street Station, where he'd catch the 18:36 Longbridge train to Five Ways Station near Frank Kalili's house. If he got much better at it, they'd probably make him a conductor.

When he returned to Yew Tree Close he spent two hours on the phone with the coach of the national team, remonstrating over the mistake it'd been to fire him, how this blight on the résumé was undeserved. The victory over Dublin, his two touch-down passes, and a handful of spirals, was vindication, and he got almost as heated as that dread vindaloo in telling it.

After celebrating, Shoop, Thornton, and I hitched a ride back to the hotel, only to be told at the front desk that we would be on the street the next morning unless our bill was paid. Yes: eviction redux. It was, Thornton snarled, Frank's bill, but still, we were astounded to learn it ran into the thousands of pounds—astounded at the amount, even with Thornton's ravenous appe-tite. What had happened to the cheap rate Frank claimed to have wheedled?

"Bill's Frank's fucking problem," Thornton repeated.

"Fraud Leadon," Shoop said. "Lied to us again."

"What are you blokes talking about?" asked one of the Bulls younger players, Davey Parkes, who'd driven us to the hotel. "You just have to know Frank for who he is—the Willy Loman of British-American football." It was one impersonation I'd never thought of, though the name, Frank Kalili-Loman, had a nice ring to it.

Afraid we wouldn't even have purple sheets to fall back into, we spent all the next day contacting real estate agents, frantic for housing. One of them got back to us with a listing that sounded promising—the location: around the corner from No. 10 Yew Tree Close.

84

Only after much prodding did Frank agree to meet us; true quoting was never more feverish than after a game. Also, he was cussing a film crew slated to shoot the game only to get lost and never make it, depriving him of a drawing-room viewing of how his attire and sideline inspiration had helped produce another Bulls victory.

Finally he waddled up, gave the house a cursory inspection, and explained to the realtor that stipulations must be met before he would agree to take it. Like sharply lowering the rent for the pioneer of Britball. The realtor agreed; the house had sat empty for almost a year. Frank signed a lease—Zark standing over his shoulder to give the transaction an official look—and promised the first few months' rent would be paid in advance.

That fine upstanding firm, F.L.A., its coffers stuffed with gate receipts, would take care of that. After its chief executive officer got what was coming to him, of course. The realtor could only smile at getting the house occupied. Had he been a follower of the team, or been familiar in the least with the Bulls, however, he'd have known not to expect a Bullrush bearing a company check.

March

21

Our expeditious move into the new house was by Mercedes limousine, the hotel manager's way of thanking us for an extended stay—and for our substantial if still outstanding bill. To get there the limo traversed a carriage road that once led to a spacious estate, whose owner through his will was a perpetual benefactor to the poor. Alas, his money ran out long before the Bulls became worthy candidates for alms giving.

Still, bona fide housing marked an emergence; at the very least the postman would no longer bombard Frank Kalili with the team's bills; that we knew because some of them almost preceded us into the house.

The address, No. 9 Star Hill, rang apropos of Yanks playing Britball. Small and postwar, the house sat next to a prep school, which owned it, in a leafy neighborhood called Edgbaston. And be it ever so humble, there's no place like a new front office. "Yeah, man!" Zark exclaimed, examining the house. "I definitely can see us living here awhile." He shimmied a toothpick. "Hell of a lot nicer than what I had in Wales. Just hope we can keep the place a little cleaner."

I was happy to hear housekeeping was another attribute, and

envisaged a new notation on the résumé: "Compartmentalized neatness at No. 9 Star Hill. Led maid drills and defended against bathtub rings. Charted vacuum cleaner routes relied on by general manager—interim head coach—emergency quarterbacks throughout the U.K."

The house's physical properties were compelling—my bedroom was eight feet by eight feet, a potential training site for any Bull expecting incarceration. It sat on the sloping end of a cul-de-sac, once another carriage road. Kin of former prime minister Neville Chamberlain trod it to attend the prep school, West House. Among more recent passersby had been the head of the United Kingdom's embalming empire, Howard Hodgson, himself an old boy.

Huckleberry trees canopied the road, and wood pigeons flitted about feasting on the berries; to me, a squab fancier, potential meals in themselves. The neighborhood atmosphere was rich and redolent; the school's compost heap sat but a few yards from my window, the spoor of red foxes was always about. Star Hill wasn't Henry James's "unmitigated England," but close. Of a morning, malt from a nearby brewery—Davenport's, the first in the country to serve bottled beer—augmented the olfactory ills of having to cohabitate with a subspecies of human given to excessive flatulence. Here I drew the line with my bad breathing, though Zark, who occupied the bedroom next to mine, wasn't very sensitive to it.

While the house signified progress for the Bulls' staff, Frank and F.L.A. still hadn't fully provided: There was a carport at the house, for instance, but no car for it (though Zark, so not to waste precious space, parked his cleats there). Nor did we have use of the old blower, meaning Frank couldn't call to check on us—real sensory deprivation, that—but Zark would pass along communiqués and our regards.

It might have been, in fact, a while before we got a telephone; British Telecom, notoriously laggard, would likely take longer on finding out that their new customer was the Birmingham Bulls. According to Denton Thomas, the team's last phone line got cut after a bill accrued by a member of the team's front office, whom he called a "phone freak," reached £6,000. But here again, as with the house lease and the hotel bill, Frank jumped right in with the magnanimous name of F.L.A.—rather James Thornton jumped in for him, forging Frank's signature on the installation voucher. Unquestionably, it was the finest signature in all Britball.

March

23

Among early visitors to Star Hill was the markets man Mr. Nice 'n Fresh, whose first vegetable run of the season included crates of spring cabbage and cauliflower. The thought of them almost made Bob Shoop green. Yuk: Brit food bagged his enthusiasm for eating. A McDonald's drive-through, the first in Brum, had opened nearby, and it buoyed him. He'd also received in the mail a cache of chewing tobacco that rounded out his diet.

Mr. Nice 'n Fresh brought enough stuff to feed the vegans of Cornwall for a year, not only quantity but finest quality: fresh, ripe, firm. Despite Shoop's protestations, to the others at Star Hill Mr. Nice 'n Fresh was the nearest thing the Bulls had to a god-send—and by his pedigree, it wasn't a bad description of him.

"Carl, can I tell you, man?" James Thornton said, referring to him by his christened name, or one of them. "Women are just unbelievable again. They're out there, cuz, are they ever."

Women? Mr. Nice 'n Fresh very much liked the sound of it. His wife had nagged him of late about monogamy, cracking down; thanks to Thornton, he'd at least get some vicarious thrills.

And make no doubt, it was withdrawal. Before moving to Brum, Mr. Nice 'n Fresh had been a devotee of the free-sex religious legend known as Baghwan Shree Rajneesh. He had first been Baghwan's gardener and later his produce manager; he and his wife had communed with Baghwan in open-boudoir colonies in Rajneeshpurham (nee Antelope), Oregon, and Poona, India.

Baghwan himself hadn't been heard from in years, even by disciples like Mr. Nice 'n Fresh; it'd been almost a decade since his deportation from America, where he had the worldly habit of wearing tea cozies as skullcaps, was protected by a private army, and owned 93 Rolls-Royces.

But how incommunicado was he? What with the ties between Mr. Nice 'n Fresh and his great friend Frank Kalili, one never knew. Frank, himself a semi-son of the Raj, had already shown how the Indian mystic/pseudo-Polynesian influence could affect the game. With Baghwan, just think of all the coupling at half-time.

And a more plangent muse: How possible that Baghwan Shree Rajneesh, with his luxury fleet of Silver Arrows, might all along have been the Rolls dealer with whom Frank was negotiating to sponsor the Bulls?

March

24

Had he been a sportswriter, Dickens would have taken the Bulls for his beat. Though our hands were out wide, we didn't always go begging. The new landlady rang the front doorbell at No. 9 Star Hill the moment we arrived. Wife of the headmaster at the neighboring school, she would come to rival Mr. Nice 'n Fresh as a goddess-send—though she personally had never heard of Baghwan Shree Rajneesh and, like 85 percent of the English people, didn't attend church services.

Matronly, her skin one of those whiter shades of pale, she spoke in bashful syllables, but with unguarded generosity; she showed up, arms loaded with blankets, linens, and a teapot.

Her name was Susan Duce, and while propriety was etched in her milky complexion, just plain Sue Duce was fine by her. "Duce," she said. She smiled and averted her eyes. "I guess you Americans would think of Florida orange juice." Her comportment was that of a favorite aunt not adverse to going dancing, so long as an early night was made of it.

In a corridor she stood, hands clasped in amazement as if four mesomorphic men—actually three mesos and one mid-morph in Bob Shoop—were the last thing one would expect to find in Great Britain. Like many, she'd never heard of the Birmingham Bulls.

She referred to us as the Bullets, though they happened to be Brum's basketball team and she'd never heard of them, either. (Besides, both teams played imported sports; moreover, it was understandable for the Brits to get big people mixed up: The Bullets had faced a 7-foot-2 center who later would line up against the Bulls at nosetackle for a gridiron team from Manchester.)

I clarified things for her: The Birmingham Braves were the local baseball team—local baseball team that played on a soccer pitch, since only one regulation diamond existed in the whole of the country. And the Brummies, yes, the Birmingham Brummies, were the city's speedway squad, giving me civic pride since I'd never lived in a city with a motorcycle racing franchise. Shameful they didn't drive the dazzling machine of yesteryear, the twin-stroked B.S.A. (Birmingham Small Arms Co.), but, alas, the company had been among the casualties of the city's industrial malaise.

She was out on Star Hill the next day taking the family's geriatric springer spaniel for what the Brits call walkies. Pausing as the dog used the bathroom in our yard, she sauntered over to ask through an open window about the Bulls' next match.

"A friendly this weekend in Bournemouth," I replied reveling in her curiosity. "Why? Might you be a spectator?"

"Er, uh, no I shan't think so," she said nervously. "Actually, I was just being polite."

"Oh."

I discerned from the set of her jaw that she'd written gridiron off as nothing more than what a British critic called "the trash of American culture." "A bit over the top, isn't it?" she declared. "I don't mean anything cruel by it, but my husband says they're all posers." She smiled. "But that might just be His Nibs. He isn't right about everything."

"She's sporty," James Thornton assessed after she repaired to her house next door. "Yup," he said with a coy smile that caused me to swallow hard, "I think we've found the woman you've been looking for."

I didn't disagree and had, in fact, invited myself into her house to watch a BBC movie titled *Defrosting the 'Fridge,* which was nothing about freon displacement, but a gridiron-à-clef, alluding to William "the Conquering Refrigerator" Perry, who was credited with launching Britball in an NFL exhibition at Wembley Stadium in London played before 80,000 people.

One of Frank Kalili's chums was the film's technical adviser, but none of the characters was endowed with a tenth of Frank's egregiousness. It dawned on me: He was the composite of several of them. The founder and owner of the team came closest, a mortician who drove a hearse in a suitably low-slung style—how better to conjure Frank's fatalism?—with a constant bleat about sponsorship: "Even synchronized swimmers have backing in Oklahoma!" He also was the team's starting quarterback, which went Frank one better, but you couldn't have reality all the time.

The coach was an American, imported straight from parole at Missouri's state penitentiary, where he'd coached the football team and boasted "every one of my defensive linemen was a convicted murderer." The Bulls had, of course, outstripped this plot device, with our imprisoned secondary, not to mention Frank's own brush with the law.

Sue Duce watched this verisimilitude unfold, when she could be disturbed from her knitting. When the coach gave an inspirational talk, gruff and midwestern, she sat particularly intent. Till now, the Duces had known only one American, an elderly Rotarian from Nebraska, who during a visit duly informed them, with plenty of flat-voiced pomp, of a vaunted team Sue called the Cornshuckers.

"Cornhuskers," I corrected.

"Well," she plowed on, "according to him they're at the center of the universe."

Our cultural exchange continued with tea in the house she called Woodbourne Manor. She was but the second Englishwoman of my acquaintance, after a romantic interest I met in Brum South. Of good looks and bearing, more captivating was how she'd been given a Welsh corgi by the actor who plays "Q" in James Bond movies.

"Hear that, Rosie?" Sue asked the old family pooch as it sprawled in a sagging chaise longue. "I think we've found a new friend here, what? You're always in dire need of someone who'll drag you along for walkies, aren't you?"

With her favorite word, the spaniel barked as if on command, only to be beset by incontinence. "Oh, Rosie, you've gone off!" Sue said without obvious embarrassment. "You're whiffy! What will this new American friend think?"

It wasn't too bad, considering what I'd been putting up with next door. For football players, imitation is the sincerest form of flatulence, and there was much among my housemates to imitate. But I didn't dare commit the indiscretion of mentioning it in Sue Duce's company.

Besides, she was too absorbed in the movie, whose climactic moment has the fictitious team exultant at having finally scored on the last play of the game in a rout by a U.S. Air Force base.

What an exaggeration of the sport; it had me fuming by the end, though I maintained decorum in Sue's presence. But such a cockamamie denouement might give Britball serious credibility problems. The sequel probably would have a championship team owned by a Don Ho impersonator trying to pick up sponsorship from a Rolls-Royce dealership.

He spoke and smoked with what syncopation a man in his shoes could muster. People asked what had gone wrong; he didn't have an answer, just mantra: "Got to find a rich American who wants a play toy." With an ironclad stipulation, no questions asked or criminal charges checked up on. Agree to those terms, Frank Kalili made it known, and you've got yourself a football team. Or maybe you didn't.

The kitman, Malcolm Byron, often brought along to practice a friend who was a businessman and had expressed an interest in buying into the team. Leave it to Malcolm; as kitman, he knew what was likely to break and best jury-rigging for it, having learned utilitarian shrewdness as a motorcycle jockey. Now he was trying to apply his touch to fixing a football team. His boyhood friend John Eyre was in the process of selling one of the companies he owned, had a sale pending, and he'd expressed to Malcolm Byron a hope of pouring the profits into a gridiron team.

For a month John Eyre sat at Moor Lane and waited for an overture from Bulls' management, a futile wait. While Denton Thomas never failed to compliment him for a Chicago Bears cap he wore, a previously unabashed Frank Kalili couldn't be bothered even to introduce himself. Odd, but then again, his reluctance, when it came to a name like John Eyre, probably stemmed from English Lit having been one of his poorer subjects in school.

But apparently, he'd also become selective over who and what kind of money he would allow for life-supporting the team. John Eyre wasn't only the prospective investor. Several British companies had inquired about taking us on, offering sponsorship, but when any of them sought the Bulls' financial records, they either got turned down by Frank or, as with John Eyre, ignored altogether. And how to explain the stalled-out Rolls-Royce deal? For three months he'd been shilling it, yet nothing materialized, not even a test ride.

Also damaging was the repercussion from the Bulls' first sponsorship deal, which came from one of the country's biggest breweries, and was meant to be a model for gridiron: a lump sum, then an annual package for as long as the team maintained solvency or showed the money was spent prudently.

The Bulls had begun as a franchise with the awarding of minority grants, a good-faith gesture for gridiron. "They came from a Labour council," the co-owner Denton Thomas recalled. "There was a lot of money around, they gave it away by the wheelbarrow load, if you were gay with one leg and needed six chin operations, you could get whatever you wanted—council's way of showing itself anti-Tory." Denton, of course, had a big hand in landing them. He was a minority, maybe more than he knew, because in the early days with the Bulls as a reserve lineman, he had been, putting it euphemistically, a shy lineman—by most accounts, the shyest player ever to put on a pair of shoulder pads.

Later the Bulls got more grant money, then acquired the brewery sponsorship, a hefty package team founder Gerry Hartman landed through slick talk and perseverance of his own. But when Frank Kalili jumped in, literally, and claimed credit, since the deal happened to be accompanied by a sizable finder's fee, there was a rift. "Frank commandeered the guy with the sponsorship check—grabbed him right up," Hartman claimed. "The guy comes in Frank's store looking for me, asks where I can be found, Frank hugs him close and says, 'Hey, babe, I think it's me you're looking for.'"

True quote?

But with Bulls' management of Hartman, Denton, and Frank, prudent spending was akin to asking a sumo wrestler to keep out of the kitchen. Sponsorship lasted just one year, before a fit of creative accounting in Frank Kalili's drawing room nixed it. When the brewery asked where its money had gone, the three of them sat up into the night making out receipts that would read the right way. "Can't you see them all, worried about going to the nick?" snickered Jess Rodgers.

"Frank was in such a state," recalled Dave Parkes, the player whose father, a brewery executive, helped secure the sponsorship. "I remember him calling me mum and going to pieces over what to do."

How wracking it had become for a man who was awaiting the call from Buckingham Palace with Queen's Birthday Honors making him the first Brit knighted for gridiron. But would there be any Birmingham Bulls left by then to attend the ceremony? We had run afoul of reality, terribly afoul of it. Rock-bottom beckoned. The Bulls were desperate, and there was a daily workout expostulating it by Frank Kalili's vocal chords.

Frank's vocal chords. Yes, vocal chords. If the team was to be saved, they were the ideal vehicle; surprising he hadn't thought of it sooner. For here was laryngeal deliverance: all the late nights he'd proudly spun his old records . . . Polynesian blasts from the past . . . indebtedness to him of Brum's vast musical community. Everything added up to high notes of hopefulness for the Bulls.

Start blowing those tiny bubbles again, babe. Frank would come out of retirement as a Don Ho impersonator, regroup the wonderful Waikikis, assemble them onstage as a lei-lined life raft for his football team, and stage a benefit concert in conjunction with our opening game.

All for Frank-Aid.

Just like Feed-the-World-Frank, even have T-shirts silk-screened with his own sallow likeness emblazoned on the front of them, except this time he'd have community spirit, not to mention the law, on his side.

Frank would impresario, the Bullrush blending with a musical cabaret, say start out having one of Brum's best acts, Ozzy Osbourne, do something outrageously akin to when he'd bitten the head off a bat on stage. Say, have Ozzy eat a layer of plastic from a pair of shoulder pads.

Maybe reassemble the Bulls cheerleaders, with the inclusion of Frank's rock star paramour—their two-week affair, remember?— surely she'd help out in this, his hour of need. Get up there on stage and sail into one of her signature songs, itself emblematic of Frank Kalili and his hopeless devotion to his football team.

Anything, for Frank-Aid.

Anything, but the reality of it, of barely staving demise. "Hold off the earth," Hamlet's pal Laertes intoned as he buried Ophelia. To which James Thornton clamored: "Fucking two-facedness of this sport's unbelievable!" and his brush of indictment swept over Yew Tree Close. Almost everyone with a British accent on the team had given up on Frank, and the Yanks fine-tuned their Brummagem epithets, too.

But then, as if he had planned it all along, maybe with a Polynesian football fertility god's divine intervention, 33 complete sets of equipment, of kit, turned up one afternoon inside his garage. The Bulls believed our fortunes had turned, were sure Uncle Frank and kismet had hit it off once again.

"I'd love to see another storybook season, and this one's got the makings!" said an inflamed James Thornton, who'd agreed to stay on at least through the regular-season opener against the archrival London Ravens.

"Hey, we're gonna survive this shit, man!" Zark proclaimed, wildly kneading his hair. "Oh, yeah!"

"Just win, baby, like the man says," came Thornton's coda. "Just win—and forget all the other shit."

But it was false hope. The kit was on consignment, Frank averred, being sold for his son, who had owned a lesser team gone defunct and who was now trying to salvage some of his investment. Though, if his ownership was anything like father, like son, maybe all that had been invested by him was someone else's signature.

Dotting the English landscape were sham castles called facades, which had once given the nobility something pretty to look at. The Bulls were a facade football franchise, if that. "We've got a few pieces of stationery with a logo, that's about it," Zark assessed.

But how much of a phantom football team were we? A solicitor engaged by James Thornton, Esq. and bête noire, looked into the Bulls' financial background and found we weren't listed on the national business register. Talk about legerdemain . . . you had to hand it to Frank: creditors damned sure couldn't collect what they couldn't find.

I began to ponder the possibility of buying into the team, buying in with the ulterior motive of securing a spot on the roster. But what, next to a nip at nosetackle, would I get for my money? Maybe, if I bargained hard enough, he'd put up his record collection as collateral.

The Bulls, meanwhile, reeled in the direction of the regular season; whether we'd reel enough to get there was not yet clear. Still, even without a stadium, the Bulls were better off than teams that played in the infields of speedways and whose players might miss a tackle, then fall and lacerate themselves on an old magneto lying about.

The rival Leicester Panthers were financially the fittest of teams, but their ownership had not yet recovered from the psychic fallout of having to mount a javelin assault against the disgruntled Steve Harvey. And another deadly weapons charge was being considered against a star running back for the London Ravens, who, after an exhibition game, invaded an opposing team's locker room, not to press high-fives, but wielding a Phillips-head screwdriver.

More discouraging yet, a player for a team called the Gateshead Senators had become British gridiron's first on-the-field fatality, when he suffered a stroke trotting out after a kickoff to retrieve a tee.

In a single week, three Budweiser League franchises had folded: the Capital (nee Cardiff) Tigers, Steel City Giants, and Luton Flyers, all of them Bulls' rivals in the Midwestern Division, which now ceased to exist.

Still another team, the Northampton Stormbringers, despite having ceremoniously signed a coach who'd led Finland to the Euro Bowl championship, was on the brink of disbanding when only five players turned out for practice just days before their opening game.

Maybe we Bulls in our stumbling roundelay weren't atypical; it could have been gridiron was a failing entity in Great Britain, even with the purest intentions of pioneers such as Frank Kalili.

March

31

Now came word Frank was quitting, and his latest cry of capitulation was starting the new league in Spain. As things stood for the Bulls, with no funding to go beyond our first game, time was riper than ever for him to get out. At last he empowered Zark to quote a sale price for ownership in the team. It was paltry; a pittance. Obviously, he wanted to see the Bulls survive more than he wanted to line his pockets—if he weren't wearing the spandex pants he was so fond of, which didn't have pockets.

He was being magnanimous, all right; and with a pooling of funds from the Americans and pledges from the players, it seemed the Bulls would be starting afresh, and in a communal spirit, not unlike the early days of the NFL. But when Zark went back to Yew Tree Close with our offer and told Frank we'd met his asking price, the price he himself had set, he turned it down.

We couldn't call him inscrutable, though, because while declining our bid, he raised his asking price thirty times over. "I'm not the brains of Britain," said Jess Rodgers, who'd been with the Bulls from the beginning, since giving up a career in military intelligence. "But he's empire building. Even I can see that."

I saw it differently: Frank Kalili's patina of misery wouldn't be complete without gridiron, the stricken face, the rheumy eyes with nothing to attune themselves to. Remove himself cold turkey from dial tones and true quotes? It'd be, for an entertainer like Frank, stageless fright. But how much longer would the Bulls provide a stage for him?

April

1

Describing the Bulls as Dickensian may have been taking it too far. How about: We were the best of teams, we were the worst of teams. British champs, we had won twenty games in a row, yet outside a pipeline of true-quotism in the gridiron press, nobody took notice of us, particularly in Brum, ironically referred to in the papers, with its plummeting soccer and rugger teams, as "success-starved second city."

During one of our first mornings at No. 9 Star Hill, James Thornton inhaled a pail of cornflakes while watching an old movie on television in which Bill Cosby, as owner of a financially ailing ambulance company, picks up a football, holds it aloft, and shouts, "It's fourth-and-twenty! Everybody else'd drop back and punt! But we're going to pass, pass, pass! This franchise is not going to go under!" Thornton's spoon tumbled from his mouth and he spewed cornflakes and shrieked wildly.

While anybody looking for a terpsichorean atmosphere was in the wrong neighborhood, gallows humor at the breakfast table was considered good etiquette. Steve Pisarkiewicz, however, barely glanced from his typewriter. "Man, ain't nothing here to be GM of," he'd decided. The plaint grew. "I mean, I ain't going to hook or crook money off the street, no way, man."

Despair at Moor Lane moved from cubicle to cubicle. Most motivated man on the pitch was Malcolm Byron, whose toolbox contained every kit accessory the Bulls owned. He lugged it around like a secular chaplain of parsimony and giving, jealous of every helmet snap. But he cared. Not only did he volunteer his services, repaid only by thankful faces when he replaced a face mask or chinstrap snap, but few Bulls realized the sacrifice he made tending their needs. Sure, he drove to practice 60 miles each way from Nottingham, not even asking gas money. "Trouble with this American football," he said, "is the season kills the best birdwatching in England. Especially the shorebirds."

Up till now, his ornithological activity had not included a region the Brits called cloud-cuckoo land. But now he was caught up in it with the Bulls. With other British sports, a team becomes champion, and the future is paved, with sure footing. The Bulls had only gotten more derelict, and demoralized. We were not a happy few. We doubted for our survival, strong doubt, odds of going under before we could defend the grotesquely lovely Budweiser Bowl trophy.

Maybe the NDMA would intervene, what with Britball's future on the line. "Nah," Zark declared. Those guys got together, wasn't an eleeomosynary molecule in the room.

James Thornton was no less disparaging toward the man with whorled hair and a withheld wallet. He had made photocopies of a tab leader charging of a cabinet minister, "YOU ARE A LIAR!" and given them to the Bulls, asking that they be mailed to No. 10 Yew Tree Close—or better yet if the player had an unsavory past and a threatening mien, delivered in person.

Thornton also began searching for a solicitor to sue the man who'd enabled him to become a star in Britball. "Minute I get my money, cuz, I'm history." He continued his hectoring, too, and plotted a departure that might coincide with a little financial gain, or regain. One morning he accompanied the other coaches into town. Flustered by what was happening with the Bulls, he wasn't sure where he wanted to go with the rest of his life, but this much he did know: He couldn't get away from Brum fast enough. But short of deportation, not a penny in his pocket, he had no way to go.

As we made our way through city center, he saw security men milling, and spotted bolted mailboxes and globs of yellow plaster that had been pressed over manhole covers—all in precaution for a rare royal visit by the queen—and then it came to him. The smile on that big, expressive face grew almost dastardly.

The queen could get James Thornton repatriated, take him away from Birmingham and the Bulls once and for all . . . without even issuing a royal decree. All HRH had to do was be complicitous—moreover, complicity that didn't require she know anything about it. Just let James Thornton act ominous toward her, passive ominousness at that.

Thornton wore a sharkskin suit and wraparound sunglasses, and carried a black briefcase as he stood on Colmore Circus, where the queen and her entourage would pass. "All I got to do is look at my watch and stare off in her direction every now and then," he said. Yes, if he really wanted to go home, he'd found a way, and most likely in handcuffs. "Just look menacing, you know, 'cause how many six-foot-five black guys you think they got around here when the queen comes to town? I'll just lurk, man."

His neosinister approach had merit. Then one of the Beefeaters guarding the queen marched past, and his face so utterly resembled Frank's scuffed Teflon complexion, that instead of wielding a pike, he might have had a Silk Cut in hand—Thornton was completely disarmed.

Maybe he'd have another entry in the *Guinness Book of World Records:* first person to fail at getting deported. Moreover, he'd failed twice at it, the first time after an encounter in a hotel lobby with Bob Preen of Sterling Management.

Preen was brought in by his crony Frank to drum up sponsorship for the Bulls but struck the Ivy Leaguers as keener on using the team for furthering Sterling's own interests. He'd made no contact with the coaching staff, none that we knew of with potential sponsors. Bob Shoop stalked him through the lobby and then confronted him. "Do you even know what a football is?" he demanded. "If I threw one and it hit you in the face, would you know? Just what the hell is Sterling Management, anyhow? Who do you manage? A third-rate P.R. company is all you are. You're—"

Preen, a prissy three-piece suit, recoiled to level the only threat he possessed. "You can't talk to me like that, young man. Why . . . why, I could have you deported."

He turned on James Thornton and bleated, "You . . . you as well."

Thornton smiled as Preen beat a retreat. But he had not yet misbehaved enough to earn the reward Preen threatened to pay him.

April

3

The peripatetic Pisarkiewicz hoped to stay in Brum, to outdo himself and put down for a few months. A noble thought, that one of these days tomorrow would have roots, and maybe this was it. But by now he could not be caught in a droning monologue as he balanced sticking with theFrank Kalili and F.L.A. against once more hitting his odyssey button.

For the moment, he was filling out a roster for the next game, correction fluid on standby. Always expanding on the GM's job, he was deciphering, as well as typing. Typical was a new lineman who, when asked on the league's player application form for his position, had written "tacal."

At one of his first stops in the United Kingdom, in Wales, he had according to his résumé told how he'd "implimented the game in it's most simpliest form." But "impliment[ing] the game in it's most simpliest form" with the Bulls constituted human relations. From the start little coziness existed at No. 9 Star Hill. Partly, the rift was how Bob Shoop and James Thornton felt at his excluding them. Or, as Ivy Leaguers, it could've been they envied him for having gotten to Oxford before they did.

Not that their whingeing was groundless. Since they'd barely been paid in a month, it irritated them Zark was making three times their salaries for a job that the Bulls as they saw it, didn't even require. GM in Britball was a sinecure if you had good earplugs and ample patience. Most teams didn't have a general manager; for those who did, it pretty much entailed finding Americans, paying Americans, and last but not least, pacifying Americans.

To the players Zark was a window wallah, talking it up, not acting it out; they also were fast coming to regard him as Britain's strangest tourist since Rudolph Hess. They'd grown more derisive toward him after he let slip a good gate for the Bulls from a friendly against the Bournemouth Bobcat. The Bobcat—they preferred the singular—was ex-Packer-slash-CIA operative Andy Capp's team, and would have been a good test following the Dublin laugher. But the game got canceled inexplicably, to the Bulls' chagrin, and mine. NDMA constraints for imports didn't apply since the game was an exhibition. Thus disappeared a prized chance for me to get into kit.

The players were angered because the Bobcat hosted the Bulls annually, paid expenses, offered not only a share of the gate but also a fete afterward in which the old operative Capp could be counted on to give one hell of a match debriefing.

Missing out on all that, the Bulls loathed Zark more than ever. He couldn't be troubled to learn their names, his practice garb shamed them, he made them run that awful lap around Moor Lane. A more subtle dislike of him reigned, whereby they sensed him as a crony of Frank Kalili, his clothes crusted with Frank's cigarette smoke. But a real anathema was having him as quarterback: If in the lineup for one game, he might want to play all season. They knew what trouble it'd been the year before to get an American quarterback, their first, and when Russ Jensen came to them, delivered by Frank Kalili, it was divine intervention— Frank's version, anyhow.

Having beaten the Irish, the Bulls were now assured a shot at the continental crown, but to win consensus we needed Jensen back, even if it meant players emptying their own wallets, which they avowed themselves willing. But would their wallets have enough left to satisfy him?

April

4

Why so sold on him? Jensen didn't have Zark's credentials, then again, he didn't snore or technologize. He was a veteran of the USFL, where he claimed to have earned $10,000 a week before he got into acting. The players fondly, frighteningly, recalled him as 6 feet 2, 225 pounds of rollicking wrath. Bob Shoop watched a Bulls' game film where he ran 50 yards to score over six broken tackles. "Tell me," he declared, "he wasn't a man among boys."

On that film he was indeed impressive. Of course, his best cinematic work he saved for Hollywood, because Russ Jensen's other career was now in pictures.

"The king," even Frank Kalili said in obeisance to him. But at the exact moment whatever was regal about him, silver screen, bedsheets, or quarterback sneaks, remained on the West Coast. Russ Jensen, what with commitments and deep-sea fishing, was still disinclined to rejoin the Bulls. He also reckoned, he'd informed several Bulls players, to be playing football in the fall for the San Diego Chargers.

But startlingly, progress had been made at fetching him back to Brum over the Chargers' offer. According to Bob Shoop, Jensen might be coming back to take himself a bride, though the woman at the moment was already married. Brum, of course, was equipped for any nuptial possibility, however, as its annual output of 50,000 wedding rings, highest in the world, attested.

That incoherent midnight call placed to him a month ago from Frank's foyer queered things for a while. But after a two-hour telephone conversation with GM Pisarkiewicz, followed by a fax-fest of contract clauses and stipulations (everything but weather reports), he was on the verge of re-signing with the Bulls, when he suddenly shouted into the phone, "Hey, this ain't right, it just ain't right. I can't come for this kind of money."

"Hey, man, you ought to sleep on it," Zark said.

"No, you ought to sleep on it," Jensen shot back.

"No, you sleep on it."

"I ain't sleeping on shit."

"Well, one way or other," Zark stated as he hung up the phone, "we're going to have ourselves a quarterback by the end of the night."

To the Bulls, his recounting the story could only mean the quarterback we'd have by the end of the night was one with a snoring condition: Zark himself.

"Ain't playing on the same side with that mouthpiece, mate!" Jess Rodgers huffed to Billy the Club Mills.

Mouthpiece?

"For bloody Frank the Wank!" Rodgers roared.

"Mates, there are horses for courses," the captain Steve Trow announced to the team after Zark left the pub at Moor Lane, "and this bloke's the wrong one for us."

"Being GM in this country," Bob Shoop declared, "is just like being queen—a fucking figurehead." But would our figurehead abdicate, be overthrown, or stay on to run the Bulls? Or were we soon to find ourselves with a new king?

April

5

Having Russ Jensen back seemed superfluous on the morning Zark folded himself atop a stairwell, defeat furrowed into his face. Ordinarily, he spoke to me only to seek expertise on the shower, a British conundrum, which could be scalding or frosty without a deft hand on the knobs. Now he unburdened himself. "Birmingham's the right place, wrong time, for football," he averred.

Nor, in his estimation, were the Bulls any longer "a happening thaaaang." He'd found out during a foray to Oxford that Sterling Management had decided to sever its ties with the team, though what, if any, benefit they had been to us was questionable, even he had to admit. But, no, their "help" couldn't be counted on.

His duress was great. Worse, perhaps, was that Frank wanted him to subvert his duties as GM to help set up a new shop, an expanded Great American Sports.

An ex-NFL starting quarterback stocking shelves? He could live with that, sure. But since the amorphous F.L.A. had taken out the loan on the new shop, and Zark, through his elaborate contract, was part owner in the company, how likely that he could be held financially liable if the shop went bust?

• • •

Increasingly concerned for his future, he skipped another practice to spend the evening at No. 10 Yew Tree Close. Regardless how the team fared, how uncertain our future, every time he went around the corner he came back having fortified his estimation of Frank, and how appallingly the players had treated his noblesse oblige. "Stole him blind, man," he said. "They'd go in his shop Saturday morning, and next thing you knew the damned shelves'd be empty."

One man's opinion, colored, of course, by blueberry brandy and, always, Tennant's Extra. But the facts were, with no sponsorship, with no owner participation, the Bulls looked none too good at surviving; we knew not where to turn. But the players determined to save the team, make it last until the Euro Bowl contest in Holland, do whatever it took. Maybe, with the proclivity for things that got some of them behind bars, they'd find an imaginative way to come up with it.

April

6

🏈

🏈

🏈

Zark pledged to meet with the players in the Moor Lane club-house, though unnerved by the thought of it. "What'd Frank say, 'Unleash the animals, or player power'? Don't do nothing but make the shit we're in deeper."

His fears came true when Femi Amu, known not only as the Bad African for his Nigerian roots, but as the Verbal Assassin, lived up to his nickname. "You know nothing about running a football team, fool," he lashed out from beneath a dilapidated cap that bore the legend RAGING BULL, "and so long as you answer to Frank, we think even less of you!"

At that exact moment, a line from Zark's résumé that compared him to another older pro quarterback and read "I certainly consider myself of the 'Don Strock' mold" might have been, "I certainly consider myself of the 'dumbstruck' mold."

Zark recoiled; Femi, worst smoker on the team, had terrible halitosis. "Why not go where you are wanted?" he said. "Else-where, man!" The meeting deteriorated from there, and I couldn't help feel this wasn't quite what Zark's résumé hailed as "meeting time productivity." When we returned home from practice that evening, the other coaches saw him through the front window in a perpetual slump over his typewriter. Maybe he was steno-graphing the team's death certificate. But the instant we walked through the front door, he jumped up exclaiming, "Man, Russ is coming!"

Never mind that the cutoff date for signing imports was now past; the NDMA was never a league to let its own rules stand in the way of anything.

It was his lone triumphant moment in the front office. "Yeah," he gushed, "Russ said he was bored back home and might as well come on over." He licked his lips. "How 'bout that?" he said again and again.

Where did Jensen's reappearance leave him? Where did it leave Frank Kalili? Antipathy between them was obvious; could Frank color over it? Everything was appearance in Britball; he was a master at manipulating it. Once, as we'd walked through Brum's city center, he flipped £1 to a well-dressed beggar. "When you see a man in coat and tie looking for handouts, it catches your eye, babe," he stated. "You know he's put some work into it." Yes, all appearance, as Frank well knew. And with the imminent return of the best player in British gridiron, "the laughable *First Down*," as Bob Shoop called it, now trumpeted another coup by the Wily Midlands Fox:

"Birmingham Bulls' supremo Frank [Kalili-] Leadon has done it again to ensure the return of superstar quarterback Russ Jensen."

Indeed he'd done it again, a passive achievement that came directly in the face of a possible literary phobia. For Russ Jensen's return and his transatlantic flight had been paid for by the American Express gold card of one John Eyre.

April

7

As if his zen weren't already impaired, James Thornton bruited: "Russ'll terrorize Zark, minute he walks into the house and decides which bedroom he wants. Biggest one, bet on it."

The flicking of his temples became chronic even before Jensen hit Star Hill. After the new American strode in wearing a black Stetson, with a bamboo flyrod wielded like a riding crop, a brooding mien and unspoken command of the house, Zark couldn't vacate quickly enough. Twenty-four hours later, the only evidence that he still lived there were his carefully typed memoranda.

It was one of those memos that would sever his hopes of hanging on in Brum. It intimated to the other Americans that a car dealer keen on the Bulls had arranged for the coaching staff to have use of a vehicle.

A half day was spent looking for the dealership, which the memo had located near the hotel where we'd been billeted by Frank Kalili. The coaches searched in a blizzard, not exactly the Californian Jensen's idea of fun abroad.

Cold and stewing when they trudged back to No. 9, they hashed out a memo of their own, its contents exceedingly stylized, as dictated by Jensen, who boasted a college degree in psychology, and written in Thornton's calligraphic hand:

"We're tired of all the fucking 'tomorrows' and the promises. How about getting something fucking done?"

They then took their cumulative anger to the Birmingham *Evening Mail,* and spent hours with a reporter on grievances against Bulls' management. The reporter had never heard such whingeing, even by Brum's high standards, and summoned her colleagues to her desk. She twigged it a great story, only one thing needed to punctuate it. But when she sought his response, Frank Kalili was forthcoming with no true quotes, no comment whatsoever.

But as GM, Zark took Frank's deft lateral, inhaled and nasally rebutted, "I really don't understand what they are complaining about. Russ Jensen and James Thornton played for the Bulls last year and knew the score." He then gave the refrain mouthed by management for three months, mastered straight from the Frank Kalili handbook of verbal prestidigitation: "There have been cash problems with the team because we are still trying to negotiate sponsorship and reorganize the management structure."

But when he put down the phone, it must have hit him how he was GM of nothing but rumor, fallacy, and a tinge of fraudulence.

Not long afterward, as Bob Shoop rifled a manila folder, looking for diagrams of Bulls plays, a yellowed clipping fell to the floor. Shoop took a moment to peruse it, then broke into laughter. "Listen to this: 'Drafting of Pisarkiewicz may have been a terrible mistake,' " he read aloud in a stilted voice. "Sound familiar, anybody?"

Bizarre-kivich, another chapter closing on him. He was gone in no time. When last we saw him, he'd reapplied his lifetime pass on that road to nowhere, a slumping figure on a train platform at the little Five Ways Station. "There's nothing here to be GM of," he'd said, echoing another newspaper story written about him in the NFL that began: "Steve Pisarkiewicz, the Big Red's forgotten man, is like a conductor without an orchestra. His music is only make-believe."

He repositioned himself for a while in the utility suite on Yew Tree Close, but it didn't have the appeal as before, curry wafting up his nostrils and dogs beneath his feet, and besides, not his nature to stay in one place too long. "I really don't know where he is now," Russ Jensen later told a sportswriter pursuing his whereabouts. "Last I heard, he was looking for a quarterback job in Italy."

It was, yes, almost that romantic. In fact, Steve Pisarkiewicz once again was pumping up his résumé, another lustrous notation, having been named coach and GM of the very team he'd helped defeat two weeks earlier. Quick crossing of the Irish Sea, and he was under new contract, of undetermined length, to the Dublin Celtics.

April

8

Frank Kalili's standoffishness toward Russ Jensen could have been deemed not only health-conscious behavior, but professional jealousy. For here was someone else in the organization with more than one illustrious identity: football player *and* relatively undiscovered star of American television.

Considering everything written about him in the gridiron press, a player of his credentials in Britball was akin to Winston Churchill's chairing a jaywalking subcommittee in Taos, New Mexico. But here he'd reappeared, had opted for an encore. Jensen, after the rigmarole he'd gone through with the Bulls and their owner, was the last Yank expected to have his passport stamped a second time. He was back, pure and simple, for the lucre.

He wasn't exactly a nobody back home; he'd had a pro football career right up there with Andy Capp's, having played in the NFL, though, not with the Packers. He could, in fact, count himself one of few NFL alumni in Great Britain who hadn't played for Green Bay, bringing himself more distinction. He'd spent most of his career with the L.A. Raiders. He just didn't have the stats to prove it. He did have, in what was equally important to a Britball player, one of those ennobling football wardrobes that utterly coordinated his heart to the Raiders' black and silver, and in Britain, if it looked good, it played good.

He also did a stint on the developmental squad of a USFL team, before the league died in debt. His having chummed with some Hollywood heavies, including the former Harvey Yeary, Jr. (nee Lee "Six Million Dollar Man" Majors, a part owner of Jensen's old team) helped him get cast in *First-and-Ten,* a cable TV series featuring a fictitious football team in weekly upheaval, coincidentally nicknamed the Bulls. From a thespian vantage, he may have been back in Brum researching his role in the show.

Jensen had to be among the most underpaid TV stars of all time, or since Flipper the dolphin. He was paid not by scene or spoken line but by body part—since he really wasn't a cast member, but a cast appendage. (As he said little, his acting style might have been called Method appendaging. Brits, of course, hate the Method, but until Jensen, had never seen it applied to football.) Only his right arm got shown on camera, it but sparingly, in a few close-ups. His spirals were what earned his TV exposure, when he managed to throw them. He made a measly $100 per show, but got a second C-note for each physical hit taken during filming.

But if he was unsung in the States, he made up for it in Britain, where he not only got raves as "the King," but where *First Down* gushed over him as the "former L.A. Raiders star" and "ex-NFL great."

All the exuberance over him was understandable, for Jensen not only consented to lengthy interviews but also gave them for free. (In Britain even third-division midfielders got a good dip into a sportswriter's wallet before saying anything.) Here was the best player in his sport syllablizing, or in Russ Jensen's case, monosyllablizing at no cost. Then again, his career NFL stats couldn't very well speak for him:

	Years	Att.	Comp.	Int.	Yards	TDs
Russ Jensen, QB	1	0	0	0	0,000	0

More amazing were stories told by the Bulls of his dexterity. He could really move around in the quarterback's pocket, and may have been even better out of it. The players and Jensen himself liked to joke how when last season ended, he'd stayed on in Brum with his girlfriend, living in a house that also happened to be occupied by her husband.

As for being Britball's best, he was nonchalant. "All that matters at the end of the damned day is getting paid," he informed fellow player-coaches. He'd rejoined the Bulls again as the highest-paid player in the game, but still it seemed puny. Jensen liked to boast to the Bulls he'd made more than $100,000 a year in the USFL—"that's ten thousand bucks a week," and a lordly sum for someone with a career limited to the developmental squad. It also bred more professional jealousy in the organization, for as the Bulls' own developmental squad, I wasn't getting a penny.

When in his first season with the Bulls he heard a rival QB in Leicester was outearning him, he'd demanded a raise. Soon, it seemed his salary was doubled every week, and from at least one account money came right out of Frank Kalili's home mortgage. That account was Frank's, of course.

The second time around, Jensen ordered the Supporters Club into the Moor Lane Lounge to set forth his contractual demands. They were enrapt by him, or frightened silly. But he couldn't scare money out of them they didn't have. Maybe if he lied and said he was doing benefit gridiron clinics in Third World countries, they'd have been more inclined to give him what he wanted.

That left the players as his best bet for lobbying. And what lengths they would go to for him were boundless. For here was a man who was an avowed enemy of politesse, who'd struck a couple of his fellow players physically, who berated them on the pitch for the sole sin of being British, who ignored them off it, and who threatened not to play in one game after another, straight through to the championship, unless his financial demands were met. Yes, many members of the team still had a lot of colonial mentality in them, for when Russ Jensen got back to Brum, they were chuffed to bits, thrilled to see him.

April

9

Until Jensen's arrival, the Bulls depended on the caffeine content of high tea to lift our spirits at practice. Now it got singsong; Jess Rodgers even told a joke:

"Bloke goes in a pub, asks for 'alf pint of bitter. Bartender says, 'Got no beer, mate, don't sell it no more.' 'What you got, then?' 'Rat,' bartender says. 'Got rat. Can get you 'alf a rat, rat wall-banger, rat and tonic . . .' 'OK, mate, 'ave 'alf a rat.' Bartender goes behind the bar, 'olds up a rat, slaps it down, cuts it in two, sticks it in a glass, and 'ands it to the customer. 'Ain't drinking that,' bloke says, 'I ain't. Got no 'ead on it.' "

Now the Bulls got ourselves a 'ead coach, and couldn't 'ave been 'appier.

The most punishing it had ever gotten for the Bulls at practice was when James Thornton shouted at an erring lineman, "You're messing up my damned aura." But with Russ Jensen running the team, not only the motivation and esprit picked up sharply, but the heavy breathing, too. And the offensive huddle, which had been a maelstrom of discontent with squawks coming from 11 different directions, grew reverential when he stepped into it.

The last practice before the regular season began against the London Ravens ended with a potato-run, another lap around

Moor Lane, a mile and a half of suffering that saw the player last in line pass the leader as the lap progresses. Billy the Club Mills, the 300-pound center, could barely drag himself around the course. Mills lapped no one, never would, never could, though the players not only encouraged him, but also always waited patiently for him at the finish. Now they went further; among those who'd completed their run, murmurs began of, "Let's go get him!" affirmed by "Aye! Aye!" and 40 Bulls dashed far into the darkness to give Billy the Club an escort.

"Hey, that's a team, man!" Bob Shoop exclaimed as Mills came into the fold. "A team, man! Oh, yeah!"

Bring on the Ravens. But first bring on the oxygen.

After practice, Jensen, outfitted in requisite black L.A. Raiders' garb, gathered the team. When he told the players, "We'll go over team rules now, so everybody listen up!" it was extraneous, since he could've asked them to eat dirt and they would have stuck out plates to have him fill them.

"No threatening or touching a coach," he began, "or you're gone. No smoking in the locker room. No smoking anything. Anything, you hear, dammit? No women on the team bus until after we win the Euro Bowl, and then you can bring 'em back with you, however many you can get on."

And then Jensen, whom they regarded as a frightful bully, despite fawning over him as player and coach, smiled through his mustache, and said, "One last thing—make sure the head coach has a beer in his hand at all times inside the bar over there." They clapped and convulsed, astonished the Bulls were, saw it as the closest he'd ever come, or was likely to come, to committing an act of human kindness.

April

10

One of Britball's largest crowds descended on Alexander Stadium for a game between the country's best teams, though some in it might have been motorway watchers who wanted to see what kind of traffic the M6 was offering that day. But many who came no doubt were aware of a continuing trend: The Sadlers Wells Royal Ballet had just moved from London to Brum, as soon would the D'Oyly Carte Opera, and now gridiron's influence was shifting, too.

The Ravens had gone five years without a loss and their first three seasons unscored on, until the Bulls put up a touchdown in a 61–6 loss that earned a notation in the team's official history. Now we had pulled even, the fans knew it, and there was a frisson in the stands reminiscent of Brum's Saturday shopping concourse. The Bulls opened the game without a huddle, a neat trick for muddling a committee-minded British defense, and Russ Jensen dropped back and passed 50 yards to Bob Shoop on the first play.

This was that razzmatazz the fans had paid to see, and it got contagious: The landlady Sue Duce, watching gridiron for the first time, complimented Shoopy for his "Maori war dance" in the end zone with fellow receiver Nizzy Nisbet after a TD catch. "I even put down my knitting to watch it," she said.

Sue also had talked her husband, the Americanophobic head-master, into attending. While she got a lot of knitting done in its three-and-a-half-hour duration, Mr. Duce, almost to his dismay, found himself enjoying the game. Perhaps his pleasure came from the treatment he got: The Duces were to have been left compli-mentary tickets at the box office by Frank Kalili, but after he forgot about it, serendipitously, they ended up in a luxury box.

Afterward, at his manor house, Kim Duce gave a postmortem that lasted nearly as long as the game itself. He didn't quite understand the penalty of face-masking, though as he also hap-pened to be a court magistrate, he cottoned to the idea of penaliz-ing teams for unsportsman-like conduct. By two o'clock next morning he still didn't feel as if his new neighbors had done enough explaining of gridiron, so he ambled over to No. 9 Star Hill. He'd just begun to hear about the shotgun formation, when his eyes were diverted. "And what's that amber liquid, if might I ask?" he said, pointing to a bottle on the dining-room table. Five enlightening shots of tequila later, he felt sure he had a better grasp of the game.

Russ Jensen really hadn't felt like explaining it for him; nothing personal, but the game against the Ravens was an outing he preferred to forget. The Bulls' unsettled finances, not to mention his own, and the team's invisible ownership so perturbed him he'd gotten victimized for four interceptions by the Ravens sec-ondary. As they were all British players, this made for one of the most embarrassing American moments abroad since that new McDonald's drive-through opened in Brum averaging only two customers per hour.

Jensen had thrown just six interceptions all last season, and most of those were spirals. But even on an off-day he was too formidable for the Ravens, him and the Bulls off and passing from the start, getting on with the scourge of the sport. Shoopy alone caught a dozen passes in the first half; all Jensen had to do was make sure the football stayed airborne. Our defense didn't fare nearly so well; these were no dumbfounded Dublin Celtics, they knew where the end zone was located, and what it was, and we had to come from behind in the fourth quarter, with two touchdowns by Trevor Carthy, before winning 26–22.

The Ravens, with an all-British backfield of Joe St. Louis and Victor Ebubedike, managed to go ahead three times against us, each time on a spectacular run. But clearly this London team was not the black and gold of old. For excuse, they didn't have to look very far, or very far back, yet to recover as they were from shock of last season's loss to Dutch champion Amsterdam Crusaders.

In this first Euro Bowl match played on British soil, the Ravens had scored an apparent winning touchdown with seconds to play, only to get too exuberant in celebrating . . . even by indigenous standards. They buried the TD maker in the end zone to cost themselves one 15-yard penalty, then, before the extra point was attempted, another celebrant booted the football into the stands for a second infraction. With the Ravens forced to kick off from their own 10-yard line, the winning points for the Dutch became mere formality.

But the Bulls too long having been the Bulls, we were conditioned against such overt displays. What ought to have been a smashing start for us, victory over the Ravens in the home opener, instead rated bittersweet at best. For we had just been informed of our eviction from Alexander Stadium for overdue rent, unless the gate from our first two games was enough to get us clear. And what with the Sterling Management having been authorized by Frank Kalili to handle gate receipts, it was a toss-up whether we would be back playing there before Buckingham Palace staged its next coronation. Still, the Bulls' season had begun on a triumphant note—or was it the first note of a funeral march?

Even with a fattened gate, the Americans were handed £50 each by Denton Thomas and told they'd have to settle for it "until receipts get sorted out." Sordid out was more like it.

As the Yanks griped with great conviction, Denton, rubbing his forehead, urged patience. "At least five Bud League teams," he rued, "have debts more substantial than the Bulls."

Of course Russ Jensen could care less about their plight. In his anaconda boots and Stetson he skulked No. 9 Star Hill. He wanted cash in hand; that was that. Only language he understood was serial numbers, or in this case, the queen's smile. Management had only a little longer to come up with it. If not, back to the fishing and the filming, a quick return trip to California.

He was hungry for it, and relentless; put in a round room and told there was a nickel in the corner, he'd have gone off to cloud-cuckoo land. Money: The mere thought was enough to transform his laconic disposition.

But his pursuit of it helped clear up, once and for all, the sponsorship situation, the team onus for months. He picked up the telephone and rang the Rolls dealership, vehemently demanding it follow through as promised. After all, every day in abeyance was an insult to his own pockets, since most of the money from it was supposed to load them down. If it meant crashing through the dealership's showroom glass, mustache bristling like a cavalry charge of cutlasses, he'd get it.

But when, after berating a secretary and melting switchboard lines with invective, he got the manager on the phone, he went stone silent. He was informed if the dealership followed through with anything that had to do with the Bulls, it would not be sponsorship but perhaps a lawsuit for false advertising.

In a desire to see the Bulls survive, undoubtedly with a nudge from his close friend Preen at Sterling Management, Frank Kalili had placed the full-page advert in the program against the Dublin Celtics, with nothing, nothing whatsoever, to back it up but his own high hopes.

Speculative advertising: another of Frank's bold concepts to further Britball. Alas, its time hadn't come. "We are not now, nor have we ever, given consideration to sponsorship of the . . . the . . . what did you say the name of your club was?" Russ Jensen was told.

Jensen, with seismic grace, slammed down the phone. "Fucking Frank again!" he shouted as the receiver bounced. His retort hung almost physically in the air; around the corner at No. 10 Yew Tree Close, Frank Kalili must have felt another coronary twinge.

The Budweiser League, with its 17 surviving members, didn't have such a strong pulse, either. Almost every team struggled. Meanwhile, neighboring minor teams in the Midlands such as the Redditch Arrows sported sponsorship patches from McDonald's while a tiny nondivision team, the Tamworth Trojans, with no Yanks on their roster to showcase the sport, got backing from an American-style amusement park. Another secured its sponsorship from the British Law Society though there was but one team qualified for that endorsement. Maybe the lawyers could have done pro bono work for our secondary, too. Or, when the Bulls went under, whisked us away to High Court for the compulsory dissolution.

The Bulls' poverty didn't go over well with James Thornton, or his stomach. He didn't want to be deported anymore—he wanted to be adopted. Or to adopt. "I'm forming my squad," he said, standing in front of a full-length mirror at No. 9 Star Hill, slipping on red suspenders. "Seven different women for seven different nights. I ain't going to go hungry in this damned town, cuz. For food, or love."

Money was the real concern. Jensen was hopeful of renewing ties with the Raiders, and Bob Shoop wasn't saying die, either.

His new stardom abroad, making touchdowns, had for the time being silenced his mantra of "I'm going home!" He'd put his Yale education to work, too, composing a visual-display package promoting the Bulls, with a dozen sheets of posterboard, chockers of facts, figures, and boyish exclamation points.

His hook was the possibility of a Brum franchise in the WLAF—the World League of American Football, the NFL offshoot. BIRMINGHAM IS A MAJOR CITY! his billboards bandied. AMERICAN FOOTBALL WILL MAKE IT EVEN BETTER! GIVE YOUR COMPANY NATIONAL EXPOSURE—SPONSOR THE BULLS! THE OTHER TEAMS IN THIS CITY ARE LOSERS! ASSOCIATE YOURSELF WITH A WINNER!

Not to be outdone, Russ Jensen sat and drafted a letter to his old boss, Al Davis, president of the Raiders, asking him to "finantuoly support the team." With the gifted Zark and his portable Corona no longer available for handling the Bulls' secretarial duties, Russ Jensen ordered me, as assistant GM, to touch up the letter and dash it off to his friend, "Mr. Davis."

Retracing his imaginative missive, I held little hope of a reply. So far, the only tangible evidence of NFL backing for Britball was a set of old San Diego Charger uniforms donated to the team's namesake from Thames Valley—and a Dallas Cowboy offensive lineman who credited his blocking technique to his father's having once been a Beefeater at Buckingham Palace—and of course the NFL's magnanimously having allowed the Budweiser League's official statistician to chart the exhibition played at Wembley Stadium. Perhaps it even had provided him with a pencil.

On a terribly newsworthy weekend, tab leaders told about a chimpanzee that tore the arm off a five-year-old boy who came too close to its cage, while in *The Sunday Sport*—the Bulls' preferred reading material—one read of a circus performer's capacity for "bonking": ELEPHANT MAN HAS HEFTY LOVE TRUNK.

But the biggest headline in Brum was WE'LL QUIT, SAY U.S. FOOT-BALLERS, which hovered atop impromptu travel plans by a trio who had "left teams in the United States to join the Birmingham Bulls." If paychecks weren't forthcoming, and quickly, the Yanks were goners. So the story went, although the players not for a second believed them, not even Russ Jensen—not with our Euro Bowl match soon upcoming; the Bulls put more credence in the elephant man's amor story.

Predictably, with his discourse about food and love, James Thornton had given in to his own animalistic urges after meeting a female advertising executive at a bar. "I did it for the team," he said the next morning at No. 9 Star Hill, "yup, for the team, I want you all to know."

"Proud of you, man," Shoop said as he sat down at breakfast to his first glass of cola.

"Atta boy, James," Jensen chimed in, which was about as verbose as he ever got.

"She said, 'I'm old enough to be your mother,' " Thornton recounted. "I said, 'Yeah, but I'd never do these things to my mother.' " He smiled. "For the team, man."

We endorsed him again, naturally, since it came off as another exciting new approach to scoring sponsorship: the utilizing of extremely free-floating libidinal urges.

But James Thornton began to find himself at the mercy of those free-floating urges, which occasionally surfaced somewhat inappropriately, too. After market man Mr. Nice 'n Fresh, whose niceness knew no bounds, invited us to his house for dinner, Thornton borrowed from him a £10 note, then carefully folded and creased it.

"Everybody—watch what the queen does," he said.

He took note in hand, gently folded it, and began moving it strategically. "Hey, is she going after the whole thing, or what?" By working the sides of the note up and down, folding it to where part of her royal garment became a phallus, Her Majesty was depicted in a licentious act. "How 'bout that, cuz?" he said. "Animal showed me."

The £10 note aside, Thornton's penury exacerbated his irreverence for the monarchy. "How fucked up are Brits," he grumbled, "that they'd pay millions just for royalty? Fergie got a sixty-nine-thousand-pound raise this year, Andrew got eight-four thousand. For fucking what?"

As for his own worsening finances, he averred, "I'm watching everything now, man. Everything, everybody." He claimed to have found six or seven loopholes in a contract Zark so meticulously put together for him. "And that's just the insurance part of it."

In what once would have been a major development, Denton Thomas finally produced applications for work permits for the Americans. But Thornton had wised up. "We can't afford to get work permits or we'll get taxed," he said. "And, hell, we ain't making any money, anyhow." He stared down Denton. "So, anybody asks, you tell 'em we're serving as volunteer coaches in return for room and board."

Thornton also enunciated where he stood as player-coach: treading quicksand. "Everything here's done by the widget system," he said with damnation. "Last year was kind of like a vacation, this year it's all business." As in doing business, doing it for the team, wherever he could pick it up. As for the Bulls, from the looks of things, we were almost out of business.

April
18

At No. 9 Star Hill, the coaches were deep in preparation for our next game, reviewing film. "Man, I can't believe that!" Bob Shoop declared boyishly. "Jeez, she's—" The sleeve from which the film came was inscribed "Blue Movies." When finally they inserted a game film, it'd gone a few plays before Russ Jensen shouted to James Thornton, holding a remote control switch: "Stop, dammit, stop it right there!"

One of the Bulls receivers, Terrence Laukum, was running a pattern on which he was wide open to make a touchdown catch, but as a defensive back converged, he let the football sail past his unstretched arms, refusing to try for one of Jensen's better-thrown passes.

"Funniest thing I ever saw!" Shoop convulsed.

"Fuckin' not funny to me!" raged Jensen. "Fucking' alligator arms!"

Unpaid, he'd become increasingly crochety; took it out on the players, coaches, even excoriated me for donating cauliflower from Mr. Nice 'n Fresh, which had become moldy, to the neighboring prep school. I figured, with rent at No. 9 two months' overdue, it was a wise goodwill gesture. But Jensen disagreed, and

134

as head coach and chief bully, ordered me to the market for fresh cauliflower.

James Thornton also took to brooding; food may have set him off, too, possible depression after the *Guinness Book of World Records* announced it was deleting 25 categories of gluttony, ending his aspiration for getting into the record book through a certified contest in which he wolfed thirty glazed doughnuts in six minutes.

Also, he and Bob Shoop had journeyed to the McDonald's drive-through, and though they were the only customers in line, they were forced to wait a half hour for their order of cheeseburgers and french fries. "They just don't get it over here," he decreed. "It's a nice country from afar, but far from nice when you have to deal with it every day."

More dismaying, our next home game was a few days away and we didn't have a home in which to play it. With uncertainty over the Bulls' future, our roster shrank, falling below 40 players, fewer than 25 of whom turned up for practice. Worse, Jensen called for a film session in the Moor Lane Lounge, to review our next opponent, the Leeds Cougars, only to find our viewing preempted by the seating of a women's bowling team.

But at least some sustenance was forthcoming; the captain Trow forked out £30 to help get the Americans through the weekend. The money, he allowed, had been collected by the Supporters Club, but who knew what motives they might have had in giving it? Maybe they only wanted to see the Bulls survive.

April

19

With Alexander Stadium denied us, the Bulls were told to go play in the traffic—the traffic of Spaghetti Junction. More specifically, we were consigned just below it, to what looked like a playing field of last resort: the condemned velodrome called Salford Park, whose infield the city kindly had given us on credit for the game against the Leeds Cougars.

Once previously the Bulls had played there, in a friendly the team's first year. Having been an upscale act at Alexander, we did not thrill to the prospects of going back, except for one: getting to play on a real 100-yard field. Scarred as it was, the pitch looked circa 1918 Marne. Dressing quarters were the size of a pantry; moreover, to the dismay of the many Bulls who'd run up against the law, boarded-over windows gave it the ambience of a holding cell.

It was St. George's Day, which broke miserable and spitting snow. "Even G-G-God is now against us," Denton Thomas muttered in the chill.

Following promotion, the Cougars were playing their first game as a member of the Budweiser League. But they proved tougher than expected, with a passing combo of Americans from the U.S. semipro championship team from Racine, Wisconsin.

One of them, doubling at defensive back, got a little close with his coverage against Bob Shoop, who retaliated by spitting tobacco juice on him. But the British officials were lenient; also, new to football, they had never seen anyone expectorate on an opposing player.

Besides our slumming back to Salford Park, there was something else of historic significance for the Bulls: For the first time in memory we made our way onto the pitch without Frank Kalili running alongside to be introduced to the crowd, or handle choreography, spot-stagecraft (with the anthem), or interviews—his absence possibly pinned on not knowing if there'd be a P.A. system at Salford Park for announcing him.

But it wasn't quite toodle-oo for Frank; he was true-quoted in the next day's newspapers, top of the sports page, calling for "British bulldog spirit" in the national team's upcoming game against France—to be played, incidentally, at Alexander Stadium, the match cosponsored by him and Sterling Management.

As for anything else in the local papers, it wasn't the Bulls; our 49–29 victory over Leeds totally got omitted. Not that the game rated as notable, except for new equipage for the Bulls that arrived just in time for the match, and what then took place with needle and thread in our locker room. The new equipage was mandatory shoulder patches from the league-sponsored brewery, and the exigency of the moment became 250-pound men sewing the patches onto tattered jerseys. Brum, city of 1,002 trades, now got its 1,003d: gridiron embroidery.

The Cougar coach, an unemployed oilfield roustabout from Alabama who parlayed his résumé into getting work as a football coach in Britball, had a flair of his own for the game. He had persuaded fans to erect scaffolding at midfield as a coaching tower, relaying his instructions by walkie-talkie—although the scaffolding stood only a few feet behind his team's bench, well within hearing distance, and was a little over head-high.

Given such a challenge, I couldn't help respond. I was, after all, Bulls' bench coach while the other Yanks were on the pitch; the coach the referee sought out when explaining, or with British officials, trying to explain a penalty. Not only was I an earnest

listener to the men in stripes, but Russ Jensen also proved receptive to my ideas. One of them was a play he credited for breaking
the game open, "49-toss," on which Trevor Carthy ran 50 yards
for a touchdown. From my vantage, the call was all too easy to
make: I noticed early on how James Thornton, blocking at the
point of the play, was exploiting a 100-pound weight advantage
over the defensive tackle opposite him.

Thornton was juiced over getting to play, reestablishing his
domination on the line of scrimmage. In the locker room before
the game, he glanced down the bench at linebacker Colin Nash,
who also was returning to action from his latest injury, an eyelash
laceration against the Ravens. "Cuz, warm that neck up," he said
as Nash rubbed Vaseline over his neckroll, "you've got to jump-
start that fucker." Some of his enthusiasm stemmed from having
received the Bulls' first new piece of kit in memory, a helmet from
the Supporters Club. He had been almost mesmerized when the
Greenwood brothers gave it to him; at his locker, he'd checked
it out thoroughly, every underfilled pocket of air in its lining a
potential brain scan nightmare.

Russ Jensen's dependence on my play calling came about after
a hit he took in the second quarter. Judging from how he walked
around in circles, he had suffered a concussion. Woozy, he came
to the sideline, eyes rolling back in his head, and said, "Find out
who we've got that can play quarterback . . . don't know if I can
make it." His bell was rung, for sure; lucid, he'd have known we
had only the tiny Rototillered punker, Jeffo, as backup.

But dazed and with a separated shoulder, he stayed in the
game. His toughness harked to what the running back and locker
room philosopher Paul Williams had remarked: "They all say
they're going after him, put him out, but instead he goes after
them. He'll call a play and run the ball right at them, and the shots
they take at him just make him angrier to give it back to them."

A Revenge of the Killer Quarterback concept; who knew but
how he might be developing it into another TV series?

April

20

Bulls' blasé play or not, I was chuffed at the outcome: For the third game in a row, my special teams excelled, although I would have been first to admit that excelling in Britball meant lining up to punt without a snap going over the punter's head or his kick getting blocked, or not having him flinch from the rush and turn around, tuck-tail, and run straight out of the end zone for a safety.

As bench coach, my responsibilities again included sideline patrol against encroachment by the Bulls' Rastafarians, and they behaved well . . . and wisely, with Russ Jensen back in Brum; the ganja stayed in their pockets, though I did chasten several of them for trying to pass beer to players during the game. (Animal Roberts refused the offer—only bubbly for him.)

Russ Jensen was too concerned by our shorthanded personnel to celebrate the victory. A new face had appeared at practice, with a promising physique to go with it, both identified by our assistant physio John McGowan as belonging to a former Bulls linebacker named Bobby Lewis. "Good player he was early on, till the game advanced faster than his brain." But brainless or not, we could have used him, thin as we'd gotten, especially at linebacker.

We were short everywhere, it seemed, but team chauffeur, where we'd begun to develop a depth chart. Son Tustin could always be counted on; he drove 120 miles round-trip to practice in his big B.M.W., so what was a few blocks out of the way— though the Yanks were reluctant to ride with him because they hated opera, which he had a propensity for playing. More promising was a spiffy chap bequeathed us by former owner Gerry Hartman; Keith Linden also doubled as backup place-kicker and bon vivant.

But when Jensen appraised it, he counted almost 20 names missing from last season's roster. Key players had quit, or retired, or were unavailable to play. It was that last description that struck him as most glaring. "They've been in prison a year," he'd said of the incarcerated secondary, "and they'd start for us tomorrow if they got out."

He hoped to persuade Frank Kalili into providing game statistics from the previous season, since the crimes alleged to have been committed occurred on Sunday afternoons, when the Bulls were playing gridiron. Jensen couldn't say whether they were innocent or not, but he definitely wanted them back with the Bulls.

But Frank, as the Brits are wont to say, didn't want to know, and shunned any importuning. And without the stats to introduce as evidence at their pretrial hearing, the three defensive backs were left in remand at Winson Green Prison.

Frank's communication with his team was not cut off, however. We heard from him through the mailslot at No. 9 Star Hill, when came a letter signed by the realtor saying that Frank and F.L.A. would no longer be paying our rent.

It was an eviction notice.

May

2

The Bulls' official logo, a splayed creature that appeared to be ripsnorting on three legs, had purportedly been copyrighted by Frank. But given how he'd run his team, the Bulls' logo should have been an abattoir.

It got gloomier. As a sportswriting or playing veteran of the World Football League, USFL, and semipro demises, I'd been witness or participant to such misery before, but desensitizing oneself to it was like getting inured to a barbed wire enema. As for how badly we were faring, an anonymous entry made its way into "Stampede," the official Supporters Club newsletter, under the humble heading of "Poem":

> We've played this funny old game
> In plenty of strange places
> Olympic Stadiums, cycle tracks
> And even air force bases.
> Last year we thought rock bottom was reached
> With Portway as our ground,
> Oh! how surprised we were to hear
> A worse place had been found.
> It has every modern convenience,

Even open-air W.C.s;
The only trouble with this is,
The water comes up to your knees.
When Dante wrote The Inferno,
About the nine levels of hell,
He couldn't have been to Salford,
Or he would have mentioned that as well.

But the Bulls got some poetic justice . . . from a magistrate, when landlord Kim Duce was kind enough to defuse the eviction notice at No. 9. Nor did I worry about a place to live, not since moving in with the Duces next door at Woodbourne Manor, as a boarder.

My fourth move in three months may have seemed declassé, going from the claustral comfort of Frank Kalili's house to a deluxe hotel to a suburban home to a dormitory room. But I found myself far too preoccupied to have regrets. For not only did headmaster Duce, old rugger man, offer personal form-tackling lessons in the Woodbourne corridors without tuition fee, but, in line with a pastime I'd acquired of dining on fine British food, he also enlightened me to gustatory grandeur.

It was called haggis, and no two more succulent syllables exist in the English language. Unknowing of it till tantalized at the table, I'd succumbed to the headmaster's scholarly yarn of haggis as an upland bird reared on a hillside, one leg shorter than the other because hunters constantly chase it around in the same direction. Did Mr. Duce take the piss on me: My delirious palate went wholly for the one-and-a-half-drumsticks-are-better-than-none theory, before he set me straight.

Haggis: While formal description is a pudding from the heart, liver, and lungs of a sheep, boiled in the animal's stomach, it might more aptly be known as offal of the gods. I loved it instantly—and instinctively, as there is a description in Le Gastronomique of how the fresh haggis resembles an overinflated football.

May

3

Frank continued purrrr-fectly inert. Co-owner Denton Thomas conveniently submerged himself in his tax books and, except for garnishing a sideline, begged for anonymity in management.

But one man still cared. Unsolicited but very aware the team was on the outs with those who in turn had ousted him, Gerry Hartman showed up at Star Hill with a detailed scouting report of our next opponent, the Nottingham Hoods.

While Frank Kalili went from waterboy to owning the team, this Hartman, the ex-pat from Philly who'd given him the job in the first place, got stark benediction for bringing gridiron to Birmingham. He got trounced all the way down to volunteer lug-nut jockey (chauffeuring coaches around town, in a borrowed car no less). Britball was an open and harsh frontier, and nobody but nobody knew it better than Gerry Hartman.

In their infancy, he operated the Bulls out of his council flat, in a block of grim dwellings called Lego-Land, where he'd been Frank Kalili's neighbor. They were still neighbors, sort of, equidistant to a burb called Five Ways, though Hartman remained denizen of a dreary orange landscape, while Frank, at Yew Tree Close, was in prime real estate.

Now he came on a mission from Lego-Land. The coaches welcomed him; we'd begun to forget what an owner—past, present, or impersonator—looked like. Bob Shoop, of course, welcomed a comparison of their crew cuts. Hartman was just as punctilious and insisted everybody call the Yanks "coach," even people who no more knew what a coach was than a cranberry. He somehow made us feel better about our status.

Also, with delivery of his first scouting report, he had scribbled some insightful remarks about the Nottingham Hoods quarterback—though as it would turn out not quite insightful enough.

Yea verily, the wolf pawed at the Bulls' portcullis. With a flat attitude and an earning disability, we nevertheless kept winning via transformation on the pitch. But while we won, we grubbed to survive. No. 9 Star Hill itself, secluded at the end of a cul-de-sac, had fund-raising possibilities as an unofficial team bordello, though the players with alleged expertise in running it were behind bars. Finally we enlisted the help of John Eyre. He'd already sprung for Russ Jensen's airfare. Now he paid Thornton's costly medical insurance and provided the coaching staff a car; he helped Malcolm Byron with kit repair, even laundered jerseys.

But first and foremost a businessman, he couldn't buy the Bulls because Frank wasn't selling. Nor, fearful of losing his estimable white windbreaker, was Denton Thomas.

So even with his help it was as another literary name, Jane Austen, had written: "One has no great hopes for Birmingham. I always say there is something direful in the sound."

Grim fact was we could manufacture team spirit only by minting money. And while, in fact, the biggest mint in the Western Hemisphere, a mint that made money for one hundred countries, was located in Brum, no one knew how to tap it for gridiron.

But there happened to be a palliative purrrr-fectly acceptable, almost as good for doing away with our financial crisis as our own license to print money, and it was betting. Betting on our own football games.

Just the thing, as Charles Dickens had put it, for recalling the Bulls to life.

Not only did the NDMA sanction it, but betting also was encouraged in program adverts and over the P.A.—the league going so far as asking coaches and GM's to pass out betting coupons to players. Moreover, the American Football Pools, as the bookmaking operation was called, numbered among the league's sponsors. And a symbiotic relationship, too, since the NDMA had cut itself in on the pools' take. "Play and support your local team. Part proceeds paid back," the pools' coupon trumpeted, "to individual clubs."

The bookie who'd begun the service, a Canadian expatriate who made his own betting lines for games, happily reported the majority of his customers were indeed players and coaches. Since most Britball scores had ceased hitting triple digits, and few games got canceled anymore at halftime because of injury, they found the odds decent.

I myself couldn't wait.

The Bulls had just been installed as 13-to-8 favorites to repeat as Britball champions, a fair play. Judiciously by this same bookie, though, there was no side betting on whether we'd manage to make it through the season.

Gambling was not only a way of life, but inspiration for the Brits. The coach of the Northampton Stormbringers, after having only a handful of players show up at practice the week the season started, enticed attendance by betting £1,000 on his team at 33 to 1 to win the Budweiser Bowl; earnings from his bet would be distributed among the players. Responding to his confidence and the incentives, the 'Bringers not only turned out but also started the season on a roll, shaving those odds to 12 to 1.

Hmmm, they might be worth a play of my own.

The Bulls were pegged 21½-point favorites against Nottingham, and while steep odds, given how we'd beaten the point spread 14 straight games, and how the star quarterback Russ Jensen could pretty well go out and name his score, it was still favorable toward us.

But when I suggested betting to the other player-coaches, to my fellow Americans, allowed to them how it just might be our vehicle, as Shakespeare elucidated in *Twelfth Night,* to "purge the air of pestilence," they treated the suggestion itself like a plague.

American consciences simply wouldn't permit or consider gambling on the game.

Bob Shoop also happened to be negotiating for a job back home with major-league baseball, and angling for it through his friend the commissioner A. Bartlett Giamatti, who at the moment was locked in an imbroglio with Pete Rose, the betting manager of the Cincinnati Reds.

Jensen might have been different with his hunger for money. But though the one player who could have broken the bank, he was too much a tightwad for the pools' coupons, and he, too, had a deterrent against it, since he aspired to play (play again, as he'd have put it) in the NFL, which always dealt swiftly with players who gambled.

I was unable to sway any of them, my notion summarily rejected. So opposed were they, moments after its arrival in the day's post, the packet of pools' coupons got discarded, unopened, into the trash.

It disappointed me, because betting football is a buddy system business, has to be, as losses can be frequent and tough to stomach. I'd been spoiled by some of the best, who knew point spreads like the Brits knew the score at Agincourt. Before committing myself to the pools' coupons I was insistent at having a partner but knew not where to turn, no idea who gave a hang about betting gridiron. Only at that moment did James Thornton's encomium about Sue Duce pop into my head: "She's sporty," he'd said, and could not have known that by sporty, he was only scratching the surface in describing her.

Sue came from a gaming family—played a lot of contract bridge and had been tiddlywinks champion at Trinity College in Dublin. Of Scottish descent, she had many ancestors from the

Highland Games and married into a family with a more famous forebear; her husband was the direct descendant of the gym teacher who had turned peach baskets into a global passion, Dr. James Naismith. Topping off the lineage was her father, a surgeon who'd rejoined the Royal Navy to become oldest veteran of the Falkland Islands conflict. He was the keenest of poker players and had won a fair amount of Her Majesty's money on troop ships.

Yes, there could be but one betting partner for me. At the kitchen table in Woodbourne Manor, I gently slid the pools' coupon in front of her, crossed my fingers, waited for a subtle indication she might be game, and when her eyes hooded slightly, I broached the suggestion of teaming up.

Sportily, she agreed.

We mapped an equitable arrangement: I would make selections, Sue'd stake the money. She also would supply the postage. We'd halve our weekly winnings. Nice arrangement, too, it was for the Bulls, to whom I planned to donate a portion of future winnings, following an altruistic precedent—from home mortgages to the sale of official team merchandise.

We picked that week's games till we hit a sticking point with the Bulls and our point spread against Nottingham. "The Hoods've got this kid at quarterback, a hotshot from California who could be troublesome," I informed her. "Maybe we ought to go with them."

"Against your own team? How . . . arch," she replied.

"No, just pragmatic. Russ Jensen's got a better tan, since he's practically just got to town, and seeing it might incite the other kid to play over his head."

"So what do we do about betting on a game in which both, èr, quarterbacks come from California?"

"If you're a sportswriter, pray you don't have to talk to either of them after the game."

.   .   .

Had we been privvy to inside information, which might have been covered in the scouting report Gerry Hartman delivered to the coaches, had not this old security man for Howard Hughes been rusty with his surveillance, no telling how much money we would have raked in.

The Hoods had gone through a disappointing season, had won only one game all year—surprisingly, since they were among preseason picks to reach the Budweiser Bowl.

Still, they had home-pitch advantage, were capable of scoring often, among the best posers in the league, and hadn't played poorly enough to rate such a huge underdog against us. Hartman's scouting report had been respectful. An upset was a possibility, he allowed. So, in making us 21½-point favorites, obviously the bookies knew something we didn't. Customs and immigration might have known, too.

Nottingham was our first road trip of the season, but the players, sensing it might be the last, seemed subdued when the team bus left city center. Or perhaps they were deep in distraction: More than for playing a football game, the Bulls were keener on Nottingham's purported 4:1 ratio of women to men. They had plenty of time to talk about exploiting those odds, as the trip, normally about 45 minutes, took 3 hours through bank holiday traffic.

Fields of rape, or goldenrod as the Brits preferred to call it, stretched far as the eye could see; we seemed stuck in a sea of yellow. Finally, Harvey Hadden Stadium hove into view; another of those 90-yard pitches in the infield of a cycling track, but hardly the typical 90-yarder, not with a hammer-throw cage in one end zone, a high-jump pit in the other, and the length of the field stippled with daisies.

Far more impressive as a natural attraction was the Hoods' 450-pound middle guard. When we'd reviewed film of an earlier game, as the referee marked off a penalty against them, an opposing fan could be heard to shout, "Illegal belly downfield!" Now Bulls' Supporters, not necessarily the most tactful bunch, picked up on the theme. "You're so fat it's un-be-LAY-vable!" they taunted as, play after play, his ill-fitting football pants unsheathed his derriere.

It didn't take long before the rest of the Hoods were rolling over against us, too. The game became a rout: We were threatened only by the distinct possibility of a receiver getting ensnared in the hammer-throw cage.

Seconds left in the first half, Russ Jensen flipped a short pass to Patrick Loftman, completely uncovered on the sideline, and he chugged 75 yards for a touchdown and a 28–7 lead. But with the spread 21½, Sue Duce and I needed another point to win with the pools' coupon, so my plea at halftime to the special teams to make Notts cough up another five or six fumbles was especially impassioned.

Trailing by three touchdowns, the Hoods chose to kick off to us to start the second half. "And I thought I was a rocket scientist," James Thornton declared. It could have been a show of British sportsmanship. But Thornton failed to consider that maybe, given the point spread, and how they trailed by 21 points, the Hoods had plopped down a few quid against themselves as well.

Maybe so; they fell farther and farther behind, continuing their tailspin. The heralded quarterback was again off-form, with four interceptions and showing no savvy, yet this was the same player who a year ago had been billed as one of the better college QBs in the United States. Another week, another woeful performance, would go by before it'd be revealed he was impersonating a quarterback.

A league with an impersonator as owner—only natural for a player to be one, too. But as it happened, the accused Hood was impersonating more than a quarterback. As reported in tabloidian terms of *First Down*, TWO WRIGHTS MAKE A WRONG. In off-season the Hoods had signed a quarterback named Paul Wright. But not long after agreeing over the telephone to play for them he received a better offer from an Italian team. He sent in his stead to Nottingham, under his name, a younger brother who'd last played football, without distinction, in high school.

If Sue Duce and I had gotten hold of an inside scoop like that with our pools' coupon, we'd have broken the Bank of England. Of course, if wishes were sashes, the Bulls would have been a team dressed for knighthood. Instead our jerseys began to look more and more like shrouds.

May

13

My new neighborhood was once home to poet A. E. Houseman, whose "To An Athlete Dying Young," for me might have been transmuted "To An Athlete Dying of Frustration." A half season gone by, and I felt conspired against by time, circumstance, and, it seemed, the Crown.

But clearly my day to play was coming, so long as the Bulls stuck around for another day: Attrition's visit on imports got heavy; all over the league, all over the country, Americans began to go down or go home, sometimes from injury, sometimes from disgust. The Yanks were head-hunted on the pitch; both in and out of kit they felt grossly mistreated or got homesick: They dropped out of Britball with alacrity.

No, often they couldn't leave quickly enough, as with a legitimate NFL draft choice from Arizona State, a quarterback named Dan Ford. Few Yanks' contracts called for medical insurance, and in Ford's case, there was the frightening corollary of having nothing that resembled an offensive line playing in front of him. He lasted two games before a neck injury made him realize risk wasn't quite commensurate with reward; he cut out and his team, the Manchester All-Stars, instantly rang up losses of 60 and 70 points.

. . .

Meanwhile, in a game whose litany bespoke lack and estranged, or just plain strange, owners, ongoing mendacity and undelivered promises, the Bulls' Americans tried to enjoy themselves, at least as long as their libidos kept them going, or even incite cultural curiosity amongst themselves. "Watched that movie *The Untouchables* yesterday," Shoop told a lineman named Mike Bailey after we'd boarded the West Midlands 113 bus to Moor Lane. "Watched it last night, too. And again this morning. And then again this afternoon."

"Was it that good?" Bailey asked.

"We were that bored," Shoop replied.

He, Thornton, and Jensen also turned creative in the front office as they awaited the team's demise, making trades. Ordinarily, trades weren't allowed in Britball, but these were different. One of them, as detailed and written in his flowery hand: "I hereby offer a 40-ish brunette with a car to Russ Jensen for 1990 draft considerations, [signed] James Thornton, director of player development."

For my own divertissement, Mr. Duce insisted I accompany him to a rugby match, where we got to watch the most prolific scorer in the history of the sport. Dusty Hare was a bald, unprepossessing chap, who though the greatest kicker and among the fiercest tacklers rugby had ever known, was, first and foremost, a sheep farmer. Moreover, he was a sheep farmer who birthed thousands of lambs every spring—Friday nights the busiest time for it—and who then shook himself free of barn straw and wool dust and went off, often without ever having gone to sleep, to play his brutally beautiful game.

I could only wonder how many brain scans he'd had.

There was little temptation for me to compare rugby to the American offshoot, but aspects of it were singularly akin to Britball. Midway through the match, a forward for the local side went down and a physician was summoned. Only with doctor's consent can a side replace an injured player, and this one gave a quick wave for a fresh substitute. "What they don't know," a friend of Mr. Duce's whispered, "is that our team doctor is a doctor, yes, but my wife works with him at the hospital and he's a gynecologist."

It wasn't a ruse the Bulls might pull, for if any medical man was coming to check on us, it was the coroner.

Even the Bulls' objective of making it through to our Euro Bowl date failed to elicit spirit. The players were disillusioned; practices became more unmemorable. Russ Jensen couldn't bully them: He could be ornery only if players appeared on the pitch, as each day fewer and fewer did. When they did show up, they serially missed assignments, had only the slightest interest in getting it right, and were full of alibis for getting it wrong. "You're a lie," James Thornton bellowed at lineman Mike Bailey, "and the truth ain't in you!"

Sue Duce forecasted her neighbors would enjoy the British summer: "Yes," she'd say, "both days of it." She was wrong; the country sweltered over a summer unlike any other. But the first summertime came not by climatic conditions, but the calendar. The Bulls' coaching staff rewound our clocks, grateful for an extra hour of daylight, hoping to glean more time for practice, but the players tenaciously stuck to their own schedule, their procrastination schedule, and simply pushed back their arrival at Moor Lane.

The coaches, with our own worries, couldn't provide an uplift. Of the Yanks, the worst mental and money fatigue always seemed foisted upon Thornton. Jensen scowled, Shoop sulked, I could have used a new set of prayer beads. But Big James gloom-ily withdrew. He did as always when things weren't to his lik-ing—ate and grew more houselike. He dropped by Woodbourne Manor to see what was on the stove, and Sue kindly offered cock-a-leekie soup. A tureen didn't whet his appetite; he made off with the crockpot.

"I'm reinstating my demand for backpay," he declared between gulps. "Irrmmemmeme—I figure at fourteen percent interest, the Bulls now owe me—irrmmemmeme—the way I figured it, about . . ."

The Americans had, in fact, come into some money. They picked up £20 apiece coaching the Bulls' youth team, an indepen-dent outfit, and anomaly, with none of the abysmal finances of the parent club. Still more sterling came when headmaster Duce let them lecture on gridiron to the boys of West House School.

Like his Kiplingesque namesake, Kim had a sense of adventure. Also, Welsh humor and a magistrate's kind of mirth. He'd intro-duced himself to me with a tale about my hometown, heard at Winson Green Prison before a speech by Archbishop Tutu of South Africa. It seemed Richard Nixon, after traveling to Ghana for a celebration marking its independence, approached a black man on the dais. "So, how does one feel upon becoming free?" he asked, clamping the man's shoulders. "Yes, you must tell me about the great feeling of independence." "Wouldn't know, sir," came the reply. "I'm from Birmingham, Alabama."

In tinny monotone Russ Jensen tried to explain gridiron, failing miserably—likely because he hadn't brought along the crib sheet he wore on his wrist during games as a prompting device. He was spared further embarrassment only when one of the boarders at Woodbourne, a bespectacled lad named Phillip Bennett Britten, gave excellent discourse on "the quarterback's options once the ball is snapped."

"Are there a lot of derby games in the NFL?" another boy asked.

"Darby . . . uh, never heard of it," Jensen replied.

Another schoolboy wanted to know: "How do they choose

which teams are in the American and National Conference? Isn't the whole country called America?"

"I used to be with the Raiders, all I know is, we were in the American Conference," Jensen informed him.

He got that much right, at least.

When the coaches asked for volunteers to present the game as occurs on the line of scrimmage, they not only got them, but within five minutes also had a functioning defense and offense run by a 10-year-old who'd never taken a snap from center making flawless handoffs to a halfback with a topknot. I had to look twice, of course, to make sure it wasn't Andrew Jefferson, his hair in yet another guise.

The West House boys caught on quickly; they probably earned the equivalent of British correspondence coaching certificates by sitting in on the lecture.

It was an informative session; the Americans even drafted the school physics teacher as a tight end, but the one pass thrown to her got batted down by a Sikh defender.

He was somebody the Bulls could have used, and not just in the secondary. Physically, in mufti, what with his topknot, he made an ideal candidate for the roster, since we wouldn't have to worry about providing him a helmet.

May

15

Our first bus to Leicester blew a tire. The next bus, when it finally rolled down one of Brum's debilitating ring roads, wasn't much bigger than a car-pool van. It came on credit, so it came small. Players got claustrophobic, tempers frayed, flatulence was epidemic. Then, upon our arrival two hours late at the stadium, a lot attendant tried to charge us to park. "Man, you're j-j-joking," said the diplomatic Denton Thomas, flashing a sleeve of his windbreaker for authentication. "Why, we're the players."

When, atop everything else, the Bulls were barred from our locker room for an hour while a women's track team occupied it, the afternoon became a rampage for Russ Jensen. He stormed into the Panther owner's office and shouted "This is fucking Leicester ridiculous! Same shit as last year!"

If animation were fungible, he'd earned his salary in a single outburst. Jensen also was miffed by the Panthers' having poached some of our better players last season, including two offensive linemen, leaving him shorn of pass protection. Bristling through his mustache got quick results: The locker room cleared in seconds. Leicester management cowered and this time, unlike with Steve Harvey, there were no spare javelins lying about to try and thwart him.

What may have figured into their acquiescence was a rumor that Harvey himself had rejoined the Bulls, and could be inserted into the lineup whenever the coaches felt prone toward violence on (or off) the pitch. And in a game like this one, between the league's only unbeaten teams, playing for first place, we had no objection to using such rumors to our advantage.

Yes, any edge we could get; we'd also sent out a phalanx of our best posers—Son Tustin, Desi Taylor, and Nizzy Nisbet—all in skullcaps and/or shiny Lycra leggings and who manfully strode again and again the length of the pitch. It was shiny AstroTurf and reflected their presence even more.

Posing, of course, was sport and art form. Since the Brits had no heroic past in football, it was for drawing attention to themselves. Football players, of course, wear who they are, and our posers put on a peacockery performance as if sporting Beefeaters.

Des Taylor was best of them: His spiraling hair, perhaps from the jolt he'd gotten last season running into a light pole, was closest the Bulls had come, tonsorially, to replacing the jailed Rastas from the secondary as an intimidation factor. He also earned from that injury the league's best nickname, Sicknote, for a propensity toward sloughing off practice. But he more than made up for it with the best stretching and striding routine in the country come game day, harlequined maneuvering. We began the day against the Panthers as 4½-point favorites; when he and the others got done, the point spread had to have gone up to a touchdown.

Far more impressive: Russ Jensen, in silver L.A. Raiders' pants, went to midfield to punctuate the posing. Ordinarily he wasn't a player who incorporated it into his game plan, but prospects of a tough game moved him to try and capitalize, and packed stands got silent at the sight of him. Nor was Jensen finished flashing his brusque side, ejecting a Dutch film crew from the Bulls' locker room as they tried to interview Trevor Carthy, or Trevor McCartney, as they called him. A bit unfair since, of all people, Russ Jensen knew the value of air time.

Maybe more professional jealousy; the cameras gave Carthy full frontal shot, while with his TV show, Jensen got only appendage angles. (Later, his judgment proved sound, the Dutch crew having been secretly deployed by the Amsterdam Crusaders to scout the Bulls, should we survive long enough to reach that Euro Bowl match against them.)

The Bulls' coach got more aggravated when Son Tustin became arguably the oldest player ever ejected from a gridiron game. Son, with an intense sense of camaraderie from 25 years of rugby, wasted no time starting a fight on the opening kickoff that drew an automatic fine (promptly paid, earning him a place in NDMA history) and a one-game suspension.

Son aside, we had the fight taken out of us in a game featuring the worst breakdown of any team with which I'd been associated. Not only associated with, but helped foist; as special teams coach and Bulls' assistant charged with running things from the bench when the other Americans were in the game, I ought to have been fired on the spot.

We were ahead 34–7 in the third quarter, coasting, and once again had stopped Leicester cold. The game was so one-sided, I got Jensen's consent to send in Andy Jefferson. Just then I glanced to see a late flag from the referee. The penalty was unmistakable: We had roughed the Panthers quarterback as he released a fourth-down desperation pass. Since we'd already put two QBs out of the game, the ref couldn't let the roughshod stuff continue. Still, an absurd play; the pass couldn't have traveled more than five yards with booster rockets, thrown by a third-string Brit. Also, the nearest receiver was in the next shire. But the penalty changed the game's complexion. Given new life, the Panthers drove downfield and scored. And scored again. And again.

Not once in the fourth quarter did the Bulls touch the football, not on offense, anyhow; we touched it only as part of a clinic on how to fumble away onside kicks.

All day our special teams play led to this fiasco, more bizarre by the minute, even by Britball standards. Players took themselves off the kickoff team without reporting to me, and we ran short of replacements for the few who did report. Others, such as Spats Lewis, were insubordinate, simply refusing to go into the game. Kicker Spider Webb, hobbled by a hamstring, had to gimp the sideline to make tackles that twice prevented kickoffs from getting run back for touchdowns. A high snap foiled an extra point attempt, two more got blocked. The wrong returner dropped back to field a punt, and fumbled it. Aaaaaargh! On the sideline, I was ready for the physio to do an impromptu tracheotomy. And such was my state even before the Panthers' progression of onside kicks.

The ball beguiled us, chimerical thing; puttering along, we weren't sure whether to pick it up and heave it back where it came from or run away from it. Falling on top of it, of course, never crossed our minds. Trying to teach a British player to recover an onside kick, to do something consequential with his hands, was like trying to coach a head of lettuce.

Leicester's onside kick was the best I'd ever seen, of the hundreds of games I'd been part of—even if it was patently illegal. The kicker lay the ball flat and dribbled it like he would in soccer—automatic penalty since once struck, the ball can't be abetted until traveling ten yards. But it went uncalled all afternoon, probably because British officials, with an ingrained sense of theatrics, weren't about to let the rulebook thwart a marvelous comeback.

Only when a pass into the end zone from our 7-yard-line on the game's last play—a natural wobbler thrown with fine imprecision by the third-string quarterback—only after that alleged pass fell incomplete by inches, was our 34–26 victory preserved.

I walked off the field flummoxed, by far my most embarrassing moment of football since I'd been spun round by a tackler after catching a pass and run the wrong way in high school. "It's a win, Mick," Andy Webb, the nosetackle and former Panther, said to shake me out of a daze as we disembarked beneath the Rotunda. "A win even if a lucky win."

Luckier than he knew: Coaching the Bulls' youth team the same week, Russ Jensen was demonstrating a pass play, only to have to crash through a 122-pound defensive tackle, who jammed Jensen's thumb into an already-ailing shoulder.

Valiant of him to play, not just because he was injured, but since he wasn't getting paid in the first place. He gained impetus from the name blazoned across the foe's jersey. Leicester was the most loathed team in the league—naturally, since it was the best financed and best outfitted team in the league.

So we stayed undefeated. Not only did the Panthers lose, but also Jensen's tirade against the front office gave them an inferiority complex from which they never recovered.

May

17

The Bulls, by our perpetual penury, had long since been vaccinated against such circumstance. We had, however, a continuing Cinderella-without-estrogen complex. We got traduced by the gridiron press, by rivals shamed at how a champion would carry on, by the NDMA. Meanwhile, trivia vultures closed in, waiting for us to become the first team to go defunct sporting an unbeaten record.

Ownerless and rudderless, we looked futureless. It all called for one of the buffer trips I often took against despair, this time to the opera. Poignant that the first line heard upon reaching my seat was about a frog "shrinking . . . like a deflating football." The composer, Sir Michael Tippett, sat a few seats away from me, and I was tempted to tell him the lyrics would be more poignant yet, had they been about a deflating football team. As for where the Bulls would play upcoming home games, including a rematch six days away against Nottingham, our only certain tenancy was nowhere. We had been removed from slummish Salford Park for falling behind in rent—not only falling behind but, typical Bulls, never having made the first payment; moreover, the league lodged a fine for insufficient seating there from an earlier game, and if it went unpaid the Bulls could be banned from the playoffs, should we survive to reach them again.

Drawing nearer to Euro Bowl and Amsterdam, we hadn't confirmed any reservations; moreover, we should have been working on the posture of our hitchhiking thumb. But if we put our hands together and prayed, then the prayers got answered for a place to play: The city relented and extended our credit for the use of Salford Park.

Another blessing: After Frank Kalili's off-song status curtailed interest from the press, we also landed a new publicity director, a diminutive fellow named Peter Biddulph, who looked a lot like Caspar Milquetoast's long-lost fourth cousin. He was extraordinarily enthusiastic about the job, too: His son happened to be a bottom-rung Bulls reserve, and by donating his time and energy to the front office, he figured to enhance the lad's chances of playing. It worked—I instantly stuck him on special teams.

Busy Biddulph, the nickname earned by his demeanor, also quickly grasped how he was expected to follow in Frank's smoke rings, dashing off one letter after another seeking sponsorship and showing versatility when he attributed James Thornton's college education to three different universities in his first three letters. As a true-quoting heir, he had a lot to live up to, but obviously we'd found our man.

The Supporters Club might also call on his savoir faire in the future. After recherché privilege in Leicester of watching the Bulls play at the nicest cycling track in the league—the Saffron Lane Velodrome, past site of the World Cycling Championships—the club had suffered a lapse in civility. The lapse was contagious: Birmingham City soccer fans, days after the Hillsborough Stadium disaster that killed 97 people, had poured onto a pitch and prompted an *Evening Mail* headline as SCUM WHO SHAMED BRUM. Our own lot? They drew an NDMA reprimand after distributing a flyer that made sport of the Panthers as perennial also-rans. "Plenty More Tears," it read, a takeoff on the Panthers' theme "No More Tears." "An always to be repeated offer!" the flyer continued. "Huge stocks for immediate dispatch. 100s and 100s of secondhand BRIDESMAIDS' DRESSES!" The NDMA was right; British sensibilities wouldn't stand for it.

The Nottingham Hoods were a last test before Euro Bowl, but not to be taken lightly, even after our earlier rout. They'd corrected their imposter problem, gone out, again by telephone, and gotten themselves a new quarterback. Another mistake: The newcomer's name was Jansen, which didn't go over well with his near-namesake on the Bulls, who wanted no part of sharing stardom due to any typographical errors. "Let's introduce that new American quarterback to British pain!" Russ Jensen exhorted as the Bulls took the pitch. "And, Boo, I want to see you hit somebody. It's been a long time . . . you oughta have it inside you after all that."

"Yah, maaan, yah!" said the newest Bulls player I'd never seen before, his eyes glazed like tombstone marble. "Yah! Yah! I will, I will kill somebody out there today!"

This was cornerback Norman "Boo" Thomas, incarcerated on assault and other charges, who had just won his release to await trial. The timing of having him back was amazing. He went out the front gate of Winson Green Prison, and not 24 hours later was in the starting lineup, reclaiming his old jersey, number 34. Not only were we pleased at his return but also the teammates who throughout the season had dangled those "Nos. 23, 32, 34— There Here" towels from their waists wouldn't have to spread their dedication so thin.

Maybe it was the name of the opponent—the Hoods—but Boo was an inspiration to my special teams as we gave them another trouncing. Clive Jackson, son of the new P.R. man Busy Biddulph, could have learned from him—should have learned. "Play skinny, dammit!" coach Jensen demanded of him after he got picked off and flattened while covering a kickoff.

Theirs was a personality clash from the outset. Clive wore a hearing aid, and Jensen didn't like shouting louder than he had to. "Play skinny or get the fuck out of there!" the coach said.

Clive looked at his waistline, subtly sucked it in; he didn't quite understand. Then Russ Jensen approximated a hula dance to try and give him a better idea.

Where we really needed Boo's bolstering, of course, was in the secondary—never more obvious than when the dysfunctional Femi Amu got scorched for another touchdown. Femi limped off the field precisely the moment the Hoods receiver reached the end zone. "Why the hell is it," James Thornton asked him, "when anything bad happens to you, you start limping?"

But the distinctive limp was his way of telling on himself. Femi hailed from a land of euphemism, Nigeria, where brassieres, for instance, are called "knickers are up." Thornton could have been kinder to him and might have recognized that the limp had by now become the Bulls' unofficial team gesture. It might even get some of us as far as Amsterdam.

May

24

If Great Britain intended becoming a classless society, gridiron only enhanced the cause. This was, all agreed, Brits and cousins alike, a classless sport. The British sporting press was always prone to wartime analogies. I had one of my own: Gridiron, most definitely, was not their finest hour.

Nevertheless, as departure to the Continent loomed, if the Americans had anything to be remotely thankful for, it was that, unless Bob Preen reentered the picture, we had no more worries of deportation. One of Russ Jensen's girlfriends, who worked in immigration, told how Indians had come to the United Kingdom as purported experts at a game called kebbadi, which "pretty much entails running the length of a rugby pitch while holding your breath." She wouldn't compare sports, only situations. "None of them file for working papers and they don't get deported. So you guys are safe."

But leaving Britain of our own volition, it was debatable whether we'd want to come back. Yes, from what we'd encountered with the Bulls, we might seek football asylum.

May

25

James Thornton's "Nice from afar, far from nice" appraisal of Britain also fit its author. To the Bulls, the coach and star lineman was many things, perpetually late one of them. As the team gathered in city center, ready to go to Euro Bowl, he went missing. Out all night on a social call, he overslept at a strange location miles from town. Next he misplaced his passport and in the predawn couldn't find a taxi to take him to the rendezvous for our departure to the Netherlands.

Of Thornton, it succinctly could be said he loathed football practice, felt the same for sticking to any schedule, and, true to the coddling of an American athlete, expected things to be handed to him. Surprise. But in Britball there was no more popular player.

Two hours late arriving, his tardiness shook the players. They looked up to Americans, hung on every utterance, and Thornton, for his wayward habits, was a compelling coach who spoke well and reassuringly. As the Bulls' new GM, he also had begun asserting himself in management, albeit personalizing it, one of those deals cut with a bedding company to provide him a futon, maybe the largest of these Japanese mattresses ever made, for endorsing its product. He'd even thought up the ad copy for it:

"I'm James Thornton. At 6 foot 5, 270 pounds, I tackle like a Bull. But on this futon, I sleep like a lamb."

Or, re the Holland excursion, overslept like one.

Some of the players' anxiety might have come from waiting all that time outside what was once Tavern on the Town, where in 1974 a dozen people were killed by an IRA blast in a case that became infamous as the Birmingham Six. The pub sat empty for years before the father of Bulls lineman Davey Parkes, a brewery executive, renamed it Bar St. Martin, and its neon trim was just beginning to pale in the dawn when Thornton's cab finally rolled up.

The scowl on the face of head coach Russ Jensen exuded anger toward his fellow American. But hesitant to vent it against Thornton, for breach of protocol, as Yanks were ostensibly equals in the eyes of the Brits, he found the nearest target in Jess Rodgers, the linebacker who had been with the Bulls since the beginning.

Jess had turned up for the trip despite having retired from the team two weeks earlier, and when Jensen went off at him, it may have been the first recorded case of a coach trashing a retired player. Also, a continuation of old carping. When he quit, Jess declared he'd gotten too old to play, had neither energy for it nor desire—bollocks; the real reason, teammates quickly twigged, a redress by Jensen over a penalty that almost cost the Bulls an earlier victory. Also, in committing it, he'd roughed a quarterback, and perhaps Jensen took it personally.

Now he wanted to go to Holland, a logical request, at least for Britball. Just because Jess had retired did not mean he was done with the team. Far from it, given the pub mentality on which gridiron was founded and surrounded by in Great Britain. Nor were his retirements anything new. Posers were always retiring, if only for effect, and Jess was one of the best. "Played five years and he's retired every season," captain Steve Trow mused. "More bloody comebacks than Sinatra," agreed Andy Webb, and Jess indeed had brought along in a travel bag, his kit; he also was first to show up at city center. And after he helped the Bulls reach Euro Bowl—in capturing the British championship, in our victory over the Dublin Celtics—he was entitled to go along with us, to have himself a hols—a holiday—even if he was no longer playing.

Of this his teammates were in unison, so they grew aghast as Jensen stormed onto the team bus and lambasted him: "What the fuck you think you're doing here?"

As Jess collected his kit and disembarked, their eyes roiled in anger. But roiling, alas, was where anger ended. In Jensen's two seasons only the parolee Boo Thomas had stood up to him, earning a three-game suspension, and now more than ever the Bulls truckled, for not only was he coach but also star quarterback, and they had gone through so much havoc and upheaval to get him back and keep him, the last thing they wanted to do was risk alienating him, especially on the eve of the big game.

As if our bon voyage hadn't too little bon to begin with, several players inexplicably failed to turn up for the bus, crucial players, among them defensive captain Colin Nash, and as a portent of how things were looking, Nash's replacement at linebacker would have been none other than Jess Rodgers.

There was more setback for us from red tape of going abroad; boyo, boyo, was there red tape, most of it in the secondary. Femi Amu, a starting defensive back, confessed he had been living in Great Britain without a visa; fearing he would be detained by immigration he shied from making the trip. (Or perhaps he couldn't limp to the consul's office.) Special teams and clothier star Son Tustin got held back by prior commitment to his job as a computer company executive. Boo Thomas was back in the starting lineup, but terms of his probation barred his leaving the country. Russ Jensen had been unsuccessful lobbying Magistrate Duce and his cohorts on the bench for furloughing Boo's fellow secondary members, and more dismaying while they remained behind bars was that the Crusaders had an accurate American quarterback and a real former NFL tight end catching his passes.

Yes, a bad bon voyage, but since when had the outlook been anything but bleak for the Bulls—an exemplary team on the field, but disastrous off it? So it was again. If we didn't go under en route to Amsterdam, figuratively go under, we were informed by

Denton Thomas that we would most likely be liquidated upon returning.

Several days before we set sail, Russ Jensen decided to try and pry Frank Kalili-Leadon's good names from the Bulls, once and for all force him to relinquish that despoliating grip he called ownership. He telephoned Frank at Yew Tree Close and demanded he "free up" his interest in the team.

Frank hadn't been heard from in weeks, save for a nasty rumor, passed along by Andy Webb, that someone had planted the head of a dead fox on his front doorstep, for having so bemired the Bulls. "Stampede," the Supporters Club newsletter, speculated over his whereabouts with the headline BULLS NEWS, OR EXIT UNCLE FRANK, STAGE LEFT, and the theatrical dismissal was about the kindest thing anyone in the Midlands had to say about him.

Jensen wasn't discreet. "Look, we're going to expose you as the fraud you are unless you turn over your shares!" he bruited. "You've lied to everybody . . . telling 'em how great you are and what all you've done—you ain't done a goddamned thing. We're going to go on television and tell the whole story."

Until then Frank had been the unflappable star of stage, screen, and self-cleaning oven. But TV? Why, babe, a different story altogether. Having to give a rebuttal to those true quotes, especially when the truth in them may have been burnished with more than a little distortion?

Frank, flustered and feeling a little fear, hung up and called his crony, Bob Preen, who in turn telephoned Denton Thomas, who rushed through the front door at No. 9 Star Hill, stammering, "Breen will have you all de-deported, unless you leave Frank alone!" His forehead gushed perspiration. "He will do it! Deport you all! Please!" he urgently advised.

Jensen grinned. Soon afterward he and Thornton strolled around the corner to Yew Tree Close and rang the doorbell at No. 10. After about five minutes in which they saw him several times peek through drawn curtains, Frank cracked a front door, which remained deadbolted and guarded by steel bars. As they told it, he was holding a large pair of garden shears; encouraging he'd finally got around to tending his garden, having neglected it so long for gridiron. "Leave me alone, I want nothing to do with you!" he said in shaky voice that almost qualified him for a falsetto comeback.

"Then give up the Bulls!" Jensen demanded.

"I'll have nothing to do with you," Frank gasped. "But I can make trouble, I warn you!"—a nod toward the ex-officio deportation officer, Preen. "G-g-go away."

"Give up those shares, damn you!" Jensen repeated.

Frank slammed the door shut and shambled to the drawing room, where from a slit in the curtains he watched until the Americans departed. What an awful fright for him. Good thing about the medicinal use for foxglove discovered in Edgbaston, not far, in fact, from Yew Tree Close, for never more had he needed a dose of digitalis.

May

27

Halfway back of the team bus Andy Webb stoked his teammates' spirits for the big match. Having been a boxing champion in Her Majesty's Service, he had seen the best of Europe. Later, for his first pro fight he'd been scheduled to face the British heavyweight contender Frank Bruno. But pugilistic exploits weren't what the players were keen to hear about at the moment. "We were on army maneuvers once in Germany," Andy said, "and I saw this bloke shit a turd, then eat it off his plate. Still steaming, it was, when it went into his mouth. Then he pissed himself a cup to wash it down with."

Players crowded round his seat, among them the young linemen Davey Parkes and Greg Cross, who cringed and tried to laugh at Andy's scatalogical motivation, or his motivational affront. "Then," he said, his brilliantly tattooed arms showing them how it was done, "he takes a newspaper, see, rolls it up, sticks it up his arse, sets it on fire, and dances around till it burns the hairs on it.

"And if we win," he pledged, "we'll take you lads out on the town and let you see a live donkey show."

After the team bus finally had broken free of bank holiday traffic, Animal Roberts gave a gruff shout from the rear, "Yo, bro',

I'm busting back here!" Others cued in with a chorus of groans, and when the battered old brown bus pulled to a stop, 41 men poured out for a colossal piss.

"We could get done for this!" Davey Parkes shouted as he climbed a shoulder of Cambridgeshire countryside. "In the nick for sure!" agreed Greg Cross.

Animal laughed wickedly while undoing his fly. The nick. Jail. No bother, bro'. He and many of the Bulls had been there, would go back again. As for himself, odds were sooner than later. He was on his way to play a ballgame, yes, but he had no football protocol to follow; if anything it juiced up his chromosomes, this man who constantly alluded to himself as a "full-time villain." Only thing that saddened him, in Amsterdam there weren't many laws to break.

He had a face only a mother could pretend to love, with nasty scars down the side of it and at the base of his neck, from having had a cocktail thrown on him by a publican. Some cocktail: Animal had been served a glass of hydrochloric acid. "Aiming for me, but got about fifteen other people, too," he said.

As I sat next to him on the bus, his Polo cologne almost acted as chloroform. But enough of my senses were retained to gather a great deal about his villainous philosophy, this man whose christened name, Locksley, was the same as Robin Hood's birthplace. He operated more by caprice than corruption. Football was diversion. He lived for villainy and drank to it, bottle after bottle of bubbly. It began as a youngster with "shoplifting, everybody does shoplifting." He led a group. "Ten-fifteen kids, gang of us, pick a shop. Somebody go in and look at a pair of pumps, somebody else go up to the clerk and say, 'Hey, he's beating up my girlfriend,' and as he tried to separate the rest of us we'd grab the goods and go."

That was enough to qualify him as permanent special teams captain of the Bulls, but his career escalated. "I was at a garden party and saw this chap across the patio looking at me real strange. A few minutes later he come up and asked if I wanted to make some money. I knew what kind of money he meant." The man was a respected businessman by day, antiques thief by night. He threw lavish parties, inviting his friends, who while making social merriment, were unaware their homes were being burgled by Animal. "Moved a lot of antiques," he said. "Made thirty-thousand quid out of it. That's why I drink champagne— got to spend all that money somehow—just not spend it in big chunks. If I buy bottles of champagne it don't leave a trail."

Animal also was awaiting financial settlement from the acid- tossing incident, which given his generosity, might be invested in the Bulls. "But because I'm a villain," he allowed, "they think they don't have to push it. The baaaas-tards."

Forget special teams captain. What he really ought to be was Bulls president and chief operating officer. Except he may have been a little too ingenuous with true quotes.

Our en masse pissing didn't end soon enough for the fussbudgety kitman Malcolm Byron; he reckoned, already running late for the ferry crossing, that the players and coaches had taken too long to empty bladders and shooed us back aboard the bus. All of us, for I whizzed away, too, and Malcolm "just like the poet" Byron, as he was apt to call himself, be damned. Here was half a Byronic quatrain for him: We weren't just taking a leak, but making a profound statement. Atop that embankment was not only relief, but enough metaphor to fill a hundred septic tanks.

On rugby tours when nature called, players removed a metal plate from the floorboard in their bus to go through it. Gridiron was more of a spectacle. And, metaphorically, a game that couldn't wait. A game where you either got pissed off or, more often, pissed on. If you made it to the top, as had the Bulls, you still got pissed on. If you were a Yank, even more of a piss was taken on you by Brits who owned teams for which you worked.

Oftentimes, an American deserved to piss back, and did, but doomed himself to a pissing contest with a skunk, though stronger odor prevails, and in Britball it was all too easy to see who had the stripes up and down their backs. Or Nehru collars around their necks.

Owners, or supremos by the British misnomer for them, weren't always responsible for what went wrong: to wit an

American whose story had been touchingly reported in *First Down* beneath a headline BRAVE TED PLAYS ON:

"Plucky Northants linebacker Ted Young has rejoined the team just weeks after suffering a nervous breakdown."—as told in the magazine's hyperbolic style and what sounded like nothing more than an acute case of home sickness. "The battling blitzer played in the Stormbringers' 20–7 division battle with the Chelmsford Cherokee. 'He misses his girlfriend, he misses playing his guitar, he's in a strange country and doesn't know his way around,' said coach Don Markham. 'But he trained all week and adjusted to things.' "

If brave Ted had adjusted and played on, he was one among many. Maybe to get over going guitarless, he'd stopped by No. 10 Yew Tree for sound studio counseling.

And what of the indigenous lads who played it, the noble savages from the twentieth century? Only benefit most Brits got for their physical trials was carte blanche to National Health Service—same privilege extended every subject of the Crown. And maybe an addendum to Kipling's remarking "the flanneled fools at the wicket and the muddied oafs at the goal," who, thanks to gridiron, could now be joined by cocooned buffoons at the 45-yard line.

Could what lay ahead in Amsterdam for the Bulls have even the slightest chance of changing all that?

May

The grim docks of Harwich hove into view, then a reassuring sight, the *Sealink St. Nicholas,* its giant stern gates down, waiting. Before we boarded, a kerfuffle ensued at customs when it couldn't be readily discerned just who the Bulls were. English football teams were banned from going abroad—soccer football teams, because of the exported hooliganism. Denton Thomas determinedly explained to an agent, "But we're a British *American* football team," causing him a start, before another official shouted over: "You know, mate, like bloody Miami Dolphins." Denton took hold of the sleeve of one of the NFL Products shirts British players always outfitted themselves in, often ensemble wear. He handled it as gingerly as if it were his own windbreaker. "See here, man," he said to the agent with his sartorial statement.

Once aboard we could count ourselves lucky British nautical laws forebade steerage. We were bled dry, so strapped that not only was per diem for the players and coaches out of the question but at the hotel where we would stay—actually a youth hostel miles outside Amsterdam—unless we brought our own, it'd cost an extra £5 per player for bed linens.

But for 24 hours we tried to shed our cynicism, helped by all that awaited in Amsterdam. We got an unexpected boost of morale when three Carolina belles, before they were numbed by bourbon and hashish, volunteered as cheerleaders against the Crusaders.

Most of the Bulls hadn't been outside the country. Novelty of the ferry further sparked their curiosity. There wasn't a lounge seat next to a woman unvisited. Michael Tulloch, a linebacker known as Badass, roamed the deck taking great glee in telling how "the team's assistant physiotherapist can't find his head; spilling his guts by the bucket."

A combination of mal de mer and lager had subdued him, and every time he got two or three steps outside the bathroom he found himself doubled over and crawling back into it. A. J. Taylor, a linebacker known as Robocop because of his shaved head and the goggles he wore on the football field, gave an imitation of the physio, arms wide as if he were clutching a sink, and went "Bluuuuu-aaaargh! And, ah, mates, his hair's all matted up with it, too."

Other players were on their way to more genuine imitations of the stricken physio. Pints of beer got turned up and thrown back with rapidity. Russ Jensen also began imbibing—imbibing heavily, to the surprise and dismay of some Bulls. But they were too timorous to say anything as he slunk further and further into a banquette next to the bar, his eyes glazing, his consciousness fading.

As in his first season with the Bulls, to the players' great irritation at the time, Jensen had reinstituted a rule of no alcohol on the team bus, which could be extended to the ferry. But now players followed his lead; had bulkheads a'tremble with their comportment. As the trip became a seven-and-a-half-hour crossing against gale winds, they had plenty of time for it, seating themselves at the bar throughout, or until they couldn't sit upright at it any longer.

Sealink St. Nicholas finally docked at Hook of Holland, and we recrammed ourselves into our bus. In the seat next to mine Errol Perkins, a veteran end, leaned against the window and smudged it with Afro-sheen, transforming my sightseeing of zees and tulip fields into a blurry vision.

Otherwise, a lovely vantage that somehow earned Davey Parkes's opprobrium. "Bloody scenery's all the same, give me Scotland any day!" he huffed. Then to the busdriver: "Get us to where we're going, mate!"

Tulips preoccupied the armchair horticulturists among us. Then it got too dark even to count windmill blades as distraction. For hours we went in circles; the driver, a little Yorkshireman named Jack, had great difficulty finding his way, even with a crucifix pinned to his lapel.

After he made another wrong turn into a cow pasture, Parkesy reblurted, "Bloody hell! Most boring country!" Fast approaching midnight, the Bulls got testy. Events of the day had left us traumatized. The scene with Jess Rodgers—nothing could have rent spirits more. Nash might spearhead the Bulls defense, but Jess was the rock. Once he'd been injured and forced to sit out a game. But he couldn't sideline his emotions, and when things weren't going the way he thought they should on the field, he'd stormed the pressbox and commandeered the P.A. "Bloody hell, ref, dodgy call!" he shouted into the tannoy. "What rubbish are you calling, eh? Give it to us fair, mate!"

The boozy glow of the ferry had long since dissipated, and after all our waywardness, the hostel was nowhere in sight. We were hungry, and our bladders taxed again, but now "getting done" could create an international incident.

We were 19 hours en route, had gone through the best of Dutch jerkwater when finally, the busdriver looped down a country road and it was almost heaven: A welcoming committee at the hostel made the theological-minded of us question the crucifix in Jack's lapel.

Yes, we were greeted by the Bulls' latest musical manifestation, a group calling themselves the World of John Denver.

And John Denver in a most worldly Dutch way, freckles painted on their faces, wearing authentic faded bib overalls. Denver was known to be a fan of space exploration, what with his having offered $10 million to the Russians if they'd send him up as a cosmonaut, but I had no idea he was an aficionado of European gridiron.

But undoubtedly so, since at the hostel, his most devoted followers, speaking and singing with Dutch hayseed accents, were there to cheer us on. Then the World of John Denver moved to the kaffeeklatsch, turning up volume and hospitality. The Bulls were inspired. "John who?" lineman Craig Wooldridge said when he failed to recognize one of music's bigger names. "I reckon them fuckers have been paid off to keep us awake all night." How awake and alert we'd stay the next day was of greater concern.

May

29

A.M.

The Crusaders were very big on game preparation, too, musical accompaniment the only thing not figuring into it. They had flown their coaches to England for scouting the Bulls on three occasions, which not only would have exhausted our budget but also required the Bulls to pawn firstborns. On native soil they were more impressive: For a month they practiced five nights a week, mandatory, the latest strategem to encamp at a rustic resort and scrimmage against the best players in the country, posing as the Bulls. And not posing as our posers, either.

The Crusaders also carried out keen reconnaissance. "So where is your number thirty-seven—Femi Amu?" one of the physios would later ask about the ailing defensive back, who'd remained behind in Brum with a case of passport phobias. "Allow me to say we were going to exploit him all day," he confessed. "He cannot cover anyone and does not wrap his arms when he tackles."

Their head coach, the man responsible for this tack, was an American who also happened to hold down the job as football coach at Richard Nixon's alma mater, Whittier College in California. He was, fittingly, secretive; besides hearsay, we knew only that they'd last year reached the semifinals of the Euro Bowl—

reached it by default, courtesy of the London Ravens' overexuberance.

We'd arrived in Holland a seriously underfed football team, and the hostel staff, knowing our straits if only because we stayed there in the first place, saw no reason to change our status. Before us they put fare for an emaciation contest instead of a training table for football players—almost imaginary food. It was not inconceivable to me, having been around Britball long enough to become a conspiracy theorist, that with the connection to Nixon, never a great friend of the British anyhow, the Cru had arranged for the Bulls to be fed starvation rations. That being the case, they were dealing with the wrong crew, Brum having been the first British city to initiate rationing during the Great War.

Game day began with a cumulative hangover for the Bulls. Stomachs growled if our competitive urge didn't. But James Thornton insisted we get in a walk-through practice before the game, in a field behind the hostel. But it proved pocked with rocks and rabbit holes, forcing us elsewhere, Thornton ordering the driver to stop along a canal near a dike. Maybe there was some symbolism in this for our defense.

The Bulls waded onto our impromptu pitch populated by Frisian cattle. Cow dung aroma wafted over our calisthenics. Carp splashed in the canal, and a man in a postman's hat ran after them. Cyclists pedaled past; in this country everyone cycled to supplement their emaciation. The scene was of a Van Gogh painting done under the influence of crankcase oil.

In the middle of it all, Bob Shoop gamely tried to preoccupy himself. Russ Jensen, as head coach, had formally announced he and Thornton were the two Americans who would kit against the Dutch. Shoopy tried not to take it too hard. If he'd put an umlaut over the double vowels in his last name, the Dutch might have reconsidered Euro Bowl rules and let him play with a repatriated-son exemption. But that would've meant altering pronunciation, which he'd never stand for.

Further hurt to his vanity awaited at Sportspark Sloten, where the game was to be played. Greeting our bus, the Cru's managing secretary almost mistook him for a waterboy; only natural, since he was the youngest-looking person in British sport next to the country's minister of sports, Colin Moynihan, who himself looked about 12 years old, especially when pictured in the tabloids alongside a former Miss India turned party girl named Pamella Bordes.

As the Bulls, fully kitted, filed past Shoopy and into the stadium, the Dutch secretary sidled over and struck up a conversation with him. She asked about the trip across, just being polite to the Bulls' British waterboy.

"Oh," she said to his reply, "but you're American!"

"Yeah, I'm a coach," Shoop said. "Got a job back in the States as a coach, too."

"But you look so very young for it," she said.

He bristled a little. "No, I'm a coach, I mean, I'm a player, too," he insisted. "I'm just not playing today."

He pulled a game program from his hindpocket, opened it, and scanned the Bulls roster with his finger, pointing to his name, which was followed by a hyphen and the "U.S.A." that denoted imports in gridiron.

"See," he informed the Dutch woman, "this is me."

Her face broke out in a hive of disbelief. "You—you are Bobby Shoop? But no, it cannot be! Then why are you not playing?" she asked in one long desperate syllable. "But you must play, you must!" she exclaimed. "All we have put in for this game is meant for stopping you!"

But Shoopy would have to placate himself with coaching comportment, stalking the sideline in starched chinos and perfectly faded Old Blue shirt with Yale blazoned over the heart—placate himself showing the Dutch how a real coach dressed. Of course, what he needed to wear, and what the Bulls really needed for him to wear, was that umlaut.

May

29

P.M.

A s the game began, players lined up sans helmets to match faces against passport photos and make sure no imposters, impersonators, or ringers tainted Euro Bowl. Somebody else was about to get a closer appraisal, too.

The Supporters Club numbers in the Netherlands rivaled the home crowd, and even Frank Kalili, with appreciation for the spoken or sung word, especially when it spilled from his own lips, would have been impressed as they rallied on their beloved Bulls. Then again, Frank had gone on record locating them at the lowest end of the food chain.

But the Club, far from the sponging, scabrous outfit Frank painted it as, endlessly came round to caulk up what management mangled. Moreover, they were almost the only thing that was not catchpenny about the Bulls.

Most diehard were L. B. Robinson, who had bought 50 percent of the team and, in a fit of foolish altruism, turned it over to Frank, and the Greenwood brothers, Ian and Terry, whose loyality went further. Ian was a mail sorter who earned £90 a week. Having become an avid gridiron fan, he'd saved for years toward an extended holiday to the States to follow the Washington Redskins.

But after the Bulls got into financial trouble, about to meet demise, he'd withdrawn the money from his savings account and given it all to enable the team to carry on to the championship.

"Serious bother to Ian," averred his brother Terry. "The Supporters already had given thousands and thousands."

So the Bulls' Supporters—parasitic, according to Frank Kalili—were in fact recurrent lifeblood transfusion for the team? There was more: what the Greenwoods called the American connection, where every Bulls' Supporter was asked to donate money weekly to help smooth international relations. "We'd give it to James Thornton," Terry said, "and he was to split it up between the other Yanks."

Big James must have had treasurer lessons from Frank, for he'd not once mentioned the club's benevolence, nor endorsed their generosity.

In Holland the Supporters Club carried on, illogically loyal as always. As the game began they passed a Bulls' cap through the stands, a whip-round. When it was totted up, they'd amassed thousands of gilders for their heroes, to guarantee win or lose we'd enjoy ourselves after the Euro Bowl.

And it was money not only come in handy but also would have to be a balm for us. For only had the World of John Denver been transformed into the starting lineup of the Denver Broncos and played for the Bulls—only then might we have stood a chance of beating the Crusaders.

Forget the alibi of boozing the day before. Forget the allure of sin city. Forget a loopy video back in the hostel, purportedly of the Cru, which featured a cameraman going into the huddle with them, a huddle of beer guts and heavy breathing. Maybe instead of a game film, they'd slipped us the Dutch version of Russ Jensen's football sitcom back in the States. Or Tricky Dick Nixon had a deeper hand than suspected.

We should have known we were in big trouble when the Cru came onto the field and there wasn't a mismatched sock to be found on the whole team. That, of course, was an intimidation factor not to be discounted in Britball. Meanwhile, the Bulls' sad spectrum of uniforms was just an outward sign of defeat. Of Jess Rodgers, of the Jensen morass, our boatload of blotto, of empty stomachs, the Dutch couldn't know. All at once, the Birmingham Bulls, British champions, undefeated, winners of 22 games in a row, ran out of picaresque relish.

The Crusaders former NFL tight end, who'd caught passes for the New York Jets and Washington Redskins, was a seine net with hands against our tiny and timorous defensive backs, catching three touchdowns. Meanwhile, with no American receiver to throw to, Jensen's passes, not crisp to begin with, sailed through British hands, and into the Crusaders'; three interceptions in the first half. By then, we trailed 25–0.

James Thornton's picayune attempt at a motivating speech at halftime—"It's a matter of hitting somebody, fellows, or of putting skirts on!"—was received with blank faces. The Bulls had come completely apart. As the second half began, it became more of a molesting. We seemed determined to let Amsterdam score one point for every dozen pints of beer we had consumed aboard the ferry.

"And on and on and on it goes," sub lineman Martin Bourne said at the end of the bench as the score climbed.

The Bulls were overwhelmed, yes, in every aspect, the game not nearly so close as the 46–15 score indicated. British leader writers and their allusion to war for almost every sporting contest, I was certain this debacle would make its way into print as the Flanders Field of gridiron. "That's what I call a bloody stuffing," said Andy Webb, the nosetackle and old Army of the Rhine soldier.

But the Bulls' fugue didn't last long. Cru players came to our sideline with invitation for postprandial deadening of any disappointment. "Smoke for you, Birmingham," one of them remarked. "All smoke you want, you come get."

"Yeah, bro'," Animal Roberts said, instantly accepting the offer. "Be right over. Just have 'em rolled."

The Bulls took our first loss in 23 games with resilience, abetted by large portions of controlled substances. Defeat was easy to forget, consciously or not. The Euro Bowl's aftermath—free hashish and a Crusaders clubhouse adorned by astonishingly hookerish-looking octaroon women—was everything a losing celebration could offer. But the real reward of the trip lay ahead in the wee hours; undoubtedly this was the best time to be a Brummie since the native son Ken Tynan came up with "Oh, Calcutta."

At every corner leading into Dam Square, players demanded the bus stop and let them decamp. They'd got stoked to learn the Cru were sponsored by a phone sex company, and spirits rose from there. Finally they cajoled the driver into pulling over and dispersed. I'd sure as hell never seen them break huddle with such determination.

But whenever the Bulls went, whatever they spent when they got there, the money would have to come from their own pockets—for Russ Jensen had single-handedly expropriated that fat wad of gilders from the Supporters.

• • •

Self-financed pleasures for them, and fun while it lasted, too, the red light foray, for headlines decrying our performance were being prepared for the Bulls' return. Back in Blighty, one correspondent would assail the Bulls' "Great hangover!" while another deplored it a "humbling event." *First Down,* in its usual understated way, blared BRITISH SCANDAL!

As the Bulls went their way, I went mine, down a wide avenue called the Damrak, where junkies and their syringes hogged the curb. I was trying hard to get custody of my own thoughts. What next for the misbegotten Fourth American? Maybe I'd soon shed the designation, once and for all. For Russ Jensen had again mouthed his threat of going home—"I'm on my bike if I'm not paid all I'm owed when we leave Amsterdam"—and his departure would open the door for me finally to play football.

But for now the appellation not only bugged the hell out of me but also put me in need of a vacation. And I damned sure didn't mean another trip with a ramshackle football team. No, drawing from personal savings, I was bound for the French countryside. The next day I was strolling through a mighty if frivolous chateau called Pierrefronds, laid to waste in the thirteenth century, restored 600 years later by Napoleon III. As for the Bulls, losers on the pitch and long laid to waste financially, no such grand restoration plan appeared available. When and if I rejoined them, would there be anything left of the team for me to go back to?

June

7

With a half-million punters, I hied off to the world's oldest horse race, the Epsom Derby. I went for a spot of royal-watching and to feast royally on race fare of jellied eels, and to try not to spend all my paycheck in one place. Yes, holy exchequeur, I'd drawn a paycheck—what's more, pay commensurate with my coaching: a £5 note, which, excluding amenities from a stint as Frank Kalili's butler, was my first compensation from the Bulls.

Among the personal items I had brought to Britain was a pair of protective prescription goggles to wear under my football helmet. My strong inclination at that moment was to make for the nearest optician for a sanguine tint.

For months we Bulls soldered ourselves together, but with the Euro Bowl loss we'd been certain demise at last had drawn a bead. Yet when the situation grew bleakest and only an act of Parliament might save the team, our saga became more a story for stretching the farfetched. As Fabian remarked in *Twelfth Night:* "If this were portrayed on stage, I would condemn it as an improbable fiction."

The Bulls, all but beleaguered out, had gotten a new owner—a putative new owner, since it was bound to go down as a contested purchase, if it constituted a purchase at all. But from looking at the situation, we'd been rescued, as the Brits put it, by one of the great and the good.

David Webb had been trying to buy into the team for weeks, but as with others, gotten absolutely nowhere negotiating with Frank Kalili. He eventually succeeded where they failed because his own pertinacity matched Frank's, who while solidifying his inertia as the Bulls foundered, continued clinging to a figure 30 times higher than his original asking price for the team.

But David Webb was quick to seize on the fact that the Bulls' majority owner owned little more than his good name(s), record collection, and risible press clippings, and moved to take over the team by eminent domain.

Certainly in his boldness, he had the law on his side, which of itself should have been enough for Feed-the-World-Frank to surrender his despoiliating grip. Yes, the law was very big on his side. For this new owner claimed to have been superintendent of the West Midlands police force. He'd once stood, moreover, as a candidate for parliament. It was almost enough to replace the dross of my cynicism, if not a cause for celebration.

As father of the nosetackle Andy Webb, he knew our needs; he was here to help, he announced, not to help himself as owner. He brought to the team egalitarianism, best evidenced when he attended his first NDMA owners meeting and didn't put anybody in handcuffs. Moreover, he was not lacking for cocksureness; after hearing how Pete the Greek, owner of the London Olympians, might be wanting to sell his team, he was quick to respond: "Fine, then, mate. We'll buy them, make them Birmingham Bulls farm team."

We threw caveats to the wind, and welcomed him.

It sure sounded good, anyhow.

Besides, Dave Webb declared, demography and people were his business, he was among the country's highest Masons and a community activist. First time the Americans sat down with him over how he planned to run the team, he cited a survey that found 24 different ethnic groups living on a single street in his neighborhood of Handsworth, where he was now a community activist. "And," he said proudly, "our streets are all of a hundred yards long."

Maybe, if things didn't work out at Salford Park, we could use one of them to play games on.

He was chuffed at taking on the Bulls. "Up till now I've only had the Rotary, mates, dealing with ninety-four-year-olds on the verge of the hereafter," he allowed. He went at his new assignment with stern singularity. He met with the Supporters Club at Moor Lane right after the deal was done, or as the case may have been, commandeered, and told them, "Everything, everybody is now going to be subjugated to the Birmingham Bulls."

As if they'd ever behaved anything to the contrary.

Again, it sounded good. Still, anybody but a former chief constable standing there, enunciating this rosy future, telling of changes to be made, this honeybear commitment of his, and it'd have come off as over the top.

But out of Dave Webb's mouth it had only the gilded ring of true-quotism. For from the outset the new owner was following at least one tradition with the Bulls: He was mighty enamored with the sound of his own voice.

The voice hadn't sung professionally, but he had yet another similarity to the old regime, what with owning a sporting goods business. Soon the official merchandiser of the Birmingham Bulls had an official change of address. He also reorganized the Bulls' front office. Unable to foreclose on Frank's foyer at No. 10 Yew Tree Close, he moved the front office elsewhere—into his own shop.

In the hasty restructuring of the team, the impuissant Denton Thomas, having sold off under pressure his own stake in the Bulls, was allowed to stay on symbolically (with his white windbreaker) and take part in the postgame confabulation along midfield. He was also put in charge of the hamburger stand for home games at Salford Park.

In a much bigger move, and to a simmering consternation from many of the players, Gerry Hartman, the disgraced founder of the team, was rehabilitated back into the Bulls' hierarchy, something of an ex-officio general manager, though a reluctant James Thornton had been bestowed by David Webb with the title.

The players, unforgiving as they were, figured having Hartman back beat going defunct, but not by much.

Meanwhile, Thornton's reluctance chiefly stemmed from still having a great deal of enmity for Frank Kalili. He felt even with Webb's claiming ownership of the Bulls, the Wily Midlands Fox had, with his Silk Cuts, lain groundsmoke and gotten away all too cleanly. He was furious at Webb's pledge to pay Frank for what he didn't own, and allow him to "retain" 5 percent of Bulls' ownership.

The new owner gave no reproof of Frank except to say, "I hear every story and make my own mind up, mate—that's how I worked as a policeman, and that's how I'll be at this gridiron." His only other comment over Frank's figurehead status was, "It's the gentlemanly thing to do."

"Pardon my French, but that's utter bullshit, Mr. Webb!" Thornton thundered. "I want him to eat his goddamned debts, choke on them. They're his debts, not the team's."

Webb nodded to the possibility, then appeased him with the first binding contract ever for a Bulls' employee, Zark's fine document notwithstanding, but Thornton hedged from putting his calligraphic signature on it.

He didn't want the responsibility of running a gridiron team that didn't "own a goddamned thing." Nor did he especially care to have to wake up and report for work on a daily basis, either. Not when he could stay out all night and sleep late on his acre of futon, and have only his presence at games on Sunday to be accounted for.

GM of his own widget system, stacking his social calendar, fine. But of a Britball team? Never.

June

9

Webb's resuscitation did not instantly make things copacetic for the Bulls. One member of the team's traveling party failed to rendezvous for the return crossing from Holland, but he was the player on whom the rest of the season hinged. Had Russ Jensen carried through with his threat to quit the Bulls?

No, he'd merely been detained by Dutch police and spent a night in jail, or more precisely inside a police station. It came about when he and a friend began looking for ways to lighten that wad of gliders from the Supporters. The buddy, a player for a team called the Hague Red Raiders, got hauled in for drunken driving, and Jensen, though not implicated, was told to follow the police in his friend's car.

When he missed the ferry, the players began to quiz Bob Shoop, whom they'd last seen in Jensen's company. Even with his denials, given their own canon of crime, they twigged he'd gotten locked up; it was this story that greeted the star quarterback when he landed back in England.

Actually, the story didn't greet him, because he arrived before the ferry docked, ahead of the players, having spent most of the gilders to fly himself to Brum.

But when he failed to board, rumor ran rampant on the ferry

that he might be held in Holland for weeks, maybe months. The Bulls promulgated it mightily, the kind of thing they wouldn't at all have minded given his Euro Bowl performance, or their own indifference to the rest of the season. Hell, by now they didn't care if the Dutch police threw away the key.

Not without complications did Jensen get back into the country. Without working papers or a viable excuse as to what he'd been doing in the United Kingdom the last three months, other than suffering from ego abuse, he'd rung his girlfriend in immigration and gotten her to spirit him through—the kind of on-his-feet thinking he'd sorely lacked in Amsterdam. Maybe the plane's inflight bar had been closed on his trip back.

The story about his incarceration also guaranteed that practice would be poorly subscribed, even though Jensen was on hand for conducting it—and predictably with less politesse than usual on the pitch. A shame, for had he been of a better disposition he might have landed personal sponsorship from a Brum automaker, which produced the vehicle that very day chosen to replace the Aston-Martin in James Bond flicks. A car not only his namesake, but that also matched his performances of late at quarterback: the Jensen Interceptor.

A slight and unmotivated turnout for practice indeed caused him to explode with a vow to bench six starters missing from the pitch when it began. "You'll probably play this week," he said, turning on and startling me. "I don't give a damn if it's too many Americans in the lineup or not."

Right-o. I didn't want to endanger our standing by breaking any rules, but I stood convinced the team's new owner would agree to it, too. As community leader he deferred to minorities. As an aspirant in his mid-30s, decked out in a football helmet almost as old I was, I'd traveled across an ocean to play, quit real life for this lark. How better to categorize myself? I could see an asterisk beside my name in the program, with the disclaimer at the bottom of the page: "Minority-Worthy Cause."

Maybe what would have cinched it was if I'd changed residences again to move into David Webb's neighborhood of Handsworth, where, defining myself as an Italo-American-dual-Birminghamian, I'd become the 25th ethnic group to be represented along one of those hundred-yard streets.

June

11

The Americans spent a Saturday morning in full kit at the Bull Ring market, promoting the Bulls by passing a football over the heads of shoppers—generally without frightening them—and handing out hundreds of complimentary tickets to our next game, trying to assure a big crowd for my debut.

But people either remained unaware of the team or were down on us after the debacle in Amsterdam, and handouts betokened nothing in increased attendance at Salford Park. Nor did I play, or dress for the game, as his old copper's propriety scotched Dave Webb's noblesse oblige. A shame, for having recommended my haggis diet, I'd never felt leaner or meaner. But David Webb, all probity, wouldn't hear it: "You're not legal, son; just won't allow it."

Nevertheless, the Bulls won a rematch with the Leicester Panthers, manhandled them 41–7, to dispel vultures and vilifiers, and move us within a game of again clinching the league's Central Conference crown.

Having to resume the British season right after losing the continental championship was another of those marvelous NDMA planning strokes. Look what had happened to the London Ravens last year, with that end zone melee that cost them the Euro Bowl game against the Dutch; when they returned to British play they were able to muster all the enthusiasm of art museum mummies. Pretty soon they were getting annihilated, 51–13, by the Bulls.

But carbon monoxide from Spaghetti Junction came down upon us like a healing zephyr. Bob Shoop caught two touchdown passes and got cheered off the field after both by his father, who was visiting (and who, it turned out, was lucky to get rid of his nervous energy pacing our sideline; driving a right-hand rental car the next day, he sideswiped a line of about 20 parked cars in one fell turn).

After Shoop's second touchdown late in the half, I ordered a squib kick to prevent the Panthers making a runback, but Spider Webb instead misfooted it into an onside attempt and we recovered. Fair boot! as the Brits say. I had no compunction at rubbing it in against the Panthers after the nightmares caused in our first game by their string of illegal onside kicks that almost cost me my job.

For this game we had a ploy of our own: Gerry Hartman as Bulls P.A. announcer. Or, should stereophonic kickback plague the tannoy: "Gerry Hartman . . . Gerry Hartman."

For a team whose management always prided itself on syllabacity, his was another resonant voice to have with the Bulls. Players weren't especially thrilled with this prodigal return, but couldn't object too much, since he had a working relationship with Dave Webb, selling donated practice jerseys and equipment he collected from America out of the new owner's sporting goods warehouse.

Yes, while the Fourth American remained on the sidelines, a fifth, expatriate though he was, energized the crowd. From scaffolding erected over the 50-yard line as his personal aerie, he gave one of the most editorially compelling public addresses in football, nay sporting history—voice thick with opinion, commending the Bulls, daring rebuff officials for unpopular penalties. "Do we care, Bulls?" he offered when we got called for defensive holding. "Hell, no! Let's go, big D. Stop 'em, defense!"

Up there in aviator sunglasses, flyboy crew cut, and A-2 pilot's jacket, his only oversight was not asking a moment of silence for James Harry "Ginger" Lacey, an ace in the Battle of Britain who shot down the only German plane that bombed Buckingham Palace, who'd died that week.

But Hartman had a scintillating surprise in store. In the third quarter, he breathed deeply, reached for his microphone, and made the Special Relationship between two countries a little more special: "We have just received word from Washington, D.C."—he paused for the sublime, or for kickback—"that President George Bush sends along his very best wishes to the Birmingham Bulls!"

Russ Jensen didn't mind Hartman's invoking the name of a president—wherever he'd gotten it, perhaps conveyed by the old CIA operative Andy Capp—but got increasingly disgruntled over his cynosure; and wanted him shushed.

He demanded that owner Webb climb the scaffolding and issue Hartman a vocal restraining order. "Right now, dammit!" When that didn't work, P.A. still full-tilt, he stepped from the huddle after another of Hartman's colorful pronouncements, and matching the tannoy's artificial amplification, shouted, "Gerry! Shut the fuck up!"

After the game David Webb got formally introduced as new owner, and promptly invited everyone associated with the Bulls to the King Edward VII pub across from Salford Park for a victory celebration. Even the Supporters were included. He also made a showy display of bestowing the American's paychecks. Webb wasn't through, though. He bought the Panthers a consolation round, which might well have been a first for largesse in the annals of the NDMA.

This gridiron football, as he called it, wasn't quite sporting homogeneity he might have taken it for, and not just because of futuristic garb and calendar rental of the matches. There were American egos and British laxity, and the un-Keynesian structure of the sport was something else again. But David Webb flatly pronounced himself prepared to deal with any possibility.

An old cockney, he was the embodiment of a man whose

greeting once was, " 'Ow's everything, guvnor?" though, sadly, nobody said governor anymore in Britain. But he was soon to learn that for the Yanks, money always governed the mood. That afternoon I got my £5 weekly salary and the others got just enough to leave them hungering for more.

June

14

O wner Dave Webb was off to a rousing start. Perhaps fearful of his close connections within the judicial system, the NDMA chose to lower no new fines for insufficient seating at Salford Park; moreover, Webb moved to double the capacity by trucking in tractor-trailers that unfolded into drop-down seats. The setup looked like a military reviewing stand but its canopy was not to be underestimated, with the sun wreaking ultraviolet havoc against sensitive British skin.

He tried his hardest to purvey integrity. He installed portable toilets at Salford, though they clogged during the game; he also halved the price of match programs to 50p, to give more people the chance to read his own true-quoting epistle placed inside the front cover.

He gave the Americans raises, doubled salaries for Bobby Shoop and James Thornton, and upped Russ Jensen's pay to where he made more than the two of them combined. But, for the moment, money was being made in the owner's head. They'd been paid, true, but not quite commensurate with how they felt about themselves.

Webb seemed unconcerned about the Bull's payroll—now the league's highest—though he had yet to square it, nor, by Jensen's

addition, come close. Inside that head of his he was already generating revenue, however. "Birmingham Bulls can really go big,"
he said of the future. "There's as much money in Brum as any
place in the country, lads, and we ought to have some of it." The
Yanks listened. If nothing else, they wanted to believe him,
though their ears, based on past experience, should have been
argumentative sentinels.

June

21

Summer wore on, the Bulls wore thin. Injuries ranged from a hurt thumb that would keep our autographing star George "T" Nisbet out of action, and from practicing his penmanship, for an entire season, to an outburst of lipomas on his lower arm for linebacker A. J. Taylor, the oddest of football injuries and a definite disadvantage for delivering forearm shivers, to torn ligaments for middle linebacker Bush James, incurred playing goalie in a soccer match. Few players turned up Saturday night for our weekly walk-through practice. When tight end Ray Malcolm arrived as it was ending, Russ Jensen shouted, "Why the hell are you late—you stoned?"

Malcolm stumbled across the artificial turf and into the huddle.

"He's got turf-toe," Errol Perkins chuckled.

"Got turf-head, too," Ray Malcolm said of himself.

Animal Roberts turned up looking a cross between Bronko Nagurski and the Sheikh of Dubai, wearing sunglasses under his helmet, with a foam knee pad taped to the back of it to protect his sun-sensitive scarred skin. Billy the Club Mills wasn't hurt, but the big center was sitting out anyhow—a one-game suspension when the referee mistook him for another player who had poked an opponent in the eye.

204

Our roster struck me as similar to something written of Franz Liszt, who played piano "with his hands, with his elbows, with his chin, with his nose. Anything that can hammer, hammers." Brits hammered away at gridiron, separating themselves from their senses.

My own bumps and bruises from practice I began to soak away in the Droitwich Brine Baths, a natural saline shrine in the Midlands, discovered by the Romans and saltiest water this side of the Red Sea. Floating about, salt riming, was ablution for the grand delusion of gridiron barnstorm where I was no closer to a lineup than were I still residing in Birmingham, Alabama.

Nor, by Webb's trademark rectitude, could I hold out a scintilla of hope for getting to play in the future. I still needed an injury, a deportation or maybe my best hope, an NDMA constitutional upheaval.

James Thornton began complaining about his oft-operated-on knees, and considered more surgery. But my plea to replace him on the roster if he went on injured reserve was preempted when Russ Jensen tried persuading Webb to hire an American friend who played for a team in Germany—played quarterback. Maybe we would run the double-barreled-shotgun offense. Further hampering my chances, Gerry Hartman peddled my helmet, sold it right out from over me.

Americans all over the league went home, or down with injury, everywhere it seemed but Birmingham. The Bulls' imports—a lineman who'd undergone five knee operations; a spindly receiver; a quarterback who'd be a millionaire if he had a nickel for every threat he made to leave—they were still playing. Protesting, but playing just the same.

I resented it, but short of tripping them down the stairs at No. 9 Star Hill or attacking them in their sleep with a kitchen knife, not much I could do. I got depressed. Asthma and its close cousin, bronchitis, known countrywide as the Birmingham disease, also bothered me that hot summer, though I did find a sympathizer and fellow sufferer in Animal Roberts.

"A spliff of hashish," he prescribed at practice, "ought to clear you right up."

A spliff was a joint, and I was given a soliloquy on its merits for restorative breathing before Thornton advised, "He don't get high, Animal."

"Yo, then try the root, bro'," Animal replied. "The Japanese root. Ginseng. Break open the capsule and sprinkle a few drops on your pillow and the asthma goes away."

Even with all his curatives, Animal himself was ever erratic at practice, that evening offering a broken finger as his latest excuse, in a shiny splint.

"How come he didn't have it on last night when we saw him dancing at Liberty's?" Bob Shoop wondered. "He was carrying a bucket of champagne around in that hand, too."

"Oh, Animal knows how to work his scam," replied Thornton, who'd then ordered the abeyant nosetackle to put shoulder pads over his black leather jacket and dress slacks and practice anyhow—also to make damned sure his splint didn't gouge anybody in the eye.

June

23

No such hesitance from another animated personality: Steve Harvey was desperate to rejoin the Bulls, having been—what else?—tarred as too violent by his new team. In a recent game an opponent had grabbed him by the face mask, an infraction officials detected and called. But Harvey, with his own code of justice, wasn't satisfied with fifteen yards, so at halftime he crossed the field to attend to it in his notoriously personalized manner.

"In the pen, mate, ain't nobody looking out for you but you," he'd once disclosed of a lengthy stint inside. "You learn fast-like to put your back to the wall. If you don't . . . might not make it." As testimony to what he'd learned behind bars, he proudly showed off a lengthy scar across his stomach where a knife had been plunged into it.

He wanted gridiron justice: He stormed the locker room, door reverberating on its hinges as he demanded "apology from that bloke, number seventy-two!"

The startled opposing coach asked him to leave. Harvey glared, repeating why he'd come. "I want it now!" he said. The coach again asked him to go away, only to have Harvey chuck him aside and strew three players in his wake before finding his quavering adversary hidden in the shower.

"I want the apology now, in front of all these!" he said with his steroid-stoked eyes.

The player covered his head after Harvey dragged him to the middle of the room.

"I'm . . . I'm sorry," he bleated.

"Again!"

"I'm s-s-sorry."

Now he was looking for a team more compatible with his kind of play. There was but one. "Been bothering me," his mate Andy Webb informed James Thornton after practice. "Going on about coming back to play with us."

"I don't know," Thornton replied. "He's trouble. Bound to be. I don't think we should take him back. But who's going to say no to him?"

"I don't want to be the one, mate," Andy Webb, 6 feet 5 and almost 270 pounds, stated. "Not to him, I ain't."

Thornton brought the team together in a pouring rain for a plebiscite. "I'm talking to you as general manager, fellows. You know we're thin. Real thin. I don't want to knock any of you guys out of a job, but somebody six-four, two-seventy comes along, he's in. But as far as this Harvey goes, we need consensus. You want him or not?"

Almost unanimously, the Bulls vetoed him from the roster. "He'll want to know 'Who? Who kept me off?' " Andy Webb said with a little distress in the dressing cubicle.

"Can't you just tell him it was the whole team?" Thornton asked.

"Nah, he'll know the team does what Yanks say."

"He's a house," Thornton said with a slight shudder. "And on the 'roids, man. He just goes off. Seems like the nicest guy in the world. But something sends him off." He spun around. "Maybe you could give him the news?"

"Me?" I gulped, bracing myself against the doorfacing.

"He don't know you, just seen you on the sideline; might think you're a league official or something."

208

"Great, when you look at his record with people in official positions. The javelins—"

"You're right. I know—we'll tell him when we put it before the league, they turned him down."

"Oh, brilliant." I didn't know who blurted the words out faster, me or Andy Webb.

But I could gleefully envisage, with Steve Harvey's handiwork, the NDMA's board of directors lined up on a 45-yard line somewhere, impaled by first-down markers.

June

24

As morning broke for a rematch with the hottest team in the league, the Leeds Cougars, the Bulls arguably became the first gridiron team whose coaches got a wakeup call from a Hindu feast.

Not a waft, but a bombardment of music, as if Frank Kalili and the Waikikis had done a mix with synthesizer and air raid siren. Frank, who spoke three Indian dialects and probably sang a couple, may have been in this festival of sound, when neighbors protested by turning their house alarms on and off. But the ceremony continued. "I was about to yell out the window and tell 'em to shut the fuck up," Russ Jensen said, "but I don't think they'd understand me."

Where the hell was Frank when he could have been helpful? Or was this something insidiously staged by the Leeds Cougars? Yorkshiremen were known to be the meanest, connivingest, cheatingest chaps in all the British Isles, and the unsettling fugue was the very thing to be expected of them.

The Cougars were playing their final home game of the season, so far successful, both on and particularly off the field. In a weekly column in the match program, their coach exclaimed,

"We have made it through another season without an American going home. What an accomplishment that is!"

The big game was set for Odsal Stadium, a former granite quarry where once turned out the largest crowd ever to see a rugby league match, more than 103,000. Yes, this was the heart of rugby country, where the cleats are three inches long and bumps on the head even higher. Rugby mentality surrounded us—we'd even get a chance to submerge ourselves in it since, instead of showers, the Bulls' locker room boasted the communal rugby bath, which in an era of communicable indiscretions, caused many of us to pass. "Okay for the rugby chaps," appraised Davey Parkes, " 'cause they fill it up with champagne, but no thanks, mate."

The first musical entertainment of the season, save for Frank's living room, was a marching band whose repertoire consisted of "Bridge Over Troubled Water," which they played for an hour before Jensen ordered them off the field so our receivers could run pass routes.

The band also staged a halftime show, a more melodic version of "Troubled Water," a treat for spectators, since usually the field in Britball went blank at halftime except for kids booting around soccer balls, or in the Bulls' case, Rastas littering it with beer cans. In Leeds, or in the outlying community of Bradford, where the game was played, such entertainment was to be expected—Bradford having been the first British locale to boast cheerleaders, to shore up a sagging Fourth Division soccer team. It didn't quite take hold. The cheerleaders were a group of 12- and 13-year-olds who'd been disbanded within three weeks after obscene chants from the team's fans.

As a sporting venue Odsal Stadium, which also hosted speedway racing, had a checkered history. It had been stopgap home for the Leeds United soccer club after its own stadium caught fire and 60 people died. Structurally, Odsal was sound, but technically, sorely lacking. The gridiron goalposts were off-center and several yards shy of regulation placement in the end zone.

Moreover, maybe two blades of grass grew the length of the

field, and for the Bulls there was a subconscious fear of getting bodyblocked to the ground and sliced up by a discarded magneto. And steps leading to the pitch were so steep, hundreds of them, we were practically knackered just in getting there, and that was a *downhill* expedition.

The first quarter was scoreless before Leeds grabbed a 3–0 lead on a 22½-yard field goal (with the shortened goalposts; it went into the books as a 25-yarder). But on the first play after kickoff, Pat Loftman was left uncovered coming out of the backfield and gathered in a swing pass from Russ Jensen for 85 yards and the go-ahead touchdown.

On the ensuing kickoff I called an onside kick, thinking a quick score might defuse the Cougars. We got the ball back and drove to the goal line, only for the dandified chauffeur, Linden, to botch a field goal and prevent us from extending the lead. It could have been, with his motorman's mentality, he'd been too immersed in the stadium's speedway attractions. More likely, from his distaff fulminations to the Americans while squiring us around, the majorettes in the marching band.

Worse than Amsterdam, it seemed we'd ordered defeat straight out of a catalog. A sweltering sun overhead was harbinger of what headmaster Kim Duce liked to call a drainlike performance. One of my top special teamers, who worked as a nightclub bouncer, got arrested for brawling and missed the game. We played without a single reserve offensive lineman. Linden kicked as if in a wheelchair. Jensen's arm went dead, limiting his passing range to about seven yards. Spats Lewis got confused by York-shire accents and was drawn offsides several times. Andy Webb went down with a wrenched knee to a hostile chorus of "Get him off! Get him off!" A few plays later Billy the Club Mills also hurt a knee, more jeers accompanying him to the sideline.

"Hear that, Bulls?" Boo Thomas shouted maniacally. "Now let's go out and dish out some pain!" Those Yorkshiremen as mean and cheating as prognosed, he meant to give it back to them in kind, or kinder.

Not only to the enemy: "Run that water, maaaan!" he'd

shouted to our waterboy during a time-out, gesturing him onto the pitch.

"Jensen didn't call for it!" hollered back the waterboy, Dave Cottrell, who doubled as youth team coach. He boldly spun around vis-à-vis Boo. Though he had no pacharan to pour, this Cottrell knew waterboying for the Bulls was a noble tradition.

"Jensen didn't call for it, I tell you!" he shouted.

"I don't care, man, get it out there! Now! Go on!" Boo threatened. He glared at the waterboy, who weighed 350 pounds and did not relish a coronary in the 90-plus degree heat. Cottrell stared back, unwilling to be belittled, and when finally Boo averted his stare, he doused him from a squirt bottle.

"Do that again, maaaan!" Boo bellowed, then caught his breath and slowly finished his sentence. "And . . . I . . . will . . . kill . . . you."

No doubt he was capable of it, though it would have meant violating his probation and could have cost him captaincy of Bulls special teams, even if the aggressiveness he'd shown was most appealing.

Alas, that aggressiveness was missing among his teammates. Worse, already minus 15 players, either through injury or absenteeism, we simply ran out of humanity. Still, we didn't so much run out of players as we ran out of or got swindled out of real estate: The winning margin in the Cougar's 20–14 victory was two field goals, neither of which would have been good if not for the goalposts squeezed onto the field. And so the Bulls' 21-game British winning streak came to a halt—helped to an end perhaps by some of that renowned Yorkshire skulduggery.

June

26

Luckily our next opponent was the weakest team in the league, if not the free world of gridiron. The Bulls led 40–0 by the first play of the second quarter. To see the Fylde Falcons bumble about, it wasn't inconceivable to me, having followed them since inception, that the Atlanta Falcons had become the first NFL team to take on a British farm club.

The first three times they touched the ball was like an impromptu audition for Russ Jensen's TV show: a lost fumble on the opening kickoff; another fumble on their first play from scrimmage; then a ballooning snap from center that cost them possession near the Fylde goal line when the punter's knee inadvertently touched down as he tried to field it.

Later it would turn out that the Falcons existed only as conduit for the finest cheerleading squad in the British Isles. When the team fell into financial trouble and was about to fold, the cheerleaders and their sponsor desperately pooled money and made a loan to keep the Falcons afloat.

Their cheerleading verve was unstinting, regardless the score, though only under duress would they even have acknowledged any affiliation with the football team. But they couldn't very well shout encouragement to a bridge club.

So embarrassing did the rout get, I asked officials to shorten the game, to keep the clock running between plays and after incomplete passes. Not a move born of compassion, but worry that the operator of our hand-scrawled scoreboard at Salford Park would run out of room to write as the score mounted, or come down with severe writer's cramp.

Our less-talented players saw their most extensive action of the season, some coming away with newfound confidence, if not, in the case of one, newfound brio. That would have been the misbegotten Clive Jackson, who was always earning Russ Jensen's ire and getting redressed by him for everything except his breathing patterns.

I'd taken a liking to Clive because he reminded me of someone I knew. Knew intimately, and had to live with, in or out of a football uniform. But I scolded him for running out of his lane covering a kickoff, and then again when he was the only player on the kickoff return team who failed to knock down or block an opponent.

These guys were marshmallows, after all, I informed him thusly.

"Why o-o-o-o always picking on me?" he demanded.

I explained it as coaching. He glared, unwilling or unable to comprehend. But as I returned my attention to the game, he mumbled angrily. With his hearing aid, he probably had no idea how far his voice carried.

"Cunt . . . a weal cunt."

I pretended not to hear as he vented his anger at his special teams coach to another player.

"Cunt, all he is . . . do one thing wrong and he—cunt."

Poor Clive, just his luck for Russ Jensen also to overhear the flap, and rush over to find out what was going on. He never passed up a chance to dress down a player, and with Clive Jackson he was always in top form stridency.

"If you ever open your mouth like that again—!" Clive cowered; who knew but his hearing aid was shattered.

·   ·   ·

Once Jensen's anger was sparked, no telling where it might rage, this day to Dave Webb. This was not unexpected. Webb had scrutinized the Bulls' operation, and to nobody's surprise found one of the team's major financial drains was the star quarterback's stonewashed pockets.

Webb called him overpaid, but Jensen countered by claiming he was unpaid, owed a month's back wages. As the players gaped in the parking lot at Salford Park the two of them traded bitter remarks and stares. They ended in a stalemate though David Webb also wore a hearing aid, so Jensen might have had the upper hand.

"Listen, you deaf bastard!" the quarterback said. "I want my damned money! And I want all of it, d'ya hear?"

Webb took umbrage; it came off as an attack on his credibility. Hadn't his noblesse been behind the takeover of the team? Wasn't he striving to save it? Some of the players already had begun to grumble he had the same impact as a safety pin on the San Andreas fault. But he promised to do more, and got in the newspaper almost daily touting the Bulls. He also had gone on television and announced high hopes for securing a Birmingham franchise in the new World League of American Football, with a new all-seater stadium of 40,000 built at Salford Park to accommodate it.

Perhaps he planned to build the stadium tiered in Victorian fashion from the overhang of Spaghetti Junction, and earn an architectural award from Prince Charles and the motorists' association AA. Whatever the stadium design, Webb had bigger designs for the Bulls. And quibbling in a parking lot with Russ Jensen, moreover having to pay him, was getting him nowhere.

David Webb spread his arms and leaned closer in his policeman's posture to try to quieten the star.

"Okay then, keep your damned money, but if I'm not paid by next week, I'm going home!" Jensen thundered.

A slight cringe registered on the owner's mooselike face.

"Do you hear me? Huh? Huh?" Jensen asked, mootly, for David Webb did have a hearing impediment, though not at a distance of approximately two and a half inches.

216

Andy Webb, the former boxer, stood by as his father got ex-coriated. "I ought to chin him!" he exclaimed but not in the vicinity of the uppity import. "Don't nobody talk to me dad like that. He reckons if he [Jensen] belonged to any of his other organizations, he'd let him go right now."

True, Russ Jensen might not have cut it in the Rotarians or the Masons, in which Webb was high-ranking, although had either seen fit to accept him and his truculence, he'd have been damned good at calling a meeting to order. Damned good at generating a whip-round, too.

But as the Brits say, "Sterling talks, the other stuff walks." And Russ Jensen, for the umpteenth time in his career with the Bulls, was again on the verge of it.

June

28

Having gone abroad in pursuit of one, I couldn't have agreed
more with the Brummie band Electric Light Orchestra's advice to
"hold on tight to your dream." But when one tires of holding on
to his dream, he exchanges it. Having done so, I could dust off
my special team's MVP plaque from the Brooklyn Mariners and
display it again with pride.

Finally given the chance, I'd not only played, but played
beyond wildest expectations—made solid licks and excelled
afield, was aggressive and always lowered my head before making contact. Now, on the nerviest scoring run of my life, far longer
than either touchdown counted as previous career highlights, I
found myself dashing downfield toward potential victory.

Eleven opposing players could but stay cemented in their foot-
steps and watch, although I may have jeopardized my chances to
score, when out of vanity I paused to adjust my helmet. Then I
lumbered away again, accelerating toward paydirt, only inches
away from it or getting smote down.

The fielder made a fine throw to the wicket, but with the ball
a shade late arriving, I managed to slide my bat across the crease
and make it in safely with another run—the objective at cricket.

Yes, I was playing cricket, and with a savvy never exhibited at gridiron . . . or with outrageous beginner's luck.

Later one of my new teammates confided, "I'd asked all around, 'Has that big bloke ever been to America? I say, his swing has loft, like he's watched a bit of that baseball.' "

We were at that moment knocking back a flurry of pints, more than one toast at the bar made to the batsman with Americanized loft in his swing, who'd posted a score of 37 in his very first innings in the crease.

I stood in swinging for an hour. Then I was retired by taking my own wicket, as shameful as running out of the baselines during a home run trot, or coming off the bench to make a tackle, or maybe coming off the bench and missing a tackle. But I didn't have time to get embarrassed when my day was done, because, oddly, teammates insisted on coming out of the pavilion one by one to shake my hand. My ears rang from the refrain of "splendid show, old chap."

Barely had I strength to reply in kind. Flailing away in requisite white flannels and sweater in the 85-degree weather I was almost dehydrated. I say, give me the gruel and tediousness of football practice, any day.

July

1

As I got an introduction to cricket and reintroduced to my sporting sanity, the Bulls met the reality of the moment. Russ Jensen's animadversion to the owner wasn't the only thing that had come to plague the team since David Webb took over. Sponsorship was still a bad dream, the players clad in tatters, and their absenteeism foretold apathy.

Too, there was the Bulls' latest musical manifestation, which, as with Dutch hayseed and Polynesian tonality, hadn't quite manifested itself, blame falling on Webb.

Lesley Price was a marketing psychologist. She also was the sister of Annette Day, who as a teenager had been plucked from a London street corner to star opposite Elvis Presley in the movie *Double Trouble.* As a marketing expert Lesley herself earned £200 per hour. The munificent John Eyre, who was one of her clients, had coaxed her into working with the Bulls—pro bona, of course.

Admixture of everything found in the first British homecoming queen, she met the Bulls' staff armed with all kinds of marketing ideas, including one with great natural appeal. Her husband was an executive with Wedgwood, the maker of fine china, and she foresaw a big ad campaign, with the Bulls kitted and festooning one of Wedgwood's china shops (and preferably, when it came to Animal Roberts, with hands held in plain sight).

But after she met with David Webb, her upbeat attitude went south. As with the Americans, Webb had frozen her out, too. "Poor man's a chauvinist," she said, "and the poor man, when you're talking to him, it's as if he's still got on that old police helmet under his scalp."

Nor, given how he'd begun to run his team, was Webb showing any inclination to take it off, or have it surgically removed. New ownership didn't stanch the Bulls' chronic want. Though the pitch at Salford Park was magnificently anointed with with red, white, and blue stripes, save for the scoreboard with a spate of 50-point victories, we were still scarcely distinguishable as a football team.

Nevertheless, James Thornton, on his new radio show on station WBRM, promised a championship was inevitable. And maybe so. It looked that way at Crystal Palace after we upended the Olympians.

With a fine stadium and accoutrements such as season tickets and indoor restrooms, cheerleaders who circled the field performing stunts, and the only American on their roster a defensive back who'd lived a decade in England and now considered himself a Brit, the Olympians were supposed to be a model of what gridiron would become in Great Britain. Thankfully, that meant everything about them appealed to the Bulls' sense of unprofessional jealousy.

"Rub their noses in it, damned cockneys!" Davey Parkes shouted as the game began. We led only 7–0 at halftime, because of the same ridiculous penalties that had all year been our bane. After the touchdown, we got flagged for the peculiarly British sin of excessive celebrating, à la Ravens this same venue a year ago, and Thornton drew a second penalty for protesting the call, which forced us to kick off from our 10-yard line, again à la Ravens.

Again we had chances to put the game away early but didn't.

Chauffeur-kicker Linden secured his career behind a steering wheel by missing a 30-yard field goal, then moments later forgot to count off players on the punting team and got us called for too many men on the field. To give him a tighter grip on the wheel, he also flubbed two extra points. After the second Russ Jensen, his holder on the snap, stormed to the sideline and swore, "Goddammit! He's cut! Get him off the field! I never want to see him again!"

At least he wasn't impugned for making an illegal U turn en route to London, when with Thornton and several of our best players in tow, he could have cost us a victory if pulled over and detained. Then again, this was a football team that had taken a lot of strange turns, the strangest yet to come.

July

4

The first player unrest of the season, not counting arrests, was evinced among the Bulls. Two receivers, Nizzy Nisbet and Mikey Price, got suspended for missing a game, and now Russ Jensen huddled their teammates at Moor Lane to discuss whether to take them back. He himself was inclined against it, yet he at least left it to a democratic vote.

"A tough decision," Jensen informed, "whether Mike Price cheated you as well as cheating himself." He paused, figuring his denigrating tone of voice would let them know which way to vote. "Now it's whether you want him back"—a flurry of hands shot up—"and you need to know how serious it is that he let you down and didn't think it was important enough"—the Bulls' hands thrust even higher—"to tell anybody why the hell he was missing a game."

Jensen scoffed; he was autocratic and couldn't disguise it. The team's unanimity for Mikey Price, only the best British receiver to play the game, grated him. He failed to see why a player missing a football game for the christening of his daughter was sufficient excuse. But the players, for once, were resolute.

No such endorsement was given Nizzy Nisbet, no support whatsoever, though at least no knocks from his teammates were made against his granite hands. "Nizzy—no way, man!" shouted safety Clive Loftman, to a thundering chorus of "Sod off!" from his now former teammates.

The Royal Navy would have been shamed hearing one of its old swabbies slagged off. Or it could have been that the Bulls' response against Nizzy was a backlash to British involvement in the Falkland Islands. But Clive Loftman confided: "Two years ago we were playing Ravens, and they were beating us bad, man, and at halftime Niz went in the dressing quarters and took off his kit and sat in the stands the second half." Now the Bulls were willing to let him stay permanently undressed.

The playoffs were about to start, but this did nothing to buoy attendance at practice. Even the coach of the Northants Storm-bringers, who bet a small fortune on his team to win the Bud-weiser Bowl, was running into motivational problems. He now wisely appealed more directly to the British mien, offering his players all the free beer they could drink if they would turn out for training.

Next night the Bulls, barely more than a dozen strong, prac-ticed alongside our youth team. "It's a two-for-one job," Bob Shoop allowed of 118-pound defensive tackles mingling with the likes of the 19-stone Andy Webb, because of player shortages.

A few minutes into practice Russ Jensen huddled with the other coaches, the two of us on hand at Moor Lane. "A scout day, dammit," he said. A scout day meant no contact work, since with so few players present we could ill afford injury. But the head coach's ire wasn't focused exclusively on absent players. "So what's Thornton's newest injury excuse for missing practice?" he asked with scorn.

"Something about his neck, I think," said Shoop.

"You sure it's not venereal disease?" Jensen joked.

"No," Shoop replied, "that penicillin in the house is for some-thing else."

Thornton of late was not acquitting himself very well; the big Yank's physical condition had finally caught up with him. In one game he'd gotten seriously winded as the Bulls offense drove up and the down the field with ease. We drew a penalty for offensive holding, and when the referee threw his flag, it went straight through a face mask and hit Davey Parkes in the eye. Parkesy wasn't hurt, however, and told the officials to play on, only to have Thornton stagger over, gasping "Take . . . the . . . damned . . . time-out!"

"Play on, mate, I'm okay," Parkes insisted.

Thornton stepped between him and the referee and spoke into Parkesy's earhole. "You NEED the time-out!"

"No, really, mate, I'm—"

"You NEED the time-out."

"But I'm—"

Thornton gave him an emphatic poke in the ribs.

"Oh, uh, I, uh, right, mate," Parkes said as he latched on to the official with his request. "I better have my contact lens looked at, then."

Per coach's orders, practice began noncontact, but when Spats Lewis collared Andy Jefferson for the third straight play, Jensen drilled him in the back of the helmet with the football.

"Who . . . whaaaa the fuck, maaaan?" Spats asked.

"You looking for me?" Jensen declared as he whirled discombobulated. "If you are, I'm here."

Almost masochistic, the players had been submissive to Jensen for two years, particularly one of the more dedicated of them, Paul Williams. His latest excoriating came from having borrowed a film of our next opponent. "Who the fuck do you think you are," Jensen railed, "walking out of our house with a game film?" The captain Steve Trow overheard it and said softly, "Hah! Last week he was the chap always well prepared for a game."

We went on to practice a drill for protecting against onside kicks, and as the little linebacker Terry Hale dived for the ball only to have it squib through his hands, Jensen flew into his face. "You ever lay out for it and miss again, I'll come onto the field and tear your goddamn head off!"

"Russ," said Bob Shoop, "is so subtle."

He was present, too, but for how much longer?

July

8

At the intersection of Salford Park and the 50-yard line was a snaky thoroughfare whose street sign identified it as Cuckoo Road. While it may have run perpendicular to the pitch on which we played, in name it traveled directly parallel to the NDMA's grand plans for gridiron.

Cuckoo Road: To get there mentally, all you had to do was reach Britball's playoffs. A team earning home field advantage got no advantage at all; no, with the league's machinations, it was posed with grave financial risk.

For our opening playoff match, we were forced to turn over to Thames Valley Chargers hundreds of complimentary tickets and most of the gate. The Bulls were always impoverished. But now we were bankrupting ourselves abiding by league bylaws.

We did manage to come away with a few bob left over— eminently better off than the Northants Stormbringers, who now faced the strong possibility of getting drummed out of the league not by defeat but by defunction from trying to pay off their payoff opponents. There was a possibility, of course, the Storm's financial straits could be attributed to their head coach's having spent too much of the team's money buying beer for his players.

· · ·

The Bulls also took a sloshing financially when a small crowd came to the game against Thames Valley. The fans who stayed away missed seeing our new fullback, an old face in a new place, and a 275-pounder who made for coach Jensen's first offensive innovation of the season. He and James Thornton had arisen early and gone out into the backyard at No. 9 Star Hill to practice handoffs for Thornton's debut in the backfield.

Never having scored at any level of football, he nevertheless was confident enough to practice celebratory skills for the end zone: "I'll do something unique. Maybe dunk the ball over the goalpost." He was near certainty to score if he could hold on to the football; maybe, to help his concentration, he'd pretend it was an oversized doughnut.

The opportunity awaited him, because Thames Valley was another puff pastry of an opponent, if a fancy puff pastry. In their dazzling uniforms, the Chargers seemed delighted just to don kit for three hours, led by the unarguable best poser in all Britball, a 6-foot-7, 272-pound tackle named Les Jackson, who was chiseled to look at, a Brobdingnagian who gave muscle blindness just from the striations, but who tackled like a truckload of cotton candy. And that was only when he mustered his courage and came across the line of scrimmage.

Of the eight-team playoff field, only Northants was a longer shot than the Chargers at the championship. The Storm, of course, had the jackpot from their coach's big bet to spur them. But even when they won a couple of games and chopped the odds down to 12 to 1, not many people were impressed. "Hah," Animal Roberts scoffed, "got a better chance of sucking Princess Di's titties."

Odds on Thornton's TD were more fancied. But given late-breaking news, it would be his coup de grace, although he'd coup de graced and come back before. "I'm quitting after this game," he yowled in the locker room. "I'm fed up. They can't pay me enough to take this bullshit anymore. Nobody but me does anything around here. Russ and Bob don't do shit. Everything comes back to me."

What prompted this outburst was his having been dispatched a half hour before game time to No. 9 to pick up the team's supply of bottled water—GM consigned to waterboy. Of course, he'd failed to recognize how it'd been a prestigious position with the Bulls. And after he got back to the stadium, Jensen accosted him for having lent out game films without permission. As if he had to answer to an equal. Then again, he may have mistakenly lent what he thought was one of the blue movies, which figured so prominently in the coaching staff's game preparations.

With the Bulls ahead 43–0 in the third quarter in our easiest game of the year and with first down and goal from our 1-yard line, Jensen tried a rapprochement by signaling him into the game and in the huddle calling his number at fullback. The play unfolded as they'd practiced it in the backyard, the cadence, sudden step toward the opening hole, the handoff—perfect as practiced, except that as Thornton dived into the line the ball did not accompany him.

"Did he spit it?" kitman Malcolm Byron asked on the sideline. "Did he spit it? Oh, the poor lad. . . ."

And while the ball stayed behind, Thornton didn't get in the end zone so quickly himself, pig's breakfast of the play, all right. Perhaps he was gassed, enervated—a conclusion based on a locker-room conversation about two women in microdot bikinis who'd paid him a visit the day before at West House School's pool, almost causing my cardial infarction to the school vicar, Rev. Pike—and then stuck around a while longer. "And he thinks he's gonna play after that much action?" Paul Williams asked. "He'd better play, maaaan, this is the playoffs!" Trevor Carthy replied, clichéd as always. "Don't see how he can," Williams said, "not after all that."

But that was only the start of it. Thornton himself, coming out of the locker room before the game began, disclosed, "I've got ten women here today to watch us." He laughed, but by no means a laugh of exaggeration.

228

All eyes had been trained as he lined up in the backfield, about to deliver as promised. The big score. But then, to have fumbled in front of them, the embarrassment of going belly up: one got the feeling his latest retirement plans were instantly scrapped— again.

July

10

Having missed the game with another indeterminate ailment, Animal Roberts had bided and divided time helping with special teams on the sideline and flirting with the women just off it. Often his intentions intermingled and caused chaos as I tried to assemble a kickoff team to keep up with our scoring parade against the Chargers. Then again some of his woman friends would have volunteered more quickly than the players I was able to send onto the pitch.

During the game I'd sought a volunteer to block a punt, and not for the first time none stepped forward. I called on Terrence Laukum, the receiver whom Russ Jensen once accused of having alligator arms, but Laukum was equally reticent at having an alligator midsection. "Me?" he clucked, grabbing his groin and scooting down the bench.

I couldn't cajole them, and I couldn't conscript them, though sometimes there were legitimate excuses, as when Animal hurt his neck during a game and at halftime got the physio to massage it with ointment. He'd gone missing from the kickoff team when the second half started, only to reappear with his head in what resembled a balaclava. " 'Ere me over blazes," he said. "That ointment set my skin on fire, bro', like getting acid thrown on me all over again."

Another injury had caused this latest absence from the lineup but it didn't deter his presence on the sideline, not to mention how he had yet a third, and more suitable, diversion besides helping to coach and carousing: Animal was merchandising. He had come earlier in the week to Moor Lane and remarked in patois, " 'Ere me now, blood clot," which translated into, "Listen up a minute, lads."

From under his leather jacket he unfurled a lovely blue lace curtain. "A thousand of 'em I'm trying to move," he announced of his job-lot sale. He took a step back and spread the curtain wider for teammates to appreciate. "Cost you twenty-five quid in the stores, I'm letting 'em go for fifteen. C'mon lads, a baaaar-gain." The players formed a queue—they hadn't seen such good material all season.

The Bulls had a more costly concern after the easy victory over Thames Valley: self-scrutiny. The players finally had begun to take a look at themselves as other than posers. As it turned out, they'd happened upon incipient self-respect.

Russ Jensen in the playoff opener had been able to give our starters some rest, but it was the unrest he provoked that this game would be remembered for. It all came about with his going berserk, or somewhat more berserk than usual.

When Badass Tulloch got called for piling-on after a kickoff, the penalty flag hadn't hit the ground before Jensen stormed onto the pitch. In plain view of the crowd and the team, he grabbed an unsuspecting Tulloch by the scruff of his shoulder pads, brought him up into the air for a vis-à-vis severe chastening, and then flung him to the ground.

The Bulls were stunned, angered; even for Jensen this went too far. If he had been Vince Lombardi, he might have gotten away with it. Of course, if he'd been Vince Lombardi, they'd never have heard of him in Great Britain.

As it was, he'd stirred foment. Paul Williams was injured and sat in the stands; the injury didn't prevent him from making one of his better blocks of the season to hold back angry supporters from coming down to sort Russ Jensen out. The Greenwood brothers in particular went scoff crazy. This ugly American business wasn't supposed to be part of paid admission for the razzmatazz they'd come to watch, and, in their case, greatly financed.

At the public belittling of a teammate, the players glared; it was palpable in their faces, this furor aforming. As Badass Tulloch hit the ground, their masochism for Russ Jensen hit a breaking point. He'd dangled their loyalty, demeaned them on the practice pitch, forsaken them in Euro Bowl, and now this. The Bulls concluded their bullying star wasn't going to cow them any longer.

Even with a new if not altogether upstanding owner, we faced somber verities. Our stadium lease was overdue, rent at No. 9 Star Hill unpaid for months, and the Bulls no longer had a functioning VCR for breaking down blue movies. David Webb's ownership was minimal; he failed even to provide a new football for games. "Either he didn't figure it'd be this hard," Bob Shoop declared of Webb, "or he just doesn't understand what an owner is. That might be it. Owner over here is just somebody who talks to the press."

Part of it, of course, yes, about 99.4 percent.

Webb planned big, but delivered little, funneling little more than syllables into the team. The coaches had gone to see him at his sporting goods business about paychecks. Irrespective of his hearing aid, they felt he suffered from selective hearing. "We couldn't get a word in edgewise. We'd start to talk and he'd break in," declared Russ Jensen. " 'Gentlemen, what I think we ought to do—' James kept saying, 'Would you please let me finish?' We finally got pissed off and left."

"I hate this damned country, with its damned widget system," James Thornton repeated after the meeting.

"Only thing I've seen that I like about Britain is a couple of nice girls," said Jensen.

"Yeah, well, twenty-two more days and I'm gone," Bob Shoop rejoindered.

"I was going to stick for a while," Jensen declared, "but now— if I stay even that long—day after the American Bowl, I'm gone."

The American Bowl was an exhibition at Wembley Stadium, one day on the calendar when 80,000 Yank wannabes misled the NFL into believing its sport was globally exportable. It was also the occasion when Britball was allowed to present its Most Valuable Player award.

Russ Jensen may or may not be staying around, but as for that MVP award, only mystery was which suitcase he'd be stuffing the trophy into. So it seemed. But the NDMA might not want to engrave Jensen's name on it just yet.

Except for Thornton, who'd begun to dream (or given his disposition toward work, have nightmares) about finding a real job in the United Kingdom, the Americans wanted only to finish the season and hasten to exercise our passports. For the first time in months we'd ridden to practice in the same car, a reunion of egos, and en route GM Thornton revealed the Bulls were thousands of pounds in arrears in rent for Salford Park, with debts not being paid off as owner Webb avowed. The city again threatened to bounce us, the irony that a playoff game against Leeds might be moved to Yorkshire, meaning while we would lose home-field advantage, we might actually make money.

Not to mention, of course, how delighted we'd feel to be treated to another concert of "Bridge Over Troubled Water."

"Mr. Webb sent Andy round to the city council today with a check," Thornton said.

"Is it gonna bounce?" Jensen asked.

He swore, the pupils in his eyes enraged sterling signs. "All I know is I'm owed three weeks' salary coming out of the weekend, I don't care where it comes from."

"Well, we ought to sit down with Webb before we do a thing

tonight on the field. Man's a fool. We're paying five hundred and forty pounds for two plumbed toilets."

"The ones at the field?"

"Yeah."

"A thousand bucks a game for two toilets?"

"Yeah."

"Christ."

But no model of fiscal turpitude, Dave Webb knew what he had to do to keep the team going. He announced, in a bid to turn our fortunes, he had entered into an agreement with a life insurance firm from which the Bulls would receive a commission on any policies the players sold.

Surprisingly, given the Yanks' enmity toward him, taking one out in the good name(s) of the fatalistic former owner of the Bulls wasn't considered, at least not openly.

The Bulls believed in the insurance scheme from the start, some with more enthusiasm than others. After practice, turning onto Star Hill, Shoop exclaimed, "Hey, everybody look, there's another new money-making venture for the team!" "Yeah," James Thornton rejoindered as he, too, caught sight of a boy pushing his lawn mower. "Hi, I play for the Birmingham Bulls, like your lawn cut?"

The Ivy Leaguers awakened game day inspired by a newspaper photo taken off St. Tropez of a horizontal Senator Ted Kennedy, on the deck of a speedboat, atop a deshabille brunette to celebrate the twentieth anniversary of Chappaquiddick. (The senator, once a Harvard tight end, now resembled two offensive tackles.) As Thornton and Shoop sat in the drawing room scads of dust fell from the ceiling above, and they discerned Russ Jensen had gone them one better; not only inspired by the photo, he was iconoclasting away against the maxim of no sex the night before a game to the morning of.

Of course, with his dominance of Britball, Jensen could have partaken of sex at halftime, in the huddle, or on the bench during a time-out, and not jeopardized the outcome of the game. So let him go with his libido. The Bulls just had to cajole and appease and hope he was paid his salary, to make sure we had him on the pitch.

The Bulls' third game against the Leeds Cougars drew to Salford Park our largest attendance of the season—largest standing crowd of the season. More surprising than the overflow was the Supporters Club's vigilante committee apprehending three people trying to sneak into the match, which might have been a first for Britball. "My daughter's a detective in Coventry," David Webb told Peter Spencer, a club officer, "and she was quite impressed with the efficiency your group had."

Every pence of revenue from the gate was greatly needed, of course, first and foremost for the rental of flush toilets at Salford Park. But when we added up the gate against expenses, it was clear any profit would have to come from Denton Thomas's hamburger stand in the end zone. But in his lone remaining responsibility with the Bulls—except for his status as a fashion plate—Denton Thomas, so absorbed in dressing smart for the occasion, had completely forgotten about it. Poor Denton, a player said of his derelicting the stand, "couldn't organize a piss-up in a brewery."

Though a playoff game, and an enlarged chance for razzmatazz, the Bulls' pregame ceremonies consisted of running back Alf Young's fiancée handing out printed invitations to their upcoming wedding. Hardly had she finished before we were inviting an upset, trailing 9–0.

The Cougars got a safety when a snap flew over the head of punter Spider Webb out of the end zone; they then scored a touchdown with a gimmick play the first time they touched the football, catching our flimsy and porous secondary in a state of numb and dumb.

Bob Shoop, who was, euphemistically, coaching the secondary, slammed down a water bottle on the sideline as still another pass was caught in front of one of our DBs. "Shit!" he shouted as Leeds' American passing combo moved effortlessly against us. "Who the hell can I put in?"

"Bob, sorry, man," James Thornton, in charge of the Bulls' defense, said confronting him along the bench, "but I'm afraid you're going to have to go in yourself."

"He's tired," head coach Russ Jensen objected, with the vested interest as quarterback of not wanting his best receiver getting winded while doubling as a defensive back.

Thornton glared at him.

"I said he's tired!" the head coach barked.

Shoop grudgingly went into the secondary and helped contain the Cougars. We made enough recovery by halftime to take a shaky 13–9 lead.

But Thorton was so unforgiving of Jensen's having dressed him down in front of the players, on top of giving him menial tasks (the waterboying and errand running) that he pulled him aside at halftime and said, "From now on you're an island out there, man! From now on, you may not know it, but you're a fucking island!"

Russ Jensen had in fact gone down to a sack late in the half, and according to Thornton not by accident. "Yeah, I let my man through," he said. "After that shit about how Bob was tireder than me. Ain't nobody 'round here does more than me! No-fucking-body!"

Midway through the fourth quarter we'd gone comfortably ahead, abiding by Gerry Hartman's enthusiastic encouragement at the tannoy, when suddenly his golden throat was overridden by something horrid from the far sideline. Bob Shoop had mis-stepped coming down with a pass and the scream, as his knee buckled beneath him, traveled through time and marrow.

Thornton was instantly at his teammate's side, barely beating a team of paramedics wielding a stretcher.

"Get the fuck away! Get away!" Shoop burst out. "Get 'em away from me, James!" As he was pushing back the paramedics, he began to convulse; it wasn't the injury causing it; the pain paled next to his fear. "I don't want that stuff!" he shouted. "Please get it the fuck away!"

But the paramedics persisted in shoving an oxygen mask in his face.

When they dropped down beside him with the mask, Shoop could see only a ghostly visage of Alf Young. It was Alf, who, after he got hurt in last year's championship game, almost became football's first player to die from oxygen overdose.

Alf, of course, served as inspiration to the Bulls, and not just by having lived. But the ghastliness, or ghostliness, of what'd happened to him was all too vivid, and Shoopy had heard the story enough to have nightmares about it. Thornton helping, he resisted the oxygen.

We seemed to have game wrapped up by the time he went down, our next stop, Crystal Palace. But then the Cougars, on some ludicrous penalties, including an interference call in the end zone, managed to close the score to 27–20 with thirteen seconds to play.

Now came an old nemesis and a paralysis that accompanied it: the receiving of an onside kick. The onsider: as Queen Elizabeth said to the eponymous Henry III, "For thou hast made this happy earth our hell." Right-o.

"Give me a hands team!" I shouted, deluding only myself. I might as well have been telling the players to form a queue for free tickets to the Black Plague. Hands team? More plausible to ask for a polo team from a prison ward.

"Okay, anybody who's even touched a ball all season," I compromised. "Yeah, even you, Laukum."

"Me?" the man of alligator arms asked in disbelief.

"Perkins, you, too."

The gulp from Errol Perkins, an end whose appendages may have been more antithetical to latching on to a football than anyone who ever played the position, was palpable enough to pop the string tying together his shoulder pads.

But finally I deployed enough players at least aware they had hands, and when that bugaboo unfolded, Terrence Laukum managed to snare the ball in midair. Or, more likely, it'd managed to defy gravity and stuck to his jersey.

In any event he smothered it and the Bulls were going back to the Budweiser Bowl. But first a Bullrush, and the players had assembled at midfield before several remembered Bob Shoop and went to give him a ride on their shoulders out onto the pitch.

Shoopy waved them off and made a valiant one-legged rush of his own. Poignant to watch, but like Femi Amu's limp, pure symbolism for what lay ahead.

240

Shoopy then was bullrushed to Birmingham Accident Hospital. Doctors there did arthroscopy, called keyhole surgery by the Brits because of the tiny incision, but next day's headline in the *Evening Mail* blared, SHOOP OP SHOCK.

Even as Shoop headed to the hospital, Russ Jensen meant to make headlines of his own. After the game he'd spent an hour whingeing about Britball to the press.

James Thornton was busy spelling out to the players his own dissatisfaction, something that made him angrier than the treatment, or mistreatment, he'd gotten at the hands of the British. "There's nothing, never, ever that can be said or done that will get me to play with Russ Jensen again!" He was voluble with anger. "Man's fucking asshole! No other way to say it! Fuck Russ! I'll never play with him again."

In the gloaming, make that the gathering gloom of Salford Park, his harsh pronouncement rang almost prophetic.

July

26

As the Bulls' team bus left for London and the championship game, Denton Thomas nimblefooted to the front of it. From the dashboard he unhooked a driver's microphone and breathily stammered: "Pfff! Pfff! Attention, Bulls, attention everyone! I am proud to announce very important news! If we win the Budweiser Bowl we have been promised an expenses-paid, two-week tour of Hawaii to play against the American semipro champion!"

The players sat almost dumbfounded. A few forged slow, knowing smiles, for only one man could arrange for us such an incentive, could reintroduce himself with such suavity: the man who'd bestrode those lei-lined stages. By now some had begun to yearn a little for the return of Frank Kalili-Leadon. The Americans, opposed as they were to British ownership altogether, were of the unanimous opinion that Frank and the current owner, David Webb, went together like oil and Welsh butter.

Webb was a man in a muddle. The Yanks hounded him over their pay, medical insurance, and expenses, as did a host of creditors, and in an ignominious fate for a former chief constable, he stood a good chance of getting taken to court for a spate of bad checks, including one for delinquent rent on No. 9 Star Hill.

Money matters were one problem with Webb, not to mention how you couldn't get through to him with a salutation of andirons. But when his picture began turning up daily on the television and in the papers, the sport and the team having become a personal platform, it seemed the Bulls' owner might be less a pillar of probity than a pillaster for making himself look good.

Certainly, he was continuing the tradition of running the Bulls like a pink-lemonade stand. Alas, he had another link to the past: He had begun to depict himself as a put-upon paterfamilias.

"So why the hell'd you ever get in, then, huh?" Jensen sneered at him. "And why don't you just get out?"

"Too many of the little people are counting on me," he replied, wearing Frank's mantle if not Nehru with a snugger fit than ever. A lot of what Webb had to say, in fact, sounded startlingly similar, except Frank was, of course, more easy listening. Frank also knew the ins and outs of getting his team, intact, to the Budweiser Bowl.

July

27

This owner, however, played it by the book—the book as he and the NDMA, with a wink between pages, read it—and he counted on the rectitude of his American imports. "He told me, 'You won't sit out Bud Bowl, because it's not professionalism, and you're a professional,' " Russ Jensen recalled after Tuesday night practice the week before the championship. "Hah! Yeah, I'm a professional, all right—a professional who ain't getting paid."

"Lookit," James Thornton told the other Americans, "we've treated him fair, done everything we're supposed to, and now he's stiffing us." He donned a baseball cap blazoned with the legend, PARDON ME, BUT OBVIOUSLY YOU'VE MISTAKEN ME FOR SOMEONE WHO GIVES A SHIT.

Thornton was frustrated with the Bulls, maybe more than ever before, which encompassed a lot of frustration. He could argue with Webb without fear of causing a coronary, but what did it matter, since the owner never heard a word he said.

"Man is outright stiffing us, it's a damned nightmare," he declared. "Promised Russ he'd have his salary and expenses by today and mine tomorrow. Nothing."

The presumably irreconcilable differences between Thornton

and Jensen had been bridged by their mutual detesting of David Webb. They'd become buddies, almost connubial, in this post-season of their discontent.

Thornton had gone so far as inviting Jensen to try a new cuisine at the Carib-b-Inn, whose menu included banana fritters and something fried and spicy called coleyfish. He'd even agreed to drive his big car, on loan to him as GM of the Bulls from a dealer in Brum, and from which he generally excluded the other coaches. En route, they drove past an infamous cul-de-sac called Cheddar Road, where women adorned front windows awaiting business calls.

"Goddamn, that's the babe Animal asked to take her top down after the championship last year," Thornton said as he spotted one of them. "Then we all signed her tits."

"I remember the tits," replied Jensen, "but I didn't sign 'em."

Streetwalk, roadside: Any distraction was now appreciated by the Americans. When David Webb seized the team, Thornton pleaded, "Just don't let us get Chernobyled again by management." But it had come to pass. Though the Bulls were again likely to win the British championship, we were in a vale of dashed hopes and disarray. For the others it was money and uncertainty over it; for me, the likelihood of becoming the first American to spend a season in Britain and not play a single down of football. I didn't even have applications for working papers to take home as a souvenir.

We worried over what David Webb would do next. He pleaded patience but that didn't wash with the team. But at his most desperate, opportunity presented itself in the form of an inquiry from Johannesburg: Would the Bulls play in South Africa?

Maybe it'd be called the Apartheid Bowl. The offer was lucrative; Webb told the Supporters Club it might be a fine thing for the Bulls to go.

When they heard this, their raised social consciousness made for swift reaction. "I know he aims to save the team," said Terry Greenwood, "but there's such thing as morals, mate, and if it ever happens, I'm done with Bulls, I don't want to know." "Got to draw the line somewhere," enjoined his brother Ian.

The protest buttons pinned to their chests practically became neon signs of anger. It'd begun to appear that Russ Jensen might not be the only member of the Bulls' organization considering a boycott of the Budweiser Bowl.

But then, divine andirons dropped from the sky onto David Webb's noggin: He located a sponsor to fund the Bulls through to the championship game, a sponsor willing to fund us sans American salaries, back bills, kit necessities, medical expenses, of course, but sponsor nonetheless. By Britball measure, we'd have the most important benefit of sponsorship: a name across our jerseys. That it'd be emblazoned on tattered and threadbare jerseys was irrelevant. Given the propensity of owners past and present for true quoting, it was that most perfect of sponsors: the Birmingham *Daily News.*

July

29

A top a nightstand in Russ Jensen's bedroom at No. 9 Star Hill sat a huge bottle of milk of magnesia. The lid was unscrewed, the bottle nearly drained. "This shit's got my stomach ulcer going again," he'd revealed. "I didn't sleep none last night, damned stomach's killing me. I just want my money. I'll decide tomorrow if I'm going to play."

He took another big swig of antacid, and it was obvious he wasn't drinking to the good health of Britball.

Jensen was taciturn, monosyllabic, but when it came to getting his way, his pay, he could kvetch with the best of them. The Bulls were formidable listeners. After announcing at our last practice of the season he probably wouldn't play in the Budweiser Bowl, he softly asserted, "I may not be there, but you can win if I play or not." He'd said the same thing to them the year before, laid it on a little thicker, only to have the Supporters come up with emergency cash before he could show how far he was willing to go with his threat.

He'd spouted off so often, the players were pretty inured to it, although at Moor Lane there was some expression of surprise among them—feigned surprise, perhaps, to show Jensen how convincingly his Method Whingeing had struck them.

But could it be that Russ Jensen had fallen too far into playing the part? Next morning at No. 9 he was up again at daybreak, pacing, staring out the front window, antacid bottle clutched as if it had laces on it. "He's really troubled now, man," Bob Shoop averred as he heaped tablespoons of sugar over a bowl of Frosted Flakes and popped open a can of Coke for breakfast. "I mean, what's the guy going to do? Look at him, he knows he's really painted himself into a corner."

That afternoon he tried again to claim his salary, demanding it in a bilious telephone call to the owner's office. Cash money, he told David Webb, was his raison d'play: "A personal guarantee," he said when Webb proposed a compromise, "that don't mean a goddamn thing to me. Because the British people have fucked me over from the start," he declared, "and I throw you right in there with 'em."

"What? Arrested? If I don't leave?" Jensen's face went volcanic. "Bullshit! You can't have me arrested because I don't have anything that belongs to the Bulls. . . . All right, I'm getting my damned stuff packed and getting out, just like you said."

Suddenly, the star quarterback donned his black Stetson, and upped and cleared out of the house with his belongings. For the second time he found himself evicted from No. 9 Star Hill; moreover, for the second time it had happened by mandate from the owner of a football team who'd had the gall to order the eviction without ever paying the rent.

Shoop tried to head him off, appeal to his better and humane judgment, but the quarterback blew past him with his boycott rollout. "A dick move, man," Shoop said as the front door slammed. "Guy makes ten times the money I make, but I'm playing." He spat in chagrin. "Andrew Jefferson's going to shit his pants when I tell him. 'Hey, Jeffo, guess who's playing quarterback in the Bud Bowl.' Damn! I mean, he really might faint over it."

Jensen left behind only a pair of foam knee pads in the front window, perhaps to symbolize a genuflection he thought ought to be made to his demands. Whoever had written his script, by Jove, was doing a damned good job of layering on the bathos.

"Think the guy's just gonna show up in London and say, 'Okay I'm here, let's win it, gang'?" Shoopy asked skeptically. "I don't believe it, I'd almost be willing to bet against it."

For weeks dispiriting comment about the season's denouement had richocheted around the little house. Within its walls—from Zark's nasal waffling, to the occupants who had been classified as football squatters, to visitation from many, many women, to the place where Animal Roberts often had gone on the lam, to a chronic shortage of toilet tissue, to the turmoil of dealing with first one, then another unresponding team owner—within those walls, well, Star Hell, it seemed.

As the Jensen saga played itself out, we were also without James Thornton, who had found another job, a job in football, and demanding a serious sense of responsibility: squiring the Philadelphia Eagles cheerleaders around London before the American Bowl exhibition.

To the players it may have seemed neglectful for the GM, associate coach, defensive coordinator, and star lineman to miss a whole week's practice before the championship, especially given how he'd been blocking and tackling of late. But he did check in daily for fiscal updates over his backpay. And besides, his argument went, and a strong one it was, the NFL was paying him in cash money, an honest day's wages for an honest day's squiring.

July

30

Before everything began to beset the Bulls the S.P., the starting price, for Britball's championship could only have been a foregone conclusion.

Our opponents were the Manchester Spartans, winners of the league's liliputian Northern Conference. They'd played in that part of the country where gridiron hadn't fully evolved, where most field goals came on dropkicks, and the best strategy from a head coach seemed to be outfitting two players in the same jersey number and playing them simultaneously. They'd then defeated the Olympians in the other semifinal game—had, judging from the score, routed them. But that rout was predictable. The Olympians had been playing at less than full strength after three of their best players sat out the game with injuries—those injuries widely thought to represent pulled boycotts and strained wallets.

The Bulls, of course, had only one wallet to worry about, and all week David Webb reassured the team it would be filled accordingly. Yet when the team bus pulled away with Crystal Palace its destination, Russ Jensen was not aboard it nor had he made any plans to be. He wasn't, to anyone's knowledge, planning to be chauffeur-driven either.

The mood on the bus, nevertheless, was upbeat. Most of the

players were still confident of victory, though most of that confidence was based on the belated appearance of the star quarterback.

The team's youngest player, 19-year-old Davey Parkes, wasn't as sure as some of his teammates. Parkesy was beyond his years not just in curmudgeonly mien. As a part-time perfume salesman he sold a lot of scent to teammates by knowing who needed it most; James Thornton was among his best customers. After the toilets at Salford Park ran out of a vital component, he hit on the idea of peddling tissue to his teammates at 10 pence per sheet. Yes, Parkesy had gumption. He'd paid a visit to the local bookmaker's shop before the season began and plunked down a wager on the Bulls to repeat as champions. Call it confidence or whatever, but he'd hastily returned to the shop the day we left for London, placing yet another bet, the same size as his first.

July

31

In the hospital after he got injured, Shoopy had seemed irrepressible even after doctors told him the knee wasn't healing as quickly as he hoped. "Been hurt before the last game of the season my last four years' playing football," he allowed during a bedside visit, "but I've still played every time."

He vowed to play in the championship, but if he couldn't, he wanted the Bulls to activate someone from the taxi squad to replace him.

Had there been a spare bed in that hospital ward when he made his nomination, I'd have fainted into it.

I had waited almost 30 years to coat over the indignity of starting out as a tackling dummy. And now I'd suffered the indignity of spending a season with a team that didn't even own a tackling dummy. Playing in a championship game would no doubt ameliorate that. "I hope you're the one, that would be the greatest," Shoop repeated.

I was ecstatic at his magnanimity, but what could I say, other than that I damned well deserved it?

I began monitoring his health, cheering his recovery, wanting him to get better with deliberate speed—say, about the time his return flight from Heathrow Airport to Pittsburgh was announcing its final boarding call.

August

3

The league spared no expense to assure this game came off as the best Budweiser Bowl in the short illusory history of Britball. For the first time and with an eye toward the future, the British championship was slated to coincide in London with the NFL exhibition played there. And what by NDMA purview was an even greater triumph, it'd been announced the pregame coin toss at Crystal Palace would be made by the distinguished career sibling Jermaine Jackson.

Alas, he wouldn't sing the national anthem, since British fans might be appalled at "God Save the Queen" in falsetto. With a little prodding, though, officials hoped he'd stick around to present the winners' medals.

Certainly, the league had done everything else to give the game a je ne sais quois all its own among British sporting spectacles. Almost everything.

The Bulls' coaching staff was reviewing films of the Manchester Spartans when the telephone rang. It sounded like a fan inquiring about Bob Shoop's health.

"Referee for the Bud Bowl," Shoopy said when he hung up the phone, "and can you believe it, he wants to know if we can help him get a scoreboard for the game. And a thirty-second play clock." Jermaine Jackson for the coin toss, check; Philadelphia Eagles cheerleader on hand, check; a ceaseless font of American beer for concessions, check. But somehow, for staging its championship game, a clock and scoreboard proved elusive.

As for the league's obsession with pageantry, the Bulls were keen on it, too. Game became secondary to occasion. Partly because of our estimation, or pronounced lack of same, for the opponents. We'd already seen what the Spartans had to offer on the playing field, and except for home-pitch goalposts that were forked and outstanding and, yes, NFL regulation, come away most unimpressed.

They had come into a regular season game against us sporting an undefeated record, had lost one game in two years, but turned out a team of paper Spartans. Tallish paper Spartans, what with a 7-foot-2 nosetackle, but no never mind. We scored on the first play and thereafter at will.

On their sideline was a befuddled Terry Smith, who also happened to be the celebrated coach of the British national team, mostly by his own celebration. (He made a bluster of himself with his own column in *First Down*, a forum for self-aggrandizement unseen since John Lennon's remark about the Beatles popularity exceeding Christ.) But judging from the outcome, it would seem his best coaching strategy for the Spartans had been to put two players into the game simultaneously wearing jersey number 22.

We won that game by six touchdowns, our offense scoring as if in a wind tunnel with the wind at our backs. Yes, the Budweiser Bowl was a cert. The most formidable thing about them, in fact, was their name. When not referred to as Spartans or Manchester, they were called, as denizens of the city they represented, Mancunians. That vaunted name, as we scouted them out, could be worth a touchdown to them.

August

5

A.M.

By now the Bulls began to fret; Russ Jensen showed no sign of reconsidering. David Webb may have felt that it would make a better statement for Britball if someone of Jensen's stature and dominance did not play in the Budweiser Bowl; damned certain for the owner, it made a better financial statement. Or perhaps this old copper was working his first gridiron sting operation. According to his son Andy, Webb had informed the Spartans' coach in a telephone conversation that because of their truculence all the Bulls' imports had been sent home.

All it took, in the end, was Webb's approaching the right person. John Eyre had never bought into the Bulls, as he'd hoped to, because he wasn't keen on investing in ongoing mendacity. But he was still a do-gooder of the first degree. On top of providing transatlantic airfare and insurance policies for players with five knee operations, he offered to reopen his wallet, yes, to accommodate the contract demands of Russ Jensen.

He wasn't alone in trying to help bring the Bulls another championship. The Supporters Club had largess at the ready, too, and that was a lot of readiness, given their past performance. Peter Spencer, known as the Mr. Feelgood of the Supporters Club, enlisted fellow members, and they approached Jensen with a check in the amount he sought. But it had become for him a vendetta against ownership, or perhaps the Anglo-Saxon people. No amount of pleading could get him to accept the Supporters' offer, or John Eyre's latest magnanimity.

This king apparently would settle only for having his tribute paid by David Webb.

During the week leading to it, the Bulls couldn't consider the big game without him. Consensus was he'd come around. But he'd waited Webb out. He remained AWOL when we got to the locker room, though the players searched every shower and stall at Crystal Palace as if he might be hiding out in one of them to heighten the suspense. But nothing; still not a sign of him.

Anxiety overrode our thoughts; whenever the locker room door flung open, 45 heads gravitated as one to see if it might be the prodigal quarterback. Would Russ Jensen capitulate? Or would he make a stand against the fraudulence of Britball? Those who doubted his return could not envision winning the championship without him. Even at personal financial loss, would he forsake the team he'd led for two seasons? Most of the players intrinsically believed he would show up. That he'd play, too. Several of them had placed wagers on it.

How I pictured it evolving: He'd dash from the dressing quarters directly into the huddle on the first play of the game, lead the Bulls to a 100–3 thrashing—the Spartans booting a dropkick, per their coach Terry Smith's strategy. Jensen would then pinch Dave Webb's hearing aid as collateral for his paycheck, and catch the first flight home.

Lights to FADE, strains of Polynesian music as the credits roll.

The Budweiser Bowl, with its attendant attractions, usually was the one day Britball's stethoscope got put away. Not today. An NDMA official, with goofy consternation furrowed into his face, began asking one Bull after another if the star QB had relented. How would it look to the NFL if the game's best player cried off the championship? Bloody hell. "Spoke with him last night," the factotum whimpered, "begged him to change his mind. Begged, mind you."

If only they'd thought of rolling out a red carpet.

Also missing at Crystal Palace was a linebacker called Lance Daw. Actually his name was Lonsdale Morris, but in their glorious inaccuracy Britball programs had bestowed him with one of the ruggedest handles ever for a gridiron player—especially somebody with the temperament of a tulip. At a recent practice he had backed away after he got assigned to the kickoff team. "Don't you want to hit somebody, goddammit?" James Thornton asked him. Lance Daw smiled through a gold inlay and shook his head with a candor seldom seen on a football field. "Then," Thornton ordered him, "go on and get the hell out of here." He had not been seen since.

His absence, however, freed a precious game jersey and—in the event Russ Jensen stayed away—freed a spot on the roster to go with it. The jersey was number 54, worn throughout his career by Jess Rodgers, before it got passed to jerseyhorse Son Tustin, who'd worn nine different shirts in 10 games, and would have had a perfect record for couture except for serving a 1-game suspension; still later it got slipped over the shoulder pads of a lineman named Paul Puffet, who'd turned up, typically, for just one game.

The shirt was about to get its fifth personnel change of the season. In the locker room I plucked it from a pile Malcolm Byron had laid out, him cheering me as I bent down to retrieve it. In spite of whoever else had worn it, and everything it had gone through, I still thought of the jersey as Jess Rodgers's, and inheriting it motivated me.

Jess's jersey and Jensen's place on the roster: What more could I ask? As I clutched it, inevitable butterflies returned for the first time in years—or else it was indigestion from too much muesli for breakfast. If they weren't butterflies, at least I wanted them to be. I stowed the jersey and my kitbag in a corner cubicle and went outside with four or five other players for a cigarette. Then I remembered I didn't smoke.

As kickoff neared I put in at a locker and began to get kitted; meticulously going about it, absorbing my first championship game. Perhaps I also had absorbed too much of the British mentality because, ostensibly taking my time to dress, I found myself procrastinating. But procrastinating with a purpose: The possibility of Russ Jensen's return deterred my going any further. How dare I the audacity to replace him on the roster? He could relent and make an appearance, and with me activated suddenly find himself an ineligible player, which in turn would cost us the championship.

Dave Webb would then use his influence with the High Court to have me brought up for treason; he had recently been named head of the NDMA's rules and advisory committee, and from the probity on his face, it meant almost as much to him as martial law (though I did relish the thought of future towels that read "Nos. 23, 32, 54-E—There Here").

Since I'd waited a season to play, a lifetime really, what harm in waiting a little longer? I was conditioned to it. I opted to give Jensen the first half to reappear, tossed the jersey into the cubicle, and slipped back into my street clothes. It was tough to reconcile; I cursed my hesitance. My name already had been penciled onto the special teams; I'd done the penciling. Now I scratched it out and told Clive Jackson he'd be playing on them instead. And playing skinny, dammit, if he knew what was best for him.

August

5

🏈

🏈

🏈

P.M.

As the Bulls waited in the tunnel at Crystal Palace for the introduction of Budweiser Bowl's starting lineups, James Thornton
launched, just when we needed it most, into an inspirational
spiel. It had been inspired the night before by a British film crew,
when he agreed to wear a tiny microphone beneath his shoulder
pads. Thornton walked and talked taller than ever, speaking ex-
aggeratedly into the mike . . . and speaking for the benefit of the
Philadelphia Eagles cheerleaders, who stood alongside ready to
accompany us when we ran onto the pitch.

Also buoying the Bulls' frazzled sangfroid was the unexpected
return of our own cheerleading squad—albeit piecemeal, just
three members and minus the pulchritude of Frank Kalili's
daughter, Debbie-Jean. (With a skin condition, she was rumored
on steroids, and bloated by them.) They met us in the runway
shaking red and black pom-poms, and one of them hugged a
starting offensive lineman and passed along tidings to him from
the baby daughter he'd fathered by her.

But without Russ Jensen, all the theatrics and the outpouring
of family support and the Bulls' best efforts might not be enough.
Who knew how we'd respond? For two seasons Jensen had taken
almost every snap of the football for the Bulls and run roughshod

260

over almost every opponent. If, as Bob Shoop often adjudged of him in Ivy League parlance, he was a man among boys, his replacement, Andy Jefferson, was just the opposite.

The Spartans won Jermaine Jackson's coin toss and opted to kick off to us. Like coast watchers of World War II, they had posted observers around Crystal Palace, and when none of them detected the arrival of Jensen, they dared us to pull him out of thin air or unveil a British quarterback.

But filling in, the team instantly uplifted by him, Jeffo got off to an astonishing start. A few days earlier, giving in to the hypochondriacal litany that often kept him out of practice, he had left Moor Lane complaining of chest pains. "Probably something with my diaphragm," he groaned. "The old man used to be top medical officer in the British army, and that's what he says, anyhow." Now he was bucking us up big time. "Hike!" with a British accent had never sounded so good, and he knew what to do when the football arrived in his tiny hands, too. Never having made more than a single completion in a game, he played out of his skin, and out of his 5-foot-5 stature, not only admitting to no pancreatic problems on the pitch, but making good on six of his first eight passes, everything on target. It was as if Anne Boleyn were looking down with her six-fingered hands cupped over him.

Jeffo was just unconscious. The voice fluctuations were gone, and the spaz haircut didn't bother his teammates, either. He still couldn't see over center, but he was immense. He lofted two touchdown passes in the first half, only to have the misfortune of throwing both to the accursed Errol Perkins, which transformed them from touchdowns to potential touchdowns to just a couple of incompletions. Dropping, of course, was all poor Perkins's hands knew how to do.

For most of a half, we outplayed and outfought and outthought the Spartans and their coach. And then—the Bulls flustered by those failures to score and by two more blown opportunities after our defense forced and recovered fumbles—the breaks began going the Mancunians' way. They got one touchdown on a play where a running back ran the wrong way, and another when a floating pass hypnotized Trevor Carthy in the secondary, and was caught right in front of him; Carthy, the game's best offensive player, was as awful on defense as the day the Dublin Celtics made their lone pass completion against him five months earlier.

Then the Spartans giant nosetackle began to use his two-foot height advantage to intimidate Jeffo's abdomen, and he cowered in the pocket, absorbing sack after sack, practically waiting for them to happen. He tossed a couple of feeble interceptions, and suddenly his confidence was shot, and so it seemed was the Bulls'.

Bob Shoop, having made good on his vow to shake off his injury and play in the championship game, lasted just four plays before his knee gave out. He came to the sideline racked by tears; it was an un-British letdown of a stiff upper lip, but a lot of other lips, and these belonging to actual Brits, started unstiffening at the sight of him, too.

Our American representation in the game was completely obliterated when Thornton, who'd grudgingly committed to playing both offense and defense, got knackered—even though his heavy breathing made a superior natural sound for his hidden microphone. But he also had to be carried from the pitch four times—not stretchered off, but lugged away by teammates, which drained our defense even more, what with his heft.

Trailing, the Bulls trudged into the locker room at halftime, hang-dog prevalent on every face. Minus our star quarterback, beset by ailing players, the Spartans' 14–0 lead looked imposing. Maybe, though, there'd be a new hero. My kit sat invitingly in a corner. Again I held up the jersey. Would vindication come at last? "Go on, then," Davey Parkes encouraged, surely thinking because I had an American birth certificate I could help him win the bets he'd placed.

I made a long appraisal of that jersey—looked at it as enthusiastically as I'd looked at any kit in all the games in all the places I had ever played, or tried to play, football.

Jensen's abdication had paved the way for a pretender, but something about it, about slipping so effortlessly into what I'd long wanted to do, didn't feel right. For a whole season, I had practiced with the Bulls, been among them, become one of them. Yet it was almost too premeditated, this planting myself on the roster. Taxi squad or not, I wanted to earn it, not inherit by default.

The referee stuck his head through the locker room door and broke through my contemplation. "Five minutes till second half, coach," he said.

Coach: That was enough for me, no matter how frustrating the job happened to be in Britball, or how inept I was at doing it. Besides, I already had the conquest of one British sport to my credit, with my storming of the cricket wicket. I spun round and tossed the jersey back atop the shoulder pads.

Why not play? To let my pretence go on living? Or to see whether the Bulls could cock a last snook on their own, without American intervention? Yes, maybe it ought to have been this way all along—Yanks joining in only to provide expertise, not dominate the sport. But that was a romantic assessment, and rather easy to make when we were down two touchdowns at halftime. Somewhat less likely, I thought Russ Jensen might make a dramatic appearance, even if it came at the two-minute warning.

My walking away also was a sop to instinct as an observer over my desire to participate. I knew at Crystal Palace that I was seeing the beginning of the end of something. This reverse colonization had not come close, wasn't about to, no matter what great expectations the NFL might have for it. Whither Britball? It didn't take a canary inside a football helmet to know where gridiron was going in Great Britain. But that was tomorrow, and tomorrow meant nothing to the Bulls. As always, we had today to get through, and a football game to win.

August

6

Some would miss Britball and all it stood for; to be more precise, would miss all it allowed them to stand for. At halftime Denton Thomas strode into the Bulls' locker room and interrupted Bob Shoop at a blackboard with the entreaty: "I have just picked up your trophy in the pressbox as the league's Most Valuable Receiver and was thinking how you and I ought to parade it in front of the stands—it would look very good." The "very" was fit for a coronation.

"No, now's not the damned time," Shoop rebuffed him, slamming down a piece of chalk. "Can't you see, we've got to get ready to play the second half?"

"Well, then, I'll go out with it myself," Denton said, "go and show it off." And he did, an inspired fit of pageantry, his white windbreaker having been replaced for the championship game by a pin-striped suit.

As for the coaches, including James Thornton as he made technical adjustments of his microphone, we indeed had better things to occupy our time. In a span of 15 minutes we managed to install the wishbone offense, whose rugbylike look supplied the Bulls with newfound resolve, and went to show how the Brits would respond, as Malcolm Byron always maintained, with their backs

264

to the wall. Running backs, in this case, what with so many of them counted on to fuel the wishbone formation.

Suddenly, the Bulls were reborn as a football team, as a molt from our third-class status. There were tears of self-discovery—many tears. Sure, we still qualified for residency in an almshouse and would never make *Burke's Peerage,* but what transpired at Crystal Palace was irrespective of all that; bloody well transcended it. The serial negligence, the mistreatment from owners, all the ugly Americanism, no never mind: We were the Birmingham Bulls now, and rather proud of it. The shaken faces of a few hours earlier were gone, replaced by a collective visage of succeeding at what we had come for.

Colin Nash and several other players started this spiritual upsurge before we went out for the second half by taking a black market and scribbling onto towels, those waist towels of the "Nos. 32, 23—There Here" variety, the number 17 for the injured Bobby Shoop . . . and he'd gotten his recognition without going to jail.

Could more inspiration possibly have coursed our veins? A grand comeback welled inside the Bulls; resounding inner thrum of 'ere we go, 'ere we go, 'ere we go, just like British soccer teams who employed it to the tune of "Stars and Stripes Forever," and the start of the half signified it. Replacing Andy Jefferson, the wiry mustachioed immigrant Pasco became an instant wishbone quarterback and expertly marched us downfield for a touchdown.

To be fair, this Pasco was a Russ Jensen creation—"When you're getting the years on you," the head coach once told him in a rare compassionate moment, twigging him, from his premature baldness and sallow Sicilian face, as much older than his age, "we'll get you in there"—and for that you had to give him credit.

Unspectacular but solid, we Bulls without Jensen may have surprised ourselves; but soon the surprise transmuted into conviction, of cocking that snook. And after trading touchdowns with the Spartans, special teams having set ours up when Trevor Carthy dashed 75 yards with a kickoff return, we knew we would again win the Budweiser Bowl.

Yes, the script, executive-produced and then abandoned by Russ Jensen, was still alive.

We were storming from behind, believing every yard of the way; confidence growing with every tough yard, every tick of the clock. Even the side judge on the officiating crew got a tear in his eye as we began to turn the game around—those British officials, by Jove, didn't they love a comeback, though? Crystal Palace became a vessel of rejuvenation, as near as Britball ever got to a glorious scrumdum.

We pushed the Spartans downfield, pushing on, too, to Blue Hawaii: For in victory there'd be more than Jermaine Jackson's awarding of medals, more than retaining that trophy on Frank Kalili's mantel—much more of a reward, from Denton's breathless exhortation on the bus. We could feel that hot sun beating down on our—on their pallid British skin. Two whole weeks in the South Pacific, grass skirts wafting while we drank those drinks with little parasols. And no telling who might turn up, in a reconciliatory way, to trill the national anthem, even throw us a luau.

Then with a tweak of our fortune those tiny bubbles began to burst. Actually, one big one.

As the team bus had been pulling out of Brum, Errol Perkins had been too devoted to making another retirement speech to hear clearly what Denton'd had to say. Alas his hands hadn't heard either, or else as always, they were hell-bent on defying dexterity.

Poor Perkins, maybe it was for the best that he'd never got his Co-Most Valuable Player trophy; holding on to it would have been a grave problem. Twice already he had dropped touchdown passes as if the football were a radioactive butler's tray. And now, in the fourth quarter, very late in the game, here was the football again coming down perfectly into his hands, coming down, down, and then, falling haplessly to the ground.

So wide open he'd been on this fateful play, everything right except for those misbegotten mortar-mixed hands of his getting in his way. They'd let yet a third and game-winning TD pass slip through them, on an uncannily thrown spiral by the halfback Trevor Carthy. In his defense, since it was Britball, maybe he'd never seen a spiral before, and certainly not one with indigenous fingerprints on it. But when the ball eluded his hands, this travesty of touch, it was the Bulls' last gasp.

When the game ended, our cheerleading squad, the three of them, crushed their pom-poms and stood sobbing against each other. More tears yet rolled down the cheek of the side judge, and Malcolm Byron's crepuscular lenses clouded more than usual, too. Hardly was it a Gainsborough canvas for the Bulls, with all this crying aloud.

There was nothing of disgrace on the pitch about the Birmingham Bulls, however. Any of those leader writers who saw it would have declared that this was our Dunkirk, victory in defeat. The players didn't fathom it right away, could not see through their gutwrench, but the loss was the closest we'd come to halcyon, the closest we would ever come, because what with Russ Jensen's staying away, Bobby Shoop sidelined, and James Thornton swept up in audio verite or having to be helped on and off the field, we'd lost by losing British. "Kind of like cheating, ain't it, mate, with somebody like a Jensen in there?" said Davey Parkes with his usual gumption.

When the gun sounded, a group of Supporters rushed onto the pitch, lifted Andy Jefferson onto their shoulders and paraded him around the grandstand. Shoop's trophy be damned, this was a genuine moment for the Bulls, and we saluted it. The stands rocked while Jeffo got passed through the crowd like a ration of heroism.

Denton Thomas, as much as he would have liked the same treatment, was too heavy for them to pick up. So he helped lead a chant begun by the Greenwood brothers: "Andy!" Clap-clap. "Andy!" Clap-clap, thousands joining in. Pasco, the second British quarterback, got borne aloft, too, and then those still holding Jeffo aloft beckoned with their free hands for more applause. It rose, up over the last row in the grandstand where Frank Kalili sat, obscure and uncomprehending that his old team had on this day become a team at last, and not for the longest time did the hosannas die down.

But all the cheers and consolation did nothing to placate many of the veteran players, among them the safety Paddy Laird, who cursed, then tossed his silver loser's medal into the grandstand. Paddy had been with the Bulls from the beginning, made many winning walks along midfield, made a lot of Bullrushes; yes, with him, with so many of them, the winning was ingrained. And when a member of the Supporters Club retrieved the medal and gave it back to him, he flung it away again, this time for good.

It also angered Paddy Laird, angered us all terribly, that the Manchester Spartans, with their whimpering coach, an extravagant sponsorship package, and a full complement of American imports in the lineup, were the new British champions—more irritating yet, they were imitation champions. "Listen," Davey Parkes said, "they've stolen our cheer." From the Spartans' side of Crystal Palace a droning chant could be heard: "We're so good it's un-be-LAY-vable."

"Bollocks!" Parkesy declared. "It's ours. We've had it since we started out in '83."

Parkesy may have been disappointed at the moment, but at least he wasn't broke. Nor dead. Had the Bulls won the Budweiser Bowl, he had planned to celebrate by attending the NFL exhibition the next day after staying overnight in London. But the hotel where he'd made reservations was no longer standing, or no longer fully standing: It had been blown up earlier in the week when a terrorist managed to kill himself between floors while trying to plant a bomb.

With his wagering Dave Parkes also came away with mixed results. After Russ Jensen had rejoined the team for a second season, Parkesy had clucked his tongue, couldn't wait to get good bob down at the neighborhood bookmaking shop on the Bulls to repeat as champions. When the team's winning streak reached 21 games, when getting through the playoffs was a formality, why, the payoff was already his. But when he paid another visit to the bookmaker shortly before the Budweiser Bowl to place another bet, he eschewed partisanship and put it firmly on the Manchester Spartans. "Four-to-one odds on the Bulls, I got," he said, almost without contrition. "They didn't know Jensen wasn't going to play."

But as this was the Britball of disowned owning, of two Wrights making a wrong, of Andy's Capptivating and other face-masked mountebanks, of a misguided American mission, of a national paranoia over kick-blocking, of Bizarre-kivich, of expatriate pioneers transformed into P.A. announcers from an Elba of Lego-Land, of Champagne Animal Roberts and odd-lot sales, of secondaries who wore prison stripes instead of football jerseys, of an endless "Bridge Over Troubled Water," of a sport with a fatality count from picking up a kicking tee—yes, as this was Britball, in all its hope and glory, Davey Parkes had won his last bet, only to lose the winning ticket.

Epilogue

As the Budweiser Bowl ended, two hundred miles away at the Twycross Zoo in the Midlands, Russ Jensen burnished a lovely afternoon strolling arm in arm past the gorilla cage with his newest girlfriend. Appalled by his behavior and the embarrassment he caused Britball on this showcase weekend, the league withdrew his MVP trophy. With an injurious sniff it also announced he was banned for life from British gridiron for reneging on his contract . . . though he never had a contract to renege on.

Jensen left the country without so much as an unkind word to the Bulls, who for two seasons had tolerated his tyranny in return for winning, though he did offer a last decree: When the other Americans returned to No. 9 Star Hill, they found in a childish scrawl on the drawing-room wall, "Webb Sucks Dicks." His spelling had improved since the letter to Al Davis.

However poignant the loss, however legitimate the Bulls had become by losing, few people would ever know about it. By now the sport had become a bad joke. The national press ignored the championship game. One newspaper's next-day edition ran lengthy accounts of croquet, gliding, hang gliding, field hockey, ice hockey, polo, yachting, speedway, triathlon, and powerboating, with nary a word of coverage devoted to gridiron, not even

270

a skewed scoreline of agate, something along the Spartans 1, Bulls 4 kind of thing the papers so often had printed in the past.

My haggis diet paid off one week later when this season of the absurd was extended at Salford Park for a friendly against the Upper Heyford U.S. Air Force Skykings. The name of the Bulls kickoff wedgebreaker was omitted from the official program, though previous print references had been made as Glodetty or Glubefty.

I sported jersey number 79, and with distinction—the distinction being it was one of the few Bulls' jerseys not worn during the season by Son Tustin. The sun had a spellbinding slant over Spaghetti Junction as I lined up for the imminent collision of opening kickoff. But picking myself off the ground, I saw at least two suns in the sky—probably the effects from the cascading carbon monoxide.

Football for me was still the felicitous world I remembered, being in the thick of things, anyhow, but when as special teams coach, I decided to replace myself in the lineup for one play with Clive Jackson, the Skykings returned a kickoff 95 yards up the middle for what proved the winning touchdown. Clive, apparently, had played a little too skinny.

The match was scheduled to retire Bulls' debts, but owner David Webb, in Britball's peculiar economics, managed to spend more than he made at the gate, most of it to pay new-coming Americans when the Bulls' imports refused to play.

Animal Roberts also sat out the game, deciding to take a break from football, or having it decided for him: the break an 18-month prison sentence for assaulting a police officer. He joined his brother the star safety at Winson Green, as the waist towels of the "there here" variety stood to be lengthened.

Various Bulls retired and unretired, though not Errol Perkins. Martyn Bourne, the tiny defensive tackle, quit with intentions to become the Bulls new kit man, though given the team's taxonomy, it was like someone announcing himself in the desert as spa manager. George "T" Nisbet, who sat out the season with a thumb injury, regained his penmanship, but not playing form; he

271

never dressed again. His brother Nizzy became one of the first Bulls to stick to retirement, though it was a forced situation—mandate of his mates, who never forgave him for shedding his kit at halftime and sitting in the stands the rest of the game. He did, however, get asked to appear on a BBC program about the Falklands conflict.

The exhibition against the USAF team was slated as a trial for prospective players and to tout improvements of the sport's indigenous talent. But the starting quarterback for the Bulls was none other than the American who'd opposed us in the Budweiser Bowl.

Playing before a handful of fans, the Supporters having spent themselves at the championship, the facsimile Bulls lost, 27–22. Not a great day for Britball—though it might have been if a short pass on the last play from an American quarterback to an American receiver covered by an American defensive back hadn't fallen incomplete in the end zone.

I came home to America demob happy, as the Brits say, ever pleased to vegetate over pro football—even started carrying around an NFL schedule in my wallet. I also was sure the critic Peter Ackroyd had Britball in mind when he called Americanism "a triumph of vulgarity over barbarism," but I saw nothing resembling triumph.

Unless it was James Thornton's having gone an entire season without a brain scan.

Thornton himself got a job with the NFL's international merchandising division. Before it came through, to fund himself, he recouped money owed him by the Bulls, most of it coming from the Supporters Club, who interrupted a meeting about democracy in Poland and let him again convince them to reempty the treasury.

Bob Shoop returned to campus, hardly mistaken anymore for a freshman, and helped coach Yale to a tie for the Ivy League championship. Coaching wasn't as rewarding as he'd anticipated, and he spoke of returning to the Bulls. But never to the disposable diaper business—though if he had, and coupled it with gridiron, one of those nappies might have read: "No. 17—He's Here, Again."

David Webb used his community stature to do battle with another of the international leagues, condemning its cheek of placing a team in Brum; he called on Bulls' Supporters to picket its games, which would be played in Villa Park, a real 55,000-seat stadium two blocks from Salford Park.

When not being true-quoted (" 'ILAF is a fix,' slams sad Dave") in the papers, the owner made his pronunciations over the new Bulls hotline, his major off-season announcement the signing of a large, talented but not-so-new player: Steve Harvey.

Baghwan Shree Rajneesh died in India, eulogized by one attorney general for "a legacy of crime left behind unparalleled in American history." His fleet of Rolls-Royces was sold off, none of the proceeds going to Britball, the Bulls, or home mortgages. His former produce manager, Mr. Nice 'n Fresh, kept attuned to James Thornton's conquests, and largess-minded as ever, made deliveries to No. 9 Star Hill til the bitter end.

No. 9 itself was converted into a vicarage, with the Reverend Mr. Pike's presence some sort of exorcism for the sybaritic damage done over six months of American occupancy.

Dick Capp (*not* aka Andy, Andie), formerly of the Green Bay Packers, is still in possession of a prized ring from having played in Super Bowl I. "Went through a few tough years in business, but nothing bad enough to make me sell it," he said. He works in Dallas in investments, and has never been to England, or hidden under an umbrella at Oxford. His near-namesake with CIA affiliation was axed as head coach of the Bournemouth Bobcats after another 1–9 season and has probably reassimilated back into the cold.

Steve Pisarkiewicz coached the Dublin Celtics into the playoffs and, tentatively—for there was no other word for him and his plans—decided to settle in Ireland. As always, chimera: The week the playoffs began, he returned stateside under the guise of a holiday. He then sent an ultimatum, self-typed of course, demanding a lump sum from the Celtics or else they could play without him. Which they did. But his résumé wasn't finished yet with its burgeoning: Zark hied off the next season to another country and became quarterback for the Barcelona Boxers.

Sterling Management's only other known account, something called the Imperial Bowl—which had been slated for Brum to be played by what the newspapers, with prodding, referred to as "two premier American gridiron powers," Southern Connecticut and Central Connecticut State—got canceled due to lack of interest.

Having so proved himself, Sterling's chief executive Bob Preen got hired by one of the new international leagues to promote gridiron in Britain.

The wonderful Waikikis went unregrouped though Frank Kalili at last went back on song, joining Preen as consultant with the new international league. Per his favorite article, that 2001 date in the Super Bowl with the Miami Dolphins—it seemed to be coming true: A local paper ran a contest, and the nickname chosen for the new team was—yes—the Birmingham Bears.

Alas, Frank never got to audition for them, whether as waterboy, owner, or vocalist; the league folded before ever playing its first game.

Frank was aggrieved, but he coped, babe. He staved off foreclosure on his house, his marriage, or VCRs and once again pacharan flowed on Yew Tree Close. True to form he went on BBC's *Clothes Show* to model football fashion, and better yet, got true-quote carte blanche as a columnist for a new gridiron tabloid. His beat: Spanish football.

We got together once more, for him to pontificate gridiron, and I was privileged to see a side of him that left me more awed than ever.

The meeting took place at a shopping mall in city center. As he made his way through it, shock registered on his face a fraction of a second before he did his impeccable best to turn into someone, or something else, folding a newspaper in front of his visage, pressing it to a storefront window. In what had to be his piece de resistance of impersonation, he was impersonating self-preservation.

At just that moment Steve Harvey rumbled past. Color drained from Frank's face, and his lifelessness worked ever so well. He was mistaken for just another quaking pane of glass.

MICHAEL GLOBETTI lives in
Boston, Massachusetts,
where he gardens and
presides over the Jack
Buchanan American
Appreciation Society.